BEHIND THE GOAL

BEHIND
THE GOAL

Sentenced to life as a Don

James Addison

Foreword by Joe Harper

MAINSTREAM
PUBLISHING

EDINBURGH AND LONDON

First published in Great Britain in 1998 by
MAINSTREAM PUBLISHING CO (EDINBURGH) LTD
7 Albany Street
Edinburgh
EH1 3UG

ISBN 1 84018 123 0

A CIP catalogue record for this book is available from
the British Library

Typeset in Garamond
Printed in Great Britain by Butler & Tanner Ltd

Contents

To my late father, John

Foreword

I'd have to recommend any book where the author puts me in the same chapter as Denis Law and Ferenc Puskas as one of his favourite strikers. But, as a former Aberdeen player, I'm just as pleased to be in there along with Benny Yorston, because I know how highly regarded he was by the players and fans who remember him – among them my old golfing companion, Matt Armstrong. I remember how proud I was to move ahead of such great players as Benny, then Harry Yorston and finally Matt in the club's all-time scoring list. *Behind the Goal* brings back many great memories for me, as I'm sure it will do for any Dons fan. It gives a fan's view of players from different decades over the whole of the Dons' history, and recalls each era in a highly entertaining way. The post-war period is just as I remember it when I was growing up, and the chapters on Bobby Clark, Willie Miller and myself are a vivid reminder of what it was like when I was playing. The 1920s and 1930s are brought to life with some well-selected newspaper quotes from the period, and I learned a lot about players like Jock Hutton and Alex Jackson, as well as an even better appreciation of how good Benny Yorston was. You may not agree with the choice of players, but then no good game was ever complete without a good argument. What I'm sure of is that Dons fans and anyone who loves the game will enjoy this book.

Joe Harper, 1998

Acknowledgements

Thanks to previous writers on Aberdeen FC and its players, mainly Jack Webster for his excellent history, *The Dons* (Stanley Paul), and Jim Rickaby for his monumental work, *Aberdeen: A Complete Record* (Breedon Books); to the numerous journalists on various newspapers, but mainly the two local papers, the *Press and Journal* and *Evening Express*, especially James Forbes; to my father, for passing on his love of the game, and to him and his cronies for all the yarns of the old days, when the sun always shone and the Dons always won, even if the record shows otherwise; to Todd McEwen, writer in residence at Aberdeen Public Library, who helped so much in the early stages of the book, and the rest of the library staff; and to my family, especially Sam, who got me out of many a computer fix, and without whose help this book would be lost somewhere in cyberspace.

Author's Preface

It started with a discussion about Aberdeen's top scorer. Joe Harper had scored 199 to Benny Yorston's 125, but at the rate Yorston scored his goals he would surely have been the top scorer if he had stayed longer. So who was the better player? How do you compare footballers who played during different eras? A few more Dons who had played at different times came to mind, and the book grew from there.

Behind the Goal is not a history, although the players do in fact cover most periods of the Dons' history (that book has already been written by Jack Webster). It starts, like a football team, from goal out, comparing players – full-backs, defenders, midfielders, strikers, wingers – and the times they lived and played in. There are also some 'guests', who never played for Aberdeen.

The players chosen are not necessarily the best who have ever played for the Dons. This is a book about players who, for one reason or another, have appealed to me. It is also about growing up and watching football in the post-war period. It is about Real Madrid, and the search for the Real Game. It is the view from the terraces, the stand – or behind the goal.

The Goalkeepers

In those days, behind the goal was where you started. The days before the all-seated stadium, when the small boys behind the goal peered over the wall (and probably peed behind it – the toilet was a long way away, but I never did that; my pal Broonser did, but I didn't) and yelled a chorus of 'Y – y – y – y – OWT!' as the goalkeeper ran up to take the goal-kick, with the final, climactic 'OWT!' timed to coincide with the thud of the goal-keeper's boot on the ball. Why, I don't know. But it was what you did, so I did it, and it was fun, especially when you didn't understand too much else of what was going on.

Goal-kicks you could understand; the goalkeeper, the one in the yellow jersey, puts the ball down, walks back, runs up to the ball, gives it a bloody great thump; it disappears up the park, and then it comes back again. Simple. The bits in between, before it came back, were a bit trickier. The ball went back and forth, the players ran here and there, and the man in black blew his whistle now and then, for obscure reasons, and quite a lot of all this took place a long way from where you were, trying to keep your head above the wall with your elbows on top of it, like a man in a rubber ring trying to keep his head above the water. After the game you'd squirm your way through the crowds, and by the time you'd had something to eat, your dad would be home with the *Green Final*, the weekly miracle with all the results and the match reports printed in the time it had taken to get home, have your tea and watch *The Lone Ranger*. You'd read about 'Dons' Triumph' or, more usually, 'Dons' Disaster', and try to relate what you'd read to what you'd seen, and hope that some day it would all make sense.

But the goalkeeper was always there, and you could understand what he was trying to do; he was there to stop the ball going in the net, and to pick it out when he didn't, and to take the goal-kicks, when you shouted 'Y – y – y – y – OWT!'. So he loomed large in your footballing life.

Fred Martin was the goalkeeper then, a great brooding presence in the foreground, pacing between the sticks when the play was at the other end and soaring above the mêlée when the crosses came in, to emerge with the ball clutched safely to his chest. Four steps, bounce, four steps, bounce, and belt it back up the park. When looking at Dons players over the years, it therefore seemed natural to start with Fred; and, having started with him, it seemed natural to begin in goal and work my way out, like a teamsheet, rather than start at the beginning, like a history. The history has been done, and anyway, for me, Fred was the beginning.

The modern status of the goalkeeper as a cult figure is a relatively recent development; possibly television close-ups and action replays have had something to do with it; possibly it reflects a general anonymity in the game, with the goalie at least identifiable by his different-coloured jersey, even if he does look like he's auditioning for *Joseph and the Amazing Technicolor Dreamcoat*. The only goalkeeper in the Scottish game to achieve any kind of popular status and lasting fame before the war was John Thomson, the Celtic goalkeeper who was so tragically killed playing against Rangers. After the war there was 'Cowan's Wembley', when Jimmy Cowan defied the English to set up a famous Scottish victory. Alas, he did not set a precedent, and Scottish goalkeepers were to be remembered for all the wrong reasons in later Wembley fixtures.

The Aberdeen goalkeepers before the war remain shadowy figures at this distance. Steve Smith was part of a defensive triumvirate along with Cooper and McGill, which gave the team such a solid foundation in the 1930s. He was succeeded by George Johnstone, who played in both the 1937 and 1947 Cup finals, and was thus an important part of the Dons' immediate post-war success.

Before the First World War there was Rab Macfarlane, who had established himself as a character by exchanging repartee with the crowd behind the goal. After the war Harry Blackwell had succeeded George Anderson and, apart from establishing himself as the regular keeper from 1921 until 1928, set a new fashion in goalkeeping attire by donning a raincoat and, finally, sheltering under an umbrella during the famous 13–0 victory over Peterhead in 1923. But, on the whole, little attention was focused on goalkeepers unless they happened to make the kind of blunder which lost a game, and the best they could hope for was anonymity. It was from Fred Martin onwards that the goalkeepers started to emerge as personalities in their own right.

After Martin there was Reggie Morrison, who, after the somewhat dour efficiency of Martin, was part of the 'You don't have to be mad to be a goalkeeper but it helps' school of custodianship. He had two specialities: saving penalties and getting caught hopelessly out of position. He also created some controversy by occasionally throwing the ball out, rather than kicking it as far up the park as he could. In those days, the idea that you could start an attacking move in your own half was regarded as something of a heresy.

After him came John 'Tubby' Ogston, who had kept goal for Banks o' Dee when they had won the Scottish Junior Cup in 1957. He had the misfortune to play behind a defence which was, to put it kindly, a mite unreliable, but he was displaced by an indubitably better goalkeeper,

Bobby Clark, and was transferred to Liverpool in 1965.

Clark's career spanned 15 seasons, which eventually saw the Dons scale the heights they had achieved with Martin, and he therefore merits a chapter in his own right. Another goalkeeper who might have merited inclusion was Jim Leighton, who formed part of the most famous defensive line-up in Aberdeen's history. Leighton, Willie Miller and Alex McLeish made scoring a goal against Aberdeen an achievement, and a matter for considerable recrimination among themselves. He went on to become part of a Scotland defence that was a substantial improvement on most of what had gone before, and did much to dispel the English belief that Scottish goalkeepers dipped their gloves in soap before every game. Until, that is, he went to Manchester United and restored the image of the Scottish goalkeeper as a man doomed to toil eternally in the back of the net, forever bending over to retrieve the ball like some mediaeval peasant tending his tiny patch of soil. This is unfair to Leighton, for he proved himself a thoroughly dependable goalkeeper over many seasons for the Dons, but his subsequent career shows how important confidence is to any sportsman, and what a fragile commodity it is. Some well-publicised mistakes at United destroyed his confidence and his reputation, and he did little later at Dundee to restore either.

It says much for his character, as well as his ability, that he was able to rebuild his career so successfully with Hibs that he recovered his place in the Scotland team. His return to Aberdeen could not have come at a more difficult time; the familiar Pittodrie he had viewed from behind the rampart of Miller and McLeish must have seemed like a strange territory overrun by marauding hordes as ever-changing defences crumbled in front of him and Aberdeen slid towards relegation. When Alex Miller arrived and made rebuilding the defence his immediate priority, Pittodrie regained some of its former reputation for impregnability, with Leighton's goalkeeping as the keystone. Even as he edges into his 40s, it is by no means certain that he is ready to write the final chapter in a remarkable career.

Leighton had overcome an initial scepticism on the part of the fans to establish himself as a highly popular figure. The gangly physique, with the question-mark legs, the wayward hair, and the general appearance of having been assembled rather hurriedly at the end of the night shift, eventually came to inspire affection, and the initial doubts were resolved by the sheer consistency of his displays during the most successful period in the club's history.

With Theo Snelders, there were never any doubts. Tall and perfectly proportioned for a goalkeeper, he inspired confidence from the outset, and, with his positioning, safe handling and agility, proved that the initial confidence was not misplaced. His meticulous work-outs before each game gave some insight into how such standards are achieved. The old ritual of 'shooty-in' just before the game started, with a few desultory shots aimed vaguely in the direction of the goal, was replaced by a routine of high shots, low shots, crosses from the left, crosses from the right, designed to ensure that he was thoroughly warmed-up and prepared for whatever the game might bring. The shots and crosses were usually provided by Drew Jarvie, who got the chance to display the accuracy which had brought him so many goals in the 1970s.

The inspiration which a team can derive from a thoroughly dependable goalkeeper was never better displayed than during the Dons' late and ultimately futile challenge for the 1990–91 championship, when Theo was in virtually unbeatable form. 'Defence hopelessly outnumbered? No problem. Theo's there.' The glory and the cruelty of goalkeeping life was exemplified in the match at Tannadice, as the mathematical possibility of catching Rangers was turning into a realistic aim, and nerves were starting to fray at the edges. Two saves in the near-impossible category kept Aberdeen in the game, while at the other end a mistake by Alan Main in the Dundee United goal allowed Aberdeen to win a game they might well have lost. I cannot remember a finer display by an Aberdeen goalkeeper.

Sadly, more fans will probably remember Snelders' mistake in the 1992 Skol Cup final, rather than the penalty save which effectively won the Scottish Cup in 1990. Such is a goalkeeper's life; the glory is fleeting, the blunders are forever.

Fred Martin

Fred Martin was born in Carnoustie, played for the local junior side Carnoustie Panmure, and was signed by Aberdeen in 1946. What makes his career unique is that he was signed not as a goalkeeper, but as an inside-forward. Many, if not most, goalkeepers have started as outfield players before being persuaded to take the gloves, the goal-kicks and, ultimately, the blame. But this is a move which usually occurs in schools or juvenile football, and the goalkeeper is usually confirmed in his lonely calling long before he reaches the senior ranks.

These were not normal times, however. A war had just ended, and the echoes could still be heard. The *Press and Journal* found it newsworthy that two Aberdeen men were to wed German girls. Less parochially, Franco had agreed to hand over 'notorious Nazis'. A retrospective article recounted how German raiders had been foiled by French bravery.

On the domestic front, austerity was the order of the day, and a ration book as essential as cash for a shopping trip. Those with enough money and petrol coupons might have considered buying a Singer Bantam Nine, only 23,000 miles on the clock, and a snip at offers over £300. For £500 you could have bought that post-war classic, the Jowett Javelin. Even the advertisements still recalled the war. Heinz announced that 'one by one the famous varieties are coming back to Civvy Street'. For home entertainment you could buy an HMV radio, with a five-volt battery and 'lovely tone' for £17.

When Fred signed for the Dons in October, he could have celebrated by going to His Majesty's Theatre to see Leslie Henson in *The Sport of Kings*. The following week had the D'Oyly Carte Opera Company, succeeded by *Antony and Cleopatra* with Edith Evans as the Egyptian temptress. If that was not enticing enough, the Tivoli had something lighter, that 'famous character comedian and impressionist' Leslie Strange, whose fame has weathered the years rather less well than that of Antony, Cleopatra, Edith Evans or, for that matter, Fred Martin, who was a better goalkeeper than any of them.

If Fred was more of a film fan, the Capitol had *Devotion*, with Ida Lupino, Olivia de Havilland and Sydney Greenstreet, who might have made not a bad goalkeeper – he was about the right width. ('Gad, Sir, but that was a well placed shot and no mistake,' as Bogie curled one into the top corner after a sneaky foul by Peter Lorre.) It also advertised a 'technicolor cartoon and F. Rowland Tims at the organ', all of which added up to a well-nigh irresistible package of entertainment.

The war was over, but young men were still required to serve their country by spending two years in the forces. Shortly after signing for Aberdeen Fred had signed for His Majesty and went to do his tour of duty. It was often said that National Servicemen went away as boys and came back as men, to the satisfaction of their fathers and dismay of their mothers – 'Oh son, what have they done to you?' Fred went away as an inside-forward and returned as a goalkeeper. His mother's reaction is not recorded, but Dave Halliday, the Aberdeen manager, liked what he saw and decided to keep him as he was.

He made his début as a goalkeeper for the first team on 14 April 1950 against East Fife. The Aberdeen team was: Martin, McKeown, Emery, Bruce, McKenzie, Harris, Kiddie, Rodger, Hamilton, Glen, Hather. Although the Dons lost 3–1, Martin was credited with a fine début in goal, until the last minute, when he caught a lob only to drop it over the line. It is the fate of goalkeepers to be remembered for their blunders rather than their triumphs, and Martin exemplifies this better than most.

He went on to become a dominating goalkeeper for the best part of the next decade. In the early-1950s he was part of one of the most successful sides in Aberdeen's history. The post-war boom in match attendances had declined slightly, but they still averaged nearly 20,000, with crowds of almost 40,000 for the visits of Rangers and Celtic. One exception was season 1953–54 when, for some unfathomable reason, the top attendance was 27,000 for Queen of the South, of all teams. Incredibly, they were top of the league at the time, but that hardly seems an adequate explanation for such a crowd. Was there a rumour that somebody had lost a tanner at the previous game, and it had never been found? During this period Aberdeen consolidated their position as one of Scotland's leading clubs, and Martin his as one of the country's top goalkeepers. He played a vital part in the league championship triumph of 1954–55. He played in three Cup finals and won six Scotland caps.

Yet, for all his great saves, for all that he achieved, for all the lost causes that he retrieved, Martin is best remembered for losing seven goals at Wembley. Indeed, he has the dubious distinction of twice losing seven goals for Scotland. The loss of such a number of goals for the national side is an achievement which few goalkeepers are invited to repeat, but the first defeat was in the World Cup, a competition for which we cared little, by Uruguay, a small, far-away country of which we knew nothing at all, so it didn't really count.

But England at Wembley was another matter. It was the game which mattered above all others. It was the only game. The 5–1 defeat of England in 1929 had convinced all the sons of Scotia's soil that they had a divine right to beat perfidious Albion, whatever the subsequent evidence to the contrary. The biennial trip to Wembley was fuelled by an optimism which made the outpourings of Ally MacLeod ('I'm no sayin' we'll win the World Cup, but . . .') sound like prophecies of doom. James Forbes, writing at that time in the *Press and Journal*, was never one to be carried away by euphoria, yet even he forecast a Scottish victory. 'If the Scots survive the expected opening onslaught, our forwards can win the game with accurate ground passing,' he wrote, under the headline: 'Scots craft is answer to English power.' Of Martin's selection, he wrote: 'Fred Martin will guard the Scots goal, and he has only to reproduce his club form to be an instant success. The chances are he will get plenty of opportunities to prove his ability.' Alas, he did not take them. How he must have wished he were at Pittodrie, where Aberdeen were defeating Rangers 4–0, or even the Gulag Archipelago, where at least there would be no one to witness or report his misery. Anywhere but Wembley.

The headline on the front page of Monday's paper said it all: 'Oh what a dreadful day!' The picture caption read: 'Lofthouse scores number four for England, while big Fred Martin looks apprehensively round'. As well he might have done. The sports page headline was: 'Matthews magic dazzles Scots.' James Forbes could perhaps defend his forecast by pointing to the proviso of surviving the opening onslaught. For the poor goalkeeper, there are no ifs or buts, only goals lost.

The match report did not make happy reading: 'Like his defensive team-mates, Martin had not a happy international. He left his charge in the first minute to cut out a high ball and lost possession. Wilshaw was quick to seize the scoring opportunity. The loss of this goal may have affected Martin's nerves. He appeared to be at fault when Revie claimed England's third.'

The report conceded that he received poor protection from the men in front of him; in particular the improbably named Harry Haddock was run ragged by the ageing but still elusive Stanley Matthews. When a team loses seven goals, however, the question is never 'Who was left-back?'.

Wembley 1955 was an albatross round Martin's neck and, not surprisingly, terminated his Scotland career. He can claim to have set a fashion for Scottish goalkeepers at Wembley, for it was only six years later that Frank Haffey allowed Martin's albatross to drop. It wasn't the only thing he allowed to drop that day, conceding no fewer than nine goals, a performance that had the Scottish press reaching for headlines of the 'Day of Shame' and 'Nine-Goal Débâcle' variety. How the headline writers loved débâcles in those days. Brickbats too. What were they? Had anyone ever seen one? Whatever they were, there were plenty of them for poor Haffey, who must have felt like a tattie howker that day. He finished his career in Australia, where he helped to resuscitate a player who nearly drowned in a puddle left by a tropical thunderstorm. He was the sort of character that things happened to. In a way, I felt glad when he let in the nine, because it got Martin off the hook. Stuart Kennedy was to follow in the great Scottish tradition in 1975. While he conceded only five, he did so with a degree of flair which stamped his performance indelibly in the collective Scottish football memory. Who can forget his swing round the goalpost as the ball sailed into the net?

If Martin felt bad at the time, he could have consoled himself with the thought that at least he wasn't Don Cockell, who was going to America to fight Rocky Marciano for the world heavyweight crown. Cockell's manager, according to the press, was 'optimistic', as well he might have been. He knew that Marciano was not going to be hitting *him*. Later that month we would listen to Raymond Glendenning giving us a round-by-round commentary, telling us how well Cockell was doing, and be mystified as to how the boxer doing all the punching could be beaten. Barrington Dalby was there to provide a more realistic, if less patriotic, view in the inter-round commentary ('Marciano's round by a mile'), and the pictures in the papers the following day told the true story.

On that Monday the *Press and Journal* forecast, rather more accurately than it had forecast the Wembley result, that Churchill would retire, to be replaced by Anthony Eden. Harold Macmillan was tipped to be the new Foreign Secretary. On the other side of the political divide, the annual conference of the Scottish Council of the Labour Party was denouncing the A-bomb as a 'threat in peace-time'.

Jack Radcliffe was appearing at the Tivoli, and the Capitol was showing *Desiree*, with Marlon Brando in the starring role as Napoleon ('I coulda bin a contender, Josephine'). Billy Graham was in the country, and would appear later that month at Pittodrie in front of a crowd of 18,000 and, according to the local wags, save more than Martin had done at Wembley. At that time, however, Graham was reported as being ill. If he was looking for an earthly cure, he might have reached for the Andrews Liver Salts, 'for inner cleanliness'. Local controversy was raging about the naming of the Justice Mill Lane baths. 'Bon-Accord Baths' was the favoured option, and eventually won the day, but not without some stiff opposition. They needn't have bothered; they were still the 'uptown baths'.

Whether he sought spiritual comfort from Billy Graham, or whether he saw what Marciano did to Cockell, or what Suez did to Eden, and reasoned that football was not, after all, a matter of life and death, Martin got over Wembley and carried on playing for another five years, although his appearances after 1957 were restricted by injury.

He played his last game for Aberdeen on 16 January 1960, against Airdrie at Pittodrie. Aberdeen had by this time declined from the league champions of 1955 to a position near the bottom of the table. It was a sign of their defensive frailty that they had tried no fewer than seven goal-keepers in the course of the season. Davie Shaw had relinquished the manager's chair to Tommy Pearson, but with no discernible improvement. By the turn of the year, the Dons were fourth from bottom of the league, and at the end of the season were happy to finish no worse than that.

The game against Airdrie was fairly typical. Before long, the relegation-threatened Aberdeen were 2–0 down. In the kind of report which had haunted him throughout his career, Martin was blamed for both goals. The first, 'when Martin fisted out, Sharkey gained possession and Baillie rammed home the winger's cross'. For the second, 'Martin failed to hold a low shot from Sharkey and again Baillie was on the spot.'

Thus he started and finished his career being blamed for lost goals. This is unfair, for he kept goal for Aberdeen during their period of post-war success, and no team ever won the league with a poor goalkeeper. More than anything, it had been a good defensive record which had won the league in 1954–55; the loss of only 26 goals in 30 games had been a remarkable performance in the relatively free-scoring 1950s, and must have been due in no small part to Martin's contribution in goal. To take but one example, there was a penalty save in a 1–0 win against Hearts which was the difference between two points and one; it is the regular accumulation of points scraped and saved in this manner which makes champions, rather than the occasional spectacular victory. It is a simple lesson, but one which Aberdeen would take the next 25 years to learn.

He dominated his goal area and was a safe pair of hands under greater physical pressure than goalkeepers are subjected to in modern times. He was the first Aberdeen goalkeeper to be capped, and thus started the tradition carried on by Bobby Clark, Ernie McGarr, Jim Leighton and Bryan Gunn. The Aberdeen team in his last game was: Martin, Caldwell, Hogg, Baird, Clunie, Kinnell, Little, Burns, Davidson, Mulhall, Hather. Of the team he had started out with in 1950, only Hather remained, and he too would be gone by the end of the season.

When Fred signed for Aberdeen in the grey years after the war, all that was left of the Palace Hotel was a hole in the ground. When he left, it had been replaced by the C&A building, which filled the hole in the ground, but left the architect little room to criticise Martin's Wembley performance. That had only lasted 90 minutes; the C&A building is still with us. At Pittodrie, Martin had seen the cover erected at the Beach End in 1958, and very welcome it had been, but of more long-term significance had been the introduction of floodlights. The first floodlit game at Pittodrie was a friendly against Luton in October 1959. This was hardly the most exciting of opposition, but the lights gave the occasion a glamour all of its own, with the Dons in a shiny new strip. Floodlights had already changed the face of football elsewhere, with midweek games against foreign opposition, first in friendlies and then in the European Cup.

We hadn't felt aggrieved when Aberdeen were denied their rightful place in the inaugural competition. The Dons were champions, but Hibs had been invited to take part in the 1955–56 European Cup. We only became dimly aware of the competition when Hibs reached the semi-final, going out to Reims. Who were they? And they were beaten in the final by Real Madrid. What sort of a name was that, for God's sake? Was there a Fake Madrid? But when the Spanish side beat Manchester United the following season we knew they were the genuine article and we had to admit that Di Stefano was a better centre-forward than Paddy Buckley, even if Paddy did have more hair. When Real reached Hampden in 1960 with Puskas in the side and put seven goals past Eintracht, who themselves had twice put six past Rangers, our own dear Rangers, we knew that they were the greatest team there had ever been, and the thought that an Aberdeen side could ever beat them in a European final was an impossible dream.

Europe had come to Glasgow and given us a glimpse of the game's possibilities. What had puzzled and frustrated me, as I slowly started to make sense of what was happening on the pitch, was that it so seldom matched my youthful ideal of the game. There were exceptions, like some moments of magic from Graham Leggat, or when the Hearts side of the late-1950s visited, with Alex Young and Dave Mackay, or when we almost beat Rangers, but usually the games at Pittodrie weren't nearly as exciting as the games we played in the playground, or the street, or down on the links. You'd see dribbling, and tricks you never saw at Pittodrie, and goals, lots of goals.

You'd get to school early, kitted out in black gymmies and khaki shorts, ready to start the playground game, which gradually grew to resemble a minor skirmish in a civil war as more players arrived. How we remembered who was on which side, I have no idea, but we did. By bell time, the main aim was keeping limbs intact while inflicting as much damage as possible on the enemy, but before then, there were some opportunities to play football.

The wall ran along one side of the pitch and, as well as forming one touchline, could be used as an ally, who would always return your pass. The goal at one end was the space between the wall and a crack running along the concrete, which gave us an exceptionally thin post, and could give rise to some controversy. The goal at the other end was the gable end of the shelter, which gave us a reasonably unambiguous target, except for the 'in-offs'. A goal could be scored off the wall at the side, but a shot which hit wall and gable end simultaneously was adjudged to have hit the post, and offered ample scope for argument and unarmed combat.

A useful time-wasting tactic when defending a narrow lead was to kick the ball into the infants' playground, an enclosed quadrangle with only a narrow entrance to the main playground. Less sensible was to kick the ball over the high wall, for it was the kicker's duty to retrieve it, and this involved a long run out of school, along the street, and into the grounds of the neighbouring college, followed by search time and the return journey. For this to happen just before the bell was tantamount to a death sentence, for it would mean you were late, and would have to face the wrath of Mr Lindsay, the assistant head. Either that, or be beaten to a pulp by your mates.

The game we played bore little relation to the game we watched at Pittodrie, but the playground tradition had much to do with the Scottish game, a hectic swirl of physical action that permitted only fleeting contact with the ball. But, now and again, a boy with more ability than the others, with balance and delicacy of touch, together with the necessary courage, would pick a way through the flailing limbs and give us a glimpse of that other game. He'd usually be small. It was this part of the tradition that gave us the wee Scottish forward, from Alan Morton and Hughie Gallacher to Willie Henderson and Jimmy Johnstone. Denis Law owed something to both sides of the playground game. He never dwelled on the ball, and could look after himself when the boots were flying, but he could also pick his way through a crowded penalty area when the occasion demanded.

There was just one occasion when Broonser and I took part in this other game, the one that existed on the higher plane. We swapped passes from our own goal-line right through to the enemy half, and I finished the move with a right-foot shot just inside the razor-thin post and just beyond the despairing fingertips of Cliffie, the goalkeeper, who must have been a good three feet high. It was Spurs' 'push and run', it was Hungary at Wembley, it was Real Madrid. And I realised why they were called Real. There was no Fake Madrid. It was just that they played the Real Game, the one that they played all the time, but which occasionally visited ordinary mortals, like it had Broonser and me, just the once.

The Aberdeen fan, rather than look to the continent and dream of the Real Game or trips to Madrid or Milan or any of those places with sunshine and stars and impossible glamour, was more likely to look downwards and dread the trips to Stenhousemuir or Cowdenbeath or any of those places with pit bings and pigeons and cloggers he had never heard of; just staying in the First Division would be quite enough, thank you very much. Bugger the Bernabeu, just let us keep going to Dens Park.

So, after the initial excitement of games under the lights had worn off, the main benefit of floodlights was to allow us to watch matches – dull, dismal, no-scoring, scrambling, scuffling games against miserable opposition – when it was really cold. Until then we had only been able to watch games in the hours of daylight, warmed by the Aberdeen winter sun. There were few recorded cases of sunstroke, and to be fair it sometimes got a bit chilly. But when the sun went down and the wind whipped off the North Sea we could really freeze.

At the start of the game there was always the hope that this time it would be different. We might have a game worth watching. There was also the warmth of a Pittodrie pie nestling somewhere in the digestive system, not the warmth of the oven (oven?) it had come out of, but the heat created by the violent chemical reaction taking place deep in the intestines. This would gradually wear off, as the pie was absorbed, converting temporary discomfort into permanent health damage. There would be some initial movement on the park, matched by some movement on the terraces, as feet were shuffled and arms swung in vain attempts to simulate a game of football on the park and stimulate the circulation off it. Eventually apathy and sub-zero temperatures would win, which is more than the Dons were ever likely to do; the blood supply to the extremities would slow to a trickle, and then the trickle would stop altogether. Blood congealed and limbs froze. The crowd began to resemble China's terracotta army, rank upon rank of immobile figures assembled together in the one place for no apparent reason.

As the blood supply to the brain started to get sluggish and gangrene of the cortex set in, it was vital to hang on to the golden rule: 'Don't touch the crush barrier! Don't touch the crush barrier!' It was rumoured that one poor bloke forgot and was instantly welded to the bare metal. It was the last game of the season before it thawed sufficiently for him to be prised away. Until then he remained on the terracing, a lone sentinel during the week, joined only on matchdays by the rest of the batallion. He got to see the matches free. So my best friend Broonser said. He was, it must be admitted, prone to exaggeration, and, on looking back on it, it does seem a little far-fetched. I mean, Aberdeen? Let him watch for free?

When the referee performed the humanitarian act of blowing the final whistle, the Shore Porters had to be brought in to wheel away the by now totally rigid spectators with those upright barrows they use for removing crates or boxes. It made a strange and ghostly sight as they were wheeled up Merkland Road East and onto King Street, and crowds would gather just to see it. So Broonser said. I never saw it myself, because I went home the Beach End way, but I believed him at the time.

Even if it isn't true – and I keep an open mind on the subject – it does serve as an example of the kind of hallucination brought on by watching the Aberdeen side of the time struggle to defeat the most moderate opposition on nights when sensible folk stayed indoors. What is definitely true is that Pittodrie on a Wednesday night in midwinter was cold and miserable; which made it an ideal place for Aberdonians to go and enjoy themselves.

From the warmth of the press-box the local journalists demanded 'new blood at Pittodrie', but still found time to praise a player from further afield, and from what seemed like another age: 'Brilliant Finney goal puts Preston on winning trail'. Outwith Aberdeen, Dr Barbara Moore was walking from John O'Groats to Lands End, and it seemed that the whole of Wick came out to see her. Perhaps she wanted to put as much distance as possible between herself and Wick, which to many people seemed to be the only sensible part of the whole enterprise. From the Kremlin, Khrushchev talked of a 'fantastic weapon' in production, and the question was not so much 'What are the 1960s going to be like?' as 'Are there going to be any 1960s?'. Anyone astute enough to foresee the boom in classic cars, and optimistic to feel that we were all going to be around long enough, could have gone to Cordiners in Menzies Road and purchased a 1936 Lanchester for £25 and a 1935 Daimler for £15. But the age of the large stately car had gone; the age of the Mini had arrived.

Fred Martin had started his career in the 1940s, in the golden age of steam radio, and finished it in the age of television. A Ferguson could be rented for ten shillings a week, and televised football highlights could be seen regularly, although live broadcasts were still rare. The 1940s had looked back to the war. As the 1960s dawned, the *Press and Journal* looked forward to the opening of the new Aberdeen Technical College and the expansion of the University. It announced 'the age of atomic fusion'. There was a feeling of change to come. The Playhouse was showing foreign films with adult themes. The Capitol was showing *The Navy Lark*.

The Dons would get worse before they got better, and it would be another five years before Bobby Clark arrived to give the team another goal-keeper of international stature. But within a few months a young man called Charlie Cooke was to arrive and bring, if not success, at least a little light into our lives, and a glimpse of the Real Game. But that is another story.

Bobby Clark

'Kirk Lashes Out at Evils of Age of Riotous Living', ran the headline. When was that, then? It could have been any time, for the age has always been a bit riotous and evil for the Kirk. It's what it's there for. The headline was from the *Press and Journal* of 4 May 1965, and I can assure you it wasn't half as much fun then as the Kirk made it sound. So the skirts had got a bit shorter, and the music a bit louder, but the Stones had still to declare Sympathy for the Devil, and for the most part it was good clean fun. After a few years it always is; the age of innocence is the one that's just gone.

If you thought you were missing out on something, and wanted to drive around looking for all the riots and a bit of evil, you could have done so for as little as £22 10s, the price of a 1953 Ford Anglia advertised in the car pages. On the back page, Basil Easterbrook was berating Leeds United's performances in the FA Cup final, when they had been beaten by Liverpool. He criticised them for stifling other teams' creativity and for lacking any of their own. 'Leeds United,' he wrote, 'are a team of limited talent, particularly in attack.' This was a side which had Johnny Giles and Billy Bremner in midfield, and Peter Lorimer and Eddie Gray in attack. To be fair to Easterbrook, they had not played well in the final, and it was to be some time before Don Revie would allow them to express their skills and develop into one of the best English club sides ever.

It was a time when Aberdeen fans would have been glad to be anywhere near a cup final, however they had played to get there. In February the Dons had been knocked out of the Scottish Cup by East Fife, the second successive season in which they had fallen to a Second Division side. It had got to the stage where their only chance of not being knocked out by a team from a lower division was to follow the old adage, 'If you can't beat 'em, join 'em'. Tommy Pearson had to go, and he went. His successor was Eddie Turnbull, who had made an impression with his Queen's Park side the previous season by taking the Dons to a replay in the second round of the Scottish Cup. The Aberdeen players had made less of an impression on him, and he made it clear from the outset that there would be an overhaul of the playing staff.

His first signings were completed in the first week of May 1965, when the *Press and Journal* reported that he was in Glasgow, pursuing three possible signings: Bobby Clark and Dave Millar of Queen's Park and Jimmy Wilson of Morton. He came back from that trip with all three players signed, and had started the process of making the Dons side his own.

He was especially lavish in his praise of Clark, describing him as 'the best young goalkeeper he had ever seen'. Clark was 19, and in normal circumstances would have expected to play for a few seasons as understudy to 'Tubby' Ogston, the established goalkeeper. It was clear, however, that Turnbull intended to mould his own side as quickly as possible, and Clark got an early chance to prove his worth in a Summer Cup game against Dundee United. Then, as now, the clubs were desperate to squeeze some more cash out of the fans, and devised this totally absurd and superfluous competition. The game hardly counts as a début, but, for the record, the Dons lost 2–1. According to the press report, Clark's handling of crosses was impressive, but he had little else to do except pick the ball out of the net. Over the previous few seasons this had become an essential skill for a Dons goalkeeper.

Ogston went to see the manager about his position at the club, but he was in his usual place at the start of the following season, despite an uninspiring defensive display by the first team in the pre-season trial. After the first four games, he was reported as injured, and Clark made his 'real' début on 28 August in a League Cup qualifying game against Clyde. It is interesting to note that there were no Danes in the side. Nothing remarkable about that, you may think; there were no Russians or Mexicans either. However, Aberdeen had three Danes on the playing staff at the time, signed by Pearson just before his resignation. Denmark had become the fashionable place to find football talent at an affordable price. Morton had started the trend, which had been followed by Hearts and Dundee United as well as Aberdeen, and had proved their business sense in buying cheap by selling Sorensen to Rangers at a healthy profit.

Aberdeen's Danes had been less successful. After scoring a few goals in his early games, Ravn, the tall centre-forward, had proved to be too slow; Mortensen, the left-winger, had made the best early impression with his speed and skill, but had failed to adapt to the rigours of Scottish football. This is a polite way of saying that defenders had found that they could kick him off the park. Jens Petersen had made less of an initial impression, but had proved to be the best of them, and, as a defensive wing-half, went on to establish the sweeper role which Martin Buchan was to make his own. He was not to make the breakthrough until later that season, though, and the team which took the field that day was: Clark, Bennett, Shewan, Burns, McMillan, Smith, Little, Winchester, White, Scott, Wilson.

The new College of Commerce was about to admit its first students. It had been built at a cost of £745,000, and, at the time of writing, is standing derelict because of the millions it would cost to pull it down. The 'timmer market', on the other hand, was temporary yet permanent. There for only a couple of days, then gone overnight; but we knew it would always be there again the next year. 'Timmer' referred to the timber of the traditional goods sold at the market. They had long been replaced by plastic junk. (If anyone reading this ever ran a timmer market stall, I do of course make an exception in your case. I remember your stall clearly; it stood out as a beacon of quality and integrity in a sea of shoddy trinkets.) The press reported the market as 'busy', with 'pluffers less in evidence'. Pluffers less in evidence? The sole reason for going to the timmer was to buy a pluffer, a thin glass tube perfectly designed for projecting split peas, along with a good healthy dose of schoolboy saliva. There was a time and a season for everything then: football, cricket, conkers – and pluffers. The pluffer season may have been a brief one, but it was devastating while it lasted.

The Tivoli had a show called *Happy as Larry*, starring 'the fabulous Anne Shelton', while His Majesty's Theatre had the *Kenneth McKellar Show*. At the cinema, the Odeon was showing *My Fair Lady*; there's evil and riot for you. You might be forgiven for thinking that the entire population of Aberdeen was over 40, but the 1960s emerged at the Majestic with the Beatles' second film, *Help!*. On the small screen, *Top of the Pops* was required viewing at 7.30 every Thursday. The top-selling record that August was 'Help!' by the inescapable Beatles. You could have watched them mime to it on the latest 19-inch television set for only 55 guineas. Guineas? Did people still use them then? No, not unless they were buying a racehorse, but 55 guineas cheaper than it really was, and classier at the same time.

If you couldn't find the required number of guineas, you could still listen to the latest hits on a transistor radio for only 50 bob, and annoy the wifies on the bus, for it was the golden age of the trannie.

As the football season got under way, the cricket season was drawing to a close, with England playing South Africa in a Test match, but the old world was rapidly ageing, and South Africa as it was would have no part in the new. In the football world, it was the dawning of the age of the football manager, with the focus of attention shifting from the players to the man in charge. In their very different ways, Bill Shankly and Don Revie had made their marks in England, and Jock Stein, having been given the credit for working miracles at Dunfermline, was about to work an even greater miracle at Parkhead. No one expected miracles of Eddie Turnbull, and he did not promise them. His promise was of the 'blood, toil, tears and sweat' variety. He made it clear from the beginning that the main ingredients of his formula for success were physical fitness and 100 per cent effort.

He had also made it clear how highly he regarded Clark's talents, and Ogston could see that his future at Pittodrie was limited under the new régime. Clark had an auspicious début with a shut-out against Clyde, and retained his place for the following game against Hearts. Ogston returned for the game against Rangers, and did his cause no good by losing four goals, despite a good performance. Clark took over again the following week, when Ogston was reported as having a muscle strain. He had been watched by Liverpool, who were looking for an understudy to Tommy Lawrence. A bid followed soon afterwards, and Ogston was on his way, leaving Clark, at the age of 19, as the undisputed tenant between the sticks.

He immediately showed himself to be an improvement on his predecessor by conceding only seven goals at Parkhead; in the previous season's corresponding fixture the Dons had lost 8–0, their worst defeat since the war. That first season was not without blemish, as Turnbull started to shape a new side. Defensive confusion between Clark and the equally untried Tommy McMillan led to a 2–1 defeat by Stirling Albion, of all sides, which meant that, following the 2–2 draw at Pittodrie earlier in the season, the Dons had failed to beat Stirling Albion. A fumble from a straightforward header contributed to a 2–1 defeat by Motherwell. Against that, there was a penalty save against Morton and a good number of solid performances. Overall, it was a satisfactory first season for such a young goalkeeper.

The following season was to bring the first hints of the success to come under Eddie Turnbull's leadership. The goals against column went down from 54 to 38, the lowest since that far-off championship season of 1954–55, and the Dons reached the Cup final. Once again, their opponents were Celtic. Only the wildest optimist believed that the Dons could actually beat them, for that was the season when they won every trophy they competed for. They had yet to win the European Cup, but the belief was growing that, with Jock Stein at the helm, anything was possible. Certainly, Aberdeen (without Eddie Turnbull, who was too ill to be at the game) gave the impression that Celtic were invincible in a Cup final. It was not an inspiring game, even for Celtic, who won 2–0 without having to play well. They scored on either side of half-time, and the game was effectively over. Once again an Aberdeen side had gone to Hampden and failed to beat an Old Firm team. Nevertheless, the season had, by recent standards, been a satisfactory one, and the foundations had been laid for future success. More immediately, the Dons were in Europe as beaten finalists.

Their improvement was maintained the following season, with another solid defensive performance in the league; they finished in fifth position, but with the third-best 'goals against' column. Clark was establishing his own reputation as one of the most reliable goalkeepers in the country, and his consistency was rewarded in November 1967 with his first cap, against Wales. There was a devaluation crisis at the time, but then there always was. It was a midweek international, which meant that Clark had to miss *Coronation Street* and *Juke Box Jury* for the honour of representing his country. His fellow sufferers were: Craig (Celtic), McReadie (Chelsea), Greig (Rangers), McKinnon (Rangers), Baxter (Sunderland), Johnstone (Celtic), Bremner (Leeds United), Gilzean (Tottenham Hotspur), Johnston (Rangers), Lennox (Celtic). They won 3–2. Clark, according to the match report, 'did not let his country down', and preserved his side's narrow lead near the end with a brilliant save from a Ron Davies header.

Another cap followed in 1968, against Holland, but before adding to those two early caps he was to lose his place in both club and international side in one of the more bizarre episodes in his career. The man who replaced him in both teams was Ernie McGarr.

To lose five goals in a game is unfortunate, but to lose six in the next looks a little like carelessness. That is what happened to Clark in successive games against Dunfermline and Hibs at the beginning of December 1968. The following Saturday, McGarr, who had been producing some spectacular displays for the reserves, was in goal against Airdrie, and was to keep his place for the following year. During that time, his good form continued for the first team, and it began to look as though Clark would have to look elsewhere for a first-team place. The feeling was reinforced when McGarr won a place in the national team, to complete one of the most meteoric rises in the Scottish game. His absence on international duty at least gave Clark the opportunity to play for the first team, in November 1969, but such was McGarr's form at the time that there seemed no chance of replacing him permanently.

This change of fortunes was strange enough, but the bizarre part of the episode came in September 1969, when Clark took the Fred Martin route in reverse, and appeared for the Dons in an outfield role. He had played for the reserves as a defender to such good effect that he was named as a substitute for the game against Rangers at Ibrox on 3 September. Coming on with about ten minutes to go, he could do little to alter the flow of a game which was always running against Aberdeen, and which was eventually lost 2–0. His presence in the squad did, however, give him the chance to see McGarr's brilliance at close quarters, for he put on a display which did more than any other to earn him a place in the Scotland team. He was described in the match report as 'hero number-one in a heroic team . . . time and again he averted danger when a goal seemed inevitable, and even the foiled Rangers attackers were forced to congratulate him on occasions'.

He was brilliant again in the match with Celtic the following week, and it began to look as though Clark's only chance of returning to the first team was as an outfield player. That was exactly what he did the following week against St Johnstone, when he appeared in the number 6 jersey. Turnbull had described him as the 'best header of a ball at Pittodrie', which makes you wonder what else they were in the habit of heading at the hallowed ground – bricks? It would have explained a lot. The match report did not question his heading skills, but raised considerable doubts about his ability to make the grade as an outfield player, his main defect being a lack of pace. He was involved in the loss of the third goal, when he was caught in possession, and he was not given the opportunity to repeat the mistake.

Faced with the task of replacing an international goalkeeper at Pittodrie, Clark was close to signing for Rangers at the beginning of 1970, when his fortunes at Pittodrie took a turn for the better. Just as quickly as he had emerged from the shadows, Ernie McGarr sank back into them. Maybe he was just a 1960s kind of guy, for as soon as the 1970s came along he seemed to lose confidence, and by February Clark was back in the side, celebrating with a win against Clydebank in the second round of the Scottish Cup, followed by four successive shut-outs.

He could not have come back at a better time, for that game against Clydebank was to be a staging post on the way to glory. It is tempting to attribute the success in the 1970 final to the experience gained in the losing final of 1967, but it was experience retained only by Clark and Tommy McMillan, such had been the turnover in players. Jim Forrest had experience of the big occasion with Rangers, but none of the other players had known anything like it; yet, faced with Celtic, one of the finest teams in Europe, in front of a crowd of almost 110,000, they rose to the occasion, just as surely as previous Dons sides had been overwhelmed by it, and produced what was at that time the greatest single moment in the club's history.

So effectively did Martin Buchan marshal the Dons defence that Clark was not seriously tested. He dealt capably with everything that came his way, although he was involved in a controversial incident when Lennox knocked the ball from his hand and put the ball in the net, only to have the goal disallowed. The referee's decision was perfectly correct, Lennox having used a hand, but a large proportion of the crowd, many of them clad in green and white, did not see it that way. Nor did they wholly agree with the referee's penalty decisions, one granted to Aberdeen, one denied to Celtic. No matter; when the whistle blew for the last time that day, the victory was Aberdeen's, and it must have tasted especially sweet to Clark and McMillan, the survivors from the disappointment of 1967.

The next day was the day I lost faith in the *Sunday Times*. According to their reporter, the Aberdeen fans had chanted, 'The cup will be ours for the first time since 1947.' Now I ask you, does that sound like a football chant? Does it sound remotely like any football chant that you have ever heard? So the piece was written in a pub from which the reporter clearly never managed to emerge. I don't mind that. I'd never want the facts to get in the way of a good match report. But I do insist that the pub should at least be on the way to the ground, and that the reporter should at least have been to a match at some time in his life. Obviously, as it was only the Scottish Cup, the *Sunday Times* gave the job to their greenest recruit, who had a theatre review to do that same evening, so he was sent off with some reference books and a trannie, so that he would at least get the result right to go along with the background information. So he went to the pub nearest the tube station that he would have used to get to Euston, which is the station he would have used to get to Glasgow if he had been going to the game, so that you *could* say the pub was on the way to the ground. Fair enough. So he was able to get some of the local atmosphere into his report, give his readers the feeling of the crowd, that sort of thing. And what was the crowd saying? Well, they chant, don't they? And what would the Aberdeen fans chant? Look up the record books. 'Last time they won the bally thing was 1947. Got it. The cup will be ours for the first time since 1947. Sounds jolly authentic. Same again, please, barman.' If I hadn't been in such a state of euphoria over the Dons' success, and if I had actually bought the paper, I would have cancelled my subscription, but in the afterglow of triumph I let it pass.

How a team reacts to success is as much a test as the reaction to failure; to some it is a pinnacle from which they can only fall, to others a hilltop offering a view of still greater heights. The last Aberdeen team to win the Cup had suffered a slump in their fortunes the following season, falling from third in the 1946–47 league campaign to tenth in 1947–48. The league champions of 1954–55 had enjoyed a reasonably successful season in 1955–56, but had then gone into a steep decline. There was no danger of that happening to Eddie Turnbull's Aberdeen side. With the vital addition of Steve Murray from Dundee, who had been ineligible to play in the final, the Hampden victory seemed to give them the self-belief which previous Aberdeen teams had lacked, and which often seemed to be the sole prerogative of the Old Firm sides. Until that successful cup run, Turnbull had followed a policy of frequent team changes, constantly seeking the right blend. Pittodrie had come to resemble Joint Station as players arrived and departed; witness the virtually complete turnover between the two Cup finals. Now he seemed at last to have the side he wanted, and the time was right to let it play. As manager, he had used as many as 26 players in the course of a season. In 1970–71 he was to use only 19, and of these George Murray, Jim Whyte and Derek 'Cup-tie'

Mackay only played a handful of games. For most of the season the line-up was virtually unchanged from week to week, and once again we had a team that rolled off the tongue, one that could be taught to the generations yet to come: Clark, Boel, Hermiston; Murray, McMillan, Buchan; Forrest, Robb, Harper, Taylor or Willoughby, Graham. It was the team which embarked on a run of 15 successive victories, starting on 10 October, that was to see them surge past Celtic by beating them at Parkhead and set a course for the championship. It was a run which also provided Clark with his finest hour.

To be more precise, it provided him with his finest nineteen and a quarter hours, for that was the playing time which elapsed between Hamilton's goal for St Mirren on 24 October and Stanton's goal for Hibs on 16 January. It was a run which broke all records, broke the hearts of the opposing forwards, and blew the minds (it was a time when minds were blown, man) of all those who had watched the profligate Dons sides of the early-1960s. It was achieved largely without heroics or panic; Martin Buchan seemed to have everything so well organised that the thought of conceding a goal was hardly allowed to intrude. On the rare occasions that the opposition were given a glimpse of goal, Clark had invariably anticipated the danger, and was in position to save with the minimum of fuss.

There were exceptions, of course. When Aberdeen beat Celtic to over-take them at the top of the league, it was largely thanks to a staunch rearguard action in the face of overwhelming pressure after Harper's goal had momentarily stunned Parkhead. There is nothing so eerie as a crowd of over 60,000 suddenly reduced to total silence; you begin to wonder if your hearing has gone. It's like the westerns: 'It's quiet. Too quiet. I don't like it. I don't like it one little bit.' Sure enough, the Injuns appeared over the ridge, and Celtic poured everything into attack. For all the pressure, the Dons seldom looked like conceding a goal until almost the last minute, when Clark was given the opportunity to prove that a team with title aspirations needs a goalkeeper as much as it needs strikers. Harper's goal had put both points in Aberdeen's grasp, but it took Clark's save from a Macari header, low down at his left-hand post, to keep them.

The rest of that memorable campaign is described in the chapter on Joe Harper. A small, select band of us followed the campaign trail, Broonser and I having been joined by Victor and Peter. Actually, we weren't all that select; all you really needed was the price of a share of the petrol and you were in.

It was a long and hard campaign. After all the excitement and the tension, the fear of failure, the dream of success, it finally fizzled out at Brockville. The only ambition we achieved that season was a pint in the Cathkin Inn on the way back from Falkirk. We had all of us, Broonser, Peter, Victor and I, passed it on the way to and from Glasgow at one time or another, and felt that we owed it to the dear departed Third Lanark to have a drink in the place called Cathkin. So we drank to them, and to the Dons, and to victory which had been in our sights, and to the success which would surely follow.

It did not. Not the next season, nor the one after that. Buchan went, then Harper, and the side which had promised so much disintegrated. Turnbull went, too, but Clark stayed, and returned to the Scotland side. Fittingly, his return was at Pittodrie, in a European Championship qualifying game against Belgium. Martin Buchan and Steve Murray also played in a game which Scotland won 1–0, but which was most notable for the introduction of Kenny Dalglish as a second-half substitute, and for the time when an Aberdeen crowd sang the praises of Jimmy Johnstone.

Broonser watched the game with his football boots hanging round his neck. When he wasn't watching Aberdeen, he was down at Inverdee, the local amateur pitches, displaying his boots to advertise his availability on a 'have boots, will play' basis, and quite often got a game. For some reason, he thought that Scotland might be short of a player that night, and hung around the players' entrance for ages, in a gesture at once gloriously hopeful, and yet utterly, utterly hopeless. I suppose that, with Johnstone in the team, and the sea near by, there was always the chance of a late emergency: 'Jimmy's whit? O'er the horizon? Hing oan, did I no' see somebody ootside wi' his boots?' As history records, the call never came, and Broonser was disappointed, not for the first time.

Clark remained as first-choice Scotland goalkeeper for the rest of that season, and had accumulated 16 caps by the time of the SFA Centenary international against England at Hampden in February 1973. As James Forbes had expressed confidence in Martin's abilities almost 20 years previously, so Colin Farquharson did for Clark: 'It will be Clark's 17th full international appearance and on his current form he won't let Scotland down.' Scotland lost 5–0. In his match report, Farquharson said that Clark was not to blame, but one of the photographs showed him flat-footed as one of Channon's goals went in. It was a cold night at Hampden, so cold that the pee froze in the lager can before it could be tipped down the terracing (we were in a middle-class section of the crowd), but it felt colder still as the English goals went in. It was hardly the most vital of games, but it was against England. Clark did not play for Scotland again.

He continued as a virtual fixture in the Dons side for the rest of the 1970s. Managers came and went after Turnbull: Bonthrone, MacLeod, McNeill and Ferguson. Clark continued to keep goal in the same manner, calm, competent, always thoroughly professional, his one concession to 'flash' goalkeeping being the ability to cut out crosses with a distinctive one-handed catch.

A League Cup medal came, somewhat fortunately, against Celtic in

1976. The Dons came close to both league and cup success under Billy McNeill in 1977–78, but, with his career drawing to a close, his chance of completing the full set of domestic medals appeared to have gone when the Dons lagged far behind Celtic at the beginning of 1980.

By the beginning of May the rest of the country was gripped by the siege of the Iranian Embassy, but on the eve of the match at Easter Road there was only one story in Aberdeen: 'The Dons can become soccer immortals', ran the headline in typically understated fashion. Aberdeen went on to destroy Hibs 5–0, and, 15 years to the day after he joined the club, Clark completed his medal collection. He was hardly mentioned in a report which was all about Aberdeen on the attack, but he would not have minded that. He was mentioned by Alex Ferguson: 'I am particularly pleased for players such as Bobby Clark and Drew Jarvie. For them the title win comes as a climax to fine football careers.'

It was not his last game for the Dons. That came the following Wednesday, when the team completed the formalities of the league pro-gramme against Partick Thistle at Firhill. The line-up that day was: Clark, Kennedy, Rougvie, McMaster, McLeish, Miller, Jarvie, Archibald, McGhee, Watson, Scanlon (Bell). After 15 years, all the players Clark had started with had long since gone, and seemed to belong to another era. He had joined Aberdeen when footballers wore short-back-and-sides haircuts, whatever the contemporary fashions; he had seen them grow long hair and moustaches and become part of the entertainment industry. In 1965, Harold Wilson's Labour government was about one year into its first term of office; in May 1980, Margaret Thatcher was completing her first year as Prime Minister. He had seen his outfield colleagues wear a far greater variety of football strips than any of his predecessors, although he was spared the more outlandish patterns of the 1990s, and was probably glad to wear a plain goalkeeper's top rather than the dazzling creations of later years. When he started, Tommy Docherty had just begun his footballing travels; when he left, Docherty was on the move again, this time from Queens Park Rangers. In 1965, the Rolling Stones were causing outrage the length of Britain with evil and riotous living; in 1980, they were still recording, still touring, and had practically become part of the establishment.

In all that time Bobby Clark played 592 games and scored not a single goal. In contrast, Marc De Clerck scored one goal in only two appearances, which makes Clark's scoring record pretty pathetic, but I don't think we'll hold that against the first player to win a full set of domestic winner's medals with Aberdeen.

The Full-backs

Full-back is the position which, perhaps more than any other, marks the boundary between the traditional and the modern game. In most positions, the old-time player has his modern counterpart: the centre-forward may have been replaced by the striker, but the stocky Benny Yorston of the 1920s was to have his 1970s successor in Joe Harper; and when goalscorers of that variety have not been available, managers have always been ready to turn to the tall, bustling centre-forward to terrorise defences.

To counter this threat, defences have usually relied on tall centre-halves or, in modern parlance, central defenders, with a commanding physical presence. There have been exceptions, such as Eddie Falloon, the Dons' centre-half of the 1930s, and Alex Young of the 1955 League Champions, but in general a Scottish defence without a tall central pillar is regarded as being of unsound construction.

Wing-halves have come in all shapes and sizes, and their transformation into midfield players has not altered their physical types; the hard-tackling ball-winner, such as Neil Simpson, had his predecessor in an earlier age – Jackie Allister, for example – just as the more slightly built ball-player has been seen down the years in the shape of Willie Mills, Bobby Wishart and Gordon Strachan. Wingers have been tall and elegant (such as Alex Jackson) and scurrying terriers (Jimmy Wilson).

In Jock Hutton, the Dons had a full-back who was not exactly unique in his physical type but who would appear as some archaeological find in the modern game. At five foot eight inches and over fifteen stone he was built for strength rather than speed. Although he is reputed to have been surprisingly nippy for one of his size, it is hard to imagine him overlapping, but this would have been regarded as no disadvantage in his playing days.

The 1948 edition of the *Encyclopaedia Britannica*, under the entry for Association Football, describes the goalkeeper's position as 'fixed' and the full-back's as 'semi-fixed'. In other words, the full-back was expected to move, but not much. What he was expected to do was to stop the opposing winger, and anything which interfered with this basic function, such as joining the attack, would have been regarded as a dereliction of duty. To this end, a bit of physical strength did not go amiss, especially when the shoulder charge was accepted as a legitimate challenge, and in this regard Jock Hutton was not found wanting.

Hutton is no more than a name to me, but it is a name I grew up with, a historical name like William the Conqueror or Napoleon, which had acquired legendary status, and for me he is an inescapable choice as one of the full-backs for this book. Who, then, is to be the other?

For most of the 1930s, the left-back spot was the property of Charlie McGill, a product of Darvel Juniors who had arrived at Pittodrie via the USA. He had a similarly uncomplicated approach to the game as Hutton, his main strategy being to boot the ball into the crowd and attempt to retain possession by claiming the resulting throw-in. It was the kind of tactic which may have worked in the Ayrshire Junior League, where the attitude to the game is, shall we say, uncompromising, but all it gained him in senior football was the nickname Oor Ba' McGill and a regular game at left-back for the Dons.

Hutton had his post-war counterpart in Don Emery, a man of similar barrel-like build and ferocious shooting power. The latter's free-kicks and penalties were eagerly anticipated by supporters and dreaded by the opposition. Any defender lining up in a wall to face one of Emery's free-kicks must have felt all of a sudden that there was a better place to be on a Saturday afternoon, such as the stand, or the pictures, or maybe the hospital. On a wet day such a defender was likely to finish up there in any case if he managed to get in the way of an Emery thunderbolt or, more accurately, failed to get out of the way. At that time, when footballs were made of absorbent leather, a player of Emery's power could transform a wet ball into a lethal weapon.

If scoring records give any clue to styles of play or tactics, Emery's record of 25 goals in 125 games appears to give the lie to the notion that the attacking full-back is a relatively recent development. However, 11 of that total were scored from penalties, and of the remainder five were scored when he was moved to the centre-forward position, with most of the others coming from his thunderous free-kicks.

The goalscoring full-back did not appear until the 1960s, with Ally Shewan and Jim Whyte scoring nine apiece in their Aberdeen careers, and Jim Hermiston getting 16. Their predecessors of the 1950s, Mitchell and Caldwell, failed to score a single goal between them in over 450 appearances, while the 1930s partnership of Cooper and McGill scored only four in over 650 games. They were full-backs who knew their place.

By way of contrast are the modern, overlapping full-backs. None was fitter or faster than Stuart Kennedy, and Gordon Strachan has acknowledged his contribution to his own attacking play. If Strachan dragged the ball inside, Kennedy was always ready to support the attack by moving into the space created on the wing, and his pace allowed him to catch many a pass that would have eluded a slower player.

After Kennedy's premature retirement, his place was taken by Stuart McKimmie. If the latter was not quite as fast as Kennedy, he was no slouch, and his wider range of skills enabled him to play at sweeper and in midfield when required. Although he consistently supported the attack, he did not score many goals, but those he did were memorable. In the 1983–84 season he scored the goal against Hearts at Tynecastle which secured the league championship; playing for Scotland against Argentina, he scored the goal which beat the world champions. Both goals were scored from well inside the penalty area, a position which would have felt distinctly alien to full-backs of an earlier era.

Together with the maturing David Robertson, McKimmie formed perhaps the finest full-back partnership Aberdeen has had since the war, with McKimmie's all-round skills and composure complemented on the other flank by Robertson's pace. Never straying far from his beat along the left flank, Robertson added to his attacking armoury a long throw which could convert the seemingly innocuous concession of a throw-in into a dangerous set-piece. He has developed his range of skills still further and become a more complete footballer, but, alas, in another place. Now that he has moved to Leeds United, we can genuinely wish him well in his future career.

If the scrawny Robertson would have seemed a strange choice of full-back to crowds accustomed to the likes of Hutton and Emery, his replacement on the other flank would have been totally unrecognisable as a member of the species. Yet the slightly built Stephen Wright, forever giving the impression that he had borrowed his big brother's football strip, looked like being the best of them all. From his first appearance he showed the confidence which marks out the international player, the kind of confidence shown in their early appearances by Charlie Cooke and Tommy Craig, and the all-round skill, the time to play the ball, which distinguishes the true footballer. In the modern game it is no longer sufficient for the full-back to have purely defensive qualities; he is required to be an all-round player. Paul Breitner of West Germany was the one who showed the way, but in an Aberdeen jersey no one epitomised the ideal better than Stephen Wright. It is unfortunate that he, too, chose to pursue his career in a jersey of another hue, and doubly unfortunate that his career should have been so seriously disrupted by injury.

In an earlier age, it was enough for the full-back to be simply a defender, although there were also players like Donald Colman and Hutton's partner, Matt Forsyth, who had a more expansive vision of the full-back's role. Conversely, the robust full-back has been a popular figure, at least with his own supporters, from the earliest period up until fairly recent times, from Hutton to Emery through to that cheerful assassin, Doug Rougvie.

But, with no full-backs of any real character emerging in the 1990s, for our other subject we go back to a period only slightly later than Hutton's, to a man who filled Aberdeen's right-back position longer than any other. The periods in which these other full-backs played are discussed in the chapters on other players in this volume. Willie Cooper represents the 1930s, the 'hungry '30s', that 'low, mean, dishonest decade'. There was never anything low, or mean, or dishonest in Willie Cooper. If he represents the 1930s, he also represents integrity, effort and loyalty.

Jock Hutton

There is nothing as vivid or as elusive as a childhood memory. Incidents recalled from many years ago can seem more real, and certainly more exciting, than the daily routine of actuality; yet we can never be sure if they really happened the way we remember them, or even if they happened at all. Are we remembering what happened, or what we have been told, so often that the tale has become an event? Reality recedes, the memory remains and becomes the story of our life as we tell it to ourselves. The stories that others recount, if well told, become part of that story too, and extend our lives to a time before we were born.

Old Jock, our downstairs neighbour, loved to talk of old times, and made the Great War part of my story. His tales were tailored to youthful sensibilities, and I didn't wake up screaming with the horrors of war or trench foot. He talked of the French villages and the wine, and shooting pears off the trees in the orchards, and made it all sound like a great adventure, no different from the 'Bang! You're dead!' games of Japs and Jerries or Cowboys and Indians we enjoyed before we started the serious business of playing football.

And a serious business it was. The first step to glory was to get into the school team, not an easy task in those huge post-war classes, especially when you had no aptitude for the game. It is in moments of doubt and crisis that a father's advice can change a young life. Mine told me to learn to kick with my left foot, because teams were always looking for left-footers. So I practised kicking with my left foot against the back-green wall, until my dad told me he meant me to kick the *ball* against the wall, but by that time I had developed a bit of strength in the left foot, so the time wasn't entirely wasted. It was about the only football Old Jock could watch by that time, as he was more or less confined to the house, and there wasn't a lot on television. So that was his football for most of the time –

me kicking the ball against the back-green wall, left foot, left foot, left foot. Sometimes I'd vary it by playing at goalies, kicking it so that I'd have to dive to save the rebound. What he couldn't see was that when I saved the rebound, I was Fred Martin, saving from Willie Bauld or Tom Finney or Ferenc Puskas, depending on the competition I was playing; when I didn't save it, I was George Niven or Bert Williams or Grosics diving vainly to save a Paddy Buckley thunderbolt, as the Dons or Scotland swept to another triumph. He probably thought I was just a crap goalkeeper. Or maybe he did know, because he'd played the same games himself, and could hear the roar of the crowd as clearly as I could.

He talked about football before the Great War, when he had played in goal for a local junior team, Parkvale. I could tell him all the facts I had learned in my swotty way about the early days of Scottish football: Queen's Park, and how they weren't beaten for years; Vale of Leven, who beat them in 1876; Renton, who beat West Bromwich Albion in 1888 and became Champions of the World. He marvelled that one small head could carry all it knew. But he had founded Parkvale, one of the great names of Aberdeen Junior football, and he could show me the lamp-post where it had been founded by him and a few of his mates. All the stuff I knew was out of books, but he had been there at the Dawn of Football. He could tell me what the Wembley Wizards looked like, Alex James, Alex Jackson, Alan Morton and all, and spoke about Scottish players before them. I don't suppose he told me he had played for Scotland, but in my mind he had, and when we were redecorating our flat, and my father and I had stripped the old varnished wallpaper down to the bare plaster, I drew a picture of him, saving a penalty, with the inscription: 'Jock Priestly saves a penalty for Scotland against England at Hampden Park, 1903. Final score 2–1 Scotland.' Pure rubbish, of course. Scotland did beat England that year, but the game was played at Bramall Lane, and Jock was not in goal. (In fact, Scotland's home games at that time were played mainly at Parkhead; Hampden did not become the international venue until 1906.)

Still, after we had stripped the walls, it was Jock, a retired decorator, who papered them, and the drawing pleased him no end. He talked, too, of Dons players of the early years, before and just after the war, players even my father didn't know about: Donald Colman and Jock Hume; Willie Lennie, Vic Milne; and one name above all others.

Jock Hutton joined Aberdeen just after the Great War. The servicemen had returned to be promised 'a land fit for heroes', but for many this meant unemployment and poverty. Football, which had established itself as the major working-class spectator sport before the war, provided one of the few escapes from the recent horrors of war and the grim reality of peace. There must have been a great need for popular heroes who did not go round killing people; Hutton fulfilled that need by stopping just short of killing opposing wingers, and became a Pittodrie legend. He could have been the model for Desperate Dan, with a large-jawed head mounted, without the intervention of a neck, on a great barrel of a body.

There were few wingers then, or at any time, who could have withstood a shoulder-charge from Hutton, and many who would rather not risk it. In his black-and-gold collarless jersey, stretched to breaking-point, he must have presented an obstacle as formidable as the Maginot Line. In contrast to the modern whippet of a full-back, forever scampering up and down the touchline in a new designer outfit every other game, Hutton stuck steadfastly to his post in a jersey that looks exactly the same in every photograph throughout his Aberdeen career. Indeed, I strongly suspect that it *was* the same jersey, and he looks the sort who wouldn't have bothered taking it off between matches. After all, stretched as it was, it must have taken a bit of effort to get it on, and if there's a match next week, why bother? It would have given wingers, a notoriously fastidious breed, another reason to give him a wide berth.

He was signed in May 1919, and made his début in the first game of the 1919–20 season, on 16 August. The front page of the local paper, then known as the *Aberdeen Daily Journal*, consisted of classified advertising, as was then the custom, but the headlines on the inside pages had a certain familiar ring: 'Chicago Race Riots'; 'With the stubborn attitude of the Yorkshire miners the industrial outlook is once again very black'. Royal reporting was frank ('The Royal party looked tired') but rather more sympathetic than its modern counterpart ('Surely it is time that Royalty enjoyed its nobly earned holiday'). 'Bolshevism Feared' was a headline very much of its time. A new rate of war pension was announced, 40 shillings per week for a single man, 50 shillings per week for a married man.

Amid the generally grim news, the annual general meeting of Aberdeen Football Club was announced. Tom Duncan, the chairman, reported that 'The directors had already signed on a team, well blended with youth and experience, to carry out the season's engagements.' His remarks were also directed towards the supporters, who were exhorted to 'consider themselves part of the team, and to make it their duty to give the players all the encouragement they could, because the knowledge that they had the sympathy of the crowd would nerve the players to better effort'. We can hear an echo of these remarks 60 years later, albeit expressed somewhat less formally, in Alex Ferguson's despairing pleas for vocal support and complaints about hearing the rustling of the sweetie papers in the South Stand. Pittodrie has seldom matched the raucous atmosphere of an Ibrox, a Parkhead, or the British Museum.

On 12 August the pre-season trial was announced, against a junior side, with a further plea to the spectators: 'The management announce that season tickets will be on sale at the ground,' expressing the hope that 'supporters of the club will avail themselves of these tickets', and announcing that 'ladies may also purchase season tickets'. It was promised that these tickets would represent a significant saving on the price of weekly admission.

Those members of the public who did not wish to see the players 'have their final test before renewing their association with the Scottish League' could have gone to His Majesty's Theatre to see *Moonstruck*, Fred Karno's latest creation described as 'entemological astronomical musical absurdity'. The Palace Theatre was showing *That's Enough*, described rather more modestly as 'that bright and breezy musical comedy'. It is not recorded how many ladies availed themselves of the opportunity to purchase season tickets, but any that did could have helped themselves squeeze into the crowd with the help of one of the six hundred pairs of ladies' corsets advertised as a 'special purchase' by Isaac Benzies, on sale at 2s.11d., with 'better quality' available at a whole shilling dearer. A teacher wishing to buy a pair would have had to find the price out of a starting salary of £80 per annum, and may well have decided to make do with the cheaper model. A head teacher could look forward to an annual salary of £390.

There were few cars advertised, but the Arcade Garage in Diamond Street was looking for a 'reliable man with a knowledge of motors'. Private transport was available in the form of a 6 h.p. Royal Enfield Sidecar Combination. Even this was available to only a few, and most of the 9,000 who went to Pittodrie on 18 August to see the Dons play Albion Rovers would have travelled there on foot or on the tram.

In Monday's paper it was reported that 'thousands upon thousands of delighted spectators were in attendance at the various league games'. The crowd at Pittodrie was taken as evidence that 'the Aberdeen public at least are resigned to the increased charge for admission'. The increased charge was one shilling, and those who paid it may have felt short-changed, for the play, according to the reporter, 'could not be described as brilliant'. How often those remarks were to be echoed down the years. The writer went on to damn with faint praise: 'The game, if quiet at times, was interesting throughout.'

This was the game in which Hutton made his début, not at full-back, but at centre-forward. With his massive physique he could only have been a centre-forward of what might euphemistically be described as the 'bustling' type; one who regarded any defender, and especially the goalkeeper, as a legitimate target. The newspaper commented favourably on his performance, reporting that the Aberdeen forwards, especially Hutton and Robertson, 'headed several incursions on the visitors' goal'. A couple of these were successful, and Aberdeen ran out 2–0 winners. The team which played in that first post-war game was: Anderson; Hannah,

Hume; Wright, Brewster, MacLachlan; Watson, Caie, Hutton, Robertson, Archibald.

The fact that 9,000 had turned out to see them play proved that the game had retained its appeal as a popular pastime. This was more or less the average crowd of the pre-war years, and was not just early season enthusiasm, for the average was to climb to 12,000 in that first post-war season and increase steadily over the following years as the game took more of a hold on the popular imagination.

Perhaps there was less money to spend on entertainment; perhaps it was a habit which needed just a little more time to grow – after all, it was only 16 years since Aberdeen FC had been formed, and five of these had been spent in war. At any rate, 9,000 was regarded as a good crowd, and that, together with the result, represented a satisfactory return to normality. The Dons were back in their black-and-gold jerseys and all was right with the world.

Well, not quite right. The League of Nations had been founded in January, but already the world was moving towards the next war. The National Socialist Party had been formed in Germany, and in February Mussolini had founded the Fascist Party in Italy. In Russia, Communism was already established, and the press thundered warnings against its onward march.

If defence remained a priority for the nation, then so it was for Aberdeen. There was only one answer: move Hutton to right-back. They did so on 1 May 1920, the last game of the 1919–20 season, and there he remained for the rest of his Aberdeen career. In that first season most of his appearances had been in the forward line, where he had not been entirely unsuccessful, with six goals to his credit. Once he moved to right-back, however, it was clear that he had found his true footballing home. He did not become a regular in that position until the middle of the following season, but from then until his transfer in 1926 he was virtually a fixture in the Aberdeen side.

The goals, naturally, dried up; they were now someone else's job. After that first season in the forward line, he scored a single goal with a penalty in season 1920–21, and had to wait until season 1925–26 before scoring with another two penalties. Then, in the first two months of the following season, he scored no fewer than five goals, including that rarity in those days, a full-back's goal from open play. To a goalkeeper, he must have been a terrifying sight from only 12 yards; almost 30 years later Don Emery was to conduct a similar campaign of terror, extended in his case to anywhere within shooting distance.

It is interesting to note that in those seven seasons before 1926–27, the Dons scored only ten penalties in 320 competitive games. Perhaps referees were more lenient, or perhaps Aberdeen were simply not in the opposition's penalty area often enough. During that period, when defences were supposedly less well organised, the club averaged little over a goal a game, and scored only six penalties in league games. Thirty years later, the post-war side consistently scored over two goals per game, and in 214 league games scored 23 penalties. Another 30 years on, and Alex Ferguson's triumphant side averaged two goals per game, despite a greater emphasis on defensive organisation, with 39 of their goals coming from the penalty-spot over a similar period.

Those who complain of the defensive nature of modern football should note that the Dons fans of that earlier period when Hutton was playing saw fewer goals per game (2.5) than the fans of the Ferguson era (2.8), the latter figure including goals conceded to the opposition by a notoriously parsimonious defence. Whenever the golden age of football was, it does not appear to have been the early-1920s.

Outwith football, and more especially across the Atlantic, the 1920s became known as the Jazz Age. The new, exciting, exotic music swept America after the war, went on to conquer Europe, and by 1926 had even reached Aberdeen. In October that year, the Tivoli was advertising *The Great Girl Show* entitled 'More Paris Nights', featuring L. Lenrap's Famous Charleston Dancers. Well, they were famous in the Tivoli that week. The Pavilion was offering the more familiar and homely fare of Harry Gordon's Entertainers. In an article in the local press, 'About This Jazz Business', Hugh S. Robertson, the conductor of the Glasgow Orpheus Choir, was not wholly dismissive of the new music – 'I even confess I cannot resist its infectious gaiety' – but it was clear that he was not thinking of introducing any Jelly Roll Morton numbers into his choir's repertoire.

Those who wanted to emulate L. Lenrap's dancers could do so at the New Palais de Danse, where a tea dance was two shillings, including 'dainty afternoon-tea'. There is no record of Sandy West's Jazzmen playing there and, given his robust image, it is difficult to imagine Jock Hutton sitting down to a dainty afternoon-tea, or even resisting the temptation to shoulder-charge a waitress. Anyone who preferred to listen to music at home could now do so, possibly on a Decca Portable Gramophone, offering 'amazing results from the new telesmatic system of sound reproduction', for only four pounds.

Alternatively, there was the BBC, broadcasting from Aberdeen, London, and a number of other stations. Nation could speak peace unto nation and London could speak to Aberdeen. There remained the question of whether London had anything to say to Aberdeen, and, in the minds of the natives, the question remains to this day. Nevertheless, there was a sense of wonder at hearing a voice announce 'This is London' over the wireless and, no doubt, for those with a wireless set, a sense of superiority over those without; yet, even while the wonder was still there that a voice which was not that of an Aberdeen fishwife could be heard over all that distance, a man called John Logie Baird had demonstrated television. It would not be so many years until the first televised football match – August 1936 – but it would be the best part of 30 years before London could be seen from Aberdeen, and, when it could, Aberdeen put London in its place; the first thing Aberdeen saw was the football from Hampden.

For the time being, however, if you wanted to see London you had to go there. If you didn't fancy the train journey by North British, the Aberdeen Steam Navigation Company Ltd offered a passenger and cargo steamer service to London. If you wanted to drive there, the 14/40 Vauxhall was a snip at £495.

The seven years Hutton had been at Pittodrie had been a time of rapid change, as the pace of the twentieth century had picked up. There had been changes, too, in football, with one of the most fundamental being brought about largely as a result of tactics developed by one of Hutton's brotherhood of full-backs, McCracken of Newcastle United. He is credited with perfecting offside tactics to such a degree that the law was changed in 1925. A player could now be onside with only two opponents between him and the goal, instead of three.

This change in the law was expected to produce more open play and, most important of all, more goals. Some games at the start of the season did produce unexpectedly large scores as defences struggled to adjust and forwards took advantage. By the end of the season the goals scored in the first division had gone up from the 1,178 of the previous season to 1,337. Fans watching Aberdeen games must have felt short-changed, for their games produced no more goals in season 1925–26 than previously, with an average of 1.29 for and 1.42 against. It was not until the following season that the Aberdeen fans, if not the goalkeepers, started to get the benefit of the new rules. In 1926–27 the average jumped to 1.92 for and 1.89 against, which gave the fans more or less another goal a game for their money, and, for Aberdeen supporters, produced a more acceptable ratio of goals scored to goals lost. Perhaps the forwards had needed a whole season to work out how best to exploit the new rules to their advantage.

Whether Hutton was the most tactically astute of backs is open to question. His strategy appears to have been to stop the opposing winger, and, preferably, the ball, and to dispatch the 'leather sphere' back into the opponents' half, the main object being distance rather than accuracy. According to his more stylish full-back partner, Matt Forsyth, such clearances would, as often as not, be sent straight back. This was football as trench warfare, but the fans loved him for it, and he was effective enough to win seven international caps for Scotland, a club record at the time.

It was during this period, in the autumn of 1926, that Stanley Baldwin reviewed the works of government, expressed faith in the future, and promised legislation to curb the trade unions. The women of the Kincardine and West Aberdeen Unionist Association, never the most forward-thinking of ladies, warned of the 'foreign danger' of socialist Sunday schools, dispensing 'Bolshevist poison' for children. The more familiar poison of alcohol was another subject of controversy. On the front page of the *Press and Journal* was a public notice warning of the dangers of alcohol to sportsmen, endorsed by Dr W.G. Grace, Jack Hobbs, Eric Liddell, and W.W. Beveridge, 'thrice amateur champion (running) and thrice international (football)', in case you didn't know, who warned readers that 'an athlete cannot use alcohol and be in good form on the cinderpath, at the wicket, or between the goals'. There have been a few since then who have tried to disprove that theory, with varying degrees of success.

Not that the prohibitionists had it all their own way. Below this notice was another advertising 'A Great Demonstration Against Prohibition'. Despite the strictures of Mr Beveridge, thrice amateur champion (running) though he was, one suspects that it was the latter message which struck the more sympathetic chord with the majority of Dons fans. What would have concerned them more than the future of the nation or the dangers of alcohol or the coming of Bolshevism was the departure of Jock Hutton. On 9 October he played his last game for Aberdeen.

The *Press and Journal* warned its readers that the Dons would have 'no easy task' in facing Kilmarnock, described as 'rather a mercurial side', which often rose to the heights of brilliance at home. The Aberdeen team that day was: Blackhall, Hutton, D. Bruce, Cosgrove, Edward, McLachlan, Reid, R. Bruce, Miller, McDermid, Smith. Of the players with whom Hutton had started his Aberdeen career, only McLachlan remained. His long-time partner at left-back, Matt Forsyth, had been one of the victims of the new offside law. His skill and positional sense had not been sufficient to compensate for a lack of speed, and he had lost his place after the first two games of the 1925–26 season, never to regain it.

On the Monday, the paper reported that Saturday's match had been spoilt by a gale, in which 'the ball accomplished many amusing cantrips'. The reporter concluded that 'a draw was a fitting result to an encounter either might have won'. One of Hutton's last contributions to Aberdeen's cause was to prevent Walker of Kilmarnock scoring when only ten yards from goal. Unfortunately, the referee judged the 'forcible' tackle to be a mite too forcible, even by the standards of the day, and awarded a penalty. It was missed, and Hutton left Aberdeen having saved the match rather than lost it.

He was transferred to Blackburn Rovers on 15 October for a reported fee of £4,000, and was in the side which won the FA Cup in 1928. He retired in 1933, but decades later the men who had seen him in his prime would tell their grandchildren and their grandchildren's friends of the deeds of the mighty Jock Hutton, and how he bestrode the field like a colossus, and how he would kick ball and winger back into the half from whence they had come, and, with every telling, young eyes would grow wider and he would grow larger, until the wonder was that one small field was large enough to hold him. Truly this was the stuff of legend.

Willie Cooper

Willie Cooper signed for Aberdeen in the year after Hutton left, in June 1927, taking the traditional route through junior football. The influence of organised schools football was beginning to be felt, however, for Cooper was a schoolboy international. In later years he would no doubt have turned professional straight from school, but at that time the junior clubs were an essential rung on the ladder; for Cooper, that rung was Muggiemoss Juniors.

He made his début at the end of the 1927–28 season, playing at right-back in the home game against Cowdenbeath on 14 April 1928. The Aberdeen team was: Blackwell; Cooper, Jackson; Black, McHale, Bruce; Love, Cheyne, MacFarlane, Yorston, Smith. He got off to a winning start in a 3–0 victory, but the local reporter was none too impressed: 'If the backs had an easy time in the second half, they were often stretched in the first period. Jackson, who tackled well, was the better of the two, Cooper being weak in that department and appearing to be slow.'

Well, no one ever accused Cooper of being too quick or too clever by half, but after that none too auspicious start he developed into a for-midable barrier for opposing wingers.

That first game was overshadowed by the Rangers *v* Celtic Scottish Cup final on the same day, in which the press reported 'tremendous interest'. Celtic won. The press also reported a collision between a liner, the *Montrose* of the Canadian Pacific line, and an iceberg: 'Almost a second *Titanic* disaster.' After the match, any fans still craving further excitement after watching Cowdenbeath could have gone to the Tivoli to see Florrie Forde and no doubt puffed a Players – ten for a tanner or twenty for elevenpence ha'penny.

It was a shrinking world; the wireless had already brought London to Aberdeen in an instant, and the previous year Charles Lindbergh had brought the *Spirit of St Louis* and the United States to Europe in just over a day and a half. The first talking feature film, *The Jazz Singer*, had come out in October 1927 and before long had queues stretching round the block to see and hear it.

Willie Cooper's horizons at that time were restricted to establishing himself in the Aberdeen side. Following his début against Cowdenbeath, he retained his place for the last game of the season, away to Motherwell, and again the result was a victory for Aberdeen, 2–1.

The start of the following season saw Jackson return to the right-back position, and Cooper played only three games that season. After a couple of short spells in the first team during 1929–30, he finished with a run of seven successive games, which continued with the first dozen games of the following season, but it was not until 1931–32 that he established himself in the team. He was Aberdeen's right-back for the rest of the decade. After missing a few games at the start of the 1932–33 season, he was an ever-present until 31 October 1937, setting a club record of 162 consecutive league appearances.

During this period the Dons consolidated their position as one of Scotland's leading clubs. During the 1920s they had climbed from the bottom half of the league to a place in the top ten, and from 1932 to 1939 they never finished outside the top six. No team performs consistently well in the league without a solid defence, and Cooper was nothing if not solid. Without the spectacular dimensions of a Hutton or an Emery, he lacked nothing in strength, and was a vital part of a defence which conceded on average fewer than 1.5 goals per game, a commendable performance in the 1930s.

Cooper was similarly unspectacular in his play, concentrating on his defensive duties and performing them with the minimum of fuss. The over-lapping full-back is not entirely a creation of the modern era but there is no doubt that the full-back was seen as a defensive stalwart, and anything else was a bonus. There were few bonuses from Cooper in the form of goals; in 327 appearances he scored only three times, but what cannot be measured is the number he stopped, and that was what he was getting paid for.

Being paid at all was a bonus in the 1930s. The career of a professional footballer has never been a secure one, and at that time was not a particularly well paid one, but it was a job, and Cooper appears to have been grateful to have had his contract renewed each season, the guarantee of another year's employment. He repaid the club with a series of con-sistent displays which helped to consolidate the Dons' position in Scottish football. The *Press and Journal* of 23 April 1934 gave him a typical accolade. Complaining of 'feckless finishing by Dons forwards in Aberdeen's 1–0 defeat by Hearts', the reporter praised the the defence, and Cooper in particular: 'Smith, Cooper and McGill were a sound rear trio with Cooper the most polished back on the field.'

By that time the press was beginning to see light at the end of the economic tunnel, what would in the 1990s be termed the 'green shoots of recovery'. 'A big fall in unemployment with general trade improvement' was reported, and LNER was confident enough to advertise 'A Continental Holiday' via Harwich to Flushing, Antwerp, or Zeebrugge for 120 shillings. The 'sturdy' Hillman Minx 10/30 saloon could be bought for only £159, but if you were a new driver you would now have to pass the driving test, introduced in March.

However, just as the home news was beginning to look a little brighter, abroad the clouds were gathering. Even the local papers reported 'Japan's startling new claims in the Pacific' and France's fears of German rearmament.

Sports reporting was of a more parochial nature. School sports days were described in detail, as were the results in the Upper Donside League. On 11 June the *Press and Journal* reported 'Victory for Buchan Bowlers'. No offence to Buchan or to its bowlers – great place, great guys – but what the paper did not mention was victory for Italy in the World Cup final on the previous day. What is the World Cup? Do they play football in Italy? Was there an NE man there? No? Not interested.

We should not be too hard on the local newspapers, for the national press was little better. None of the home countries participated in the competition, which, apart from the final, was therefore ignored by the press, just as the inaugural competition had been ignored four years earlier. The trophy was presented to the home country by *Il Duce*, Mussolini, who described their triumph as a victory for Fascism.

This intrusion of politics into sport was largely ignored at the time by both political and sports journalists. And if the political writers failed to see the evils of the new political régime, their sports colleagues, at a less serious level, failed to see the growing power of the foreign game. Even such an august newspaper as the *Manchester Guardian* saw fit to describe the event as the world football 'championship', putting inverted commas round a championship which no right-thinking Englishman would recognise as such without the participation of their national side. England, as everyone knew, were the true world champions, and had no need to take part in a competition to prove it.

Later that year, England got the chance to prove it by playing Italy at Wembley. The tabloids demanded a ten-goal victory, but had to be satisfied with a 3–2 win over an Italian side reduced to ten men. Four years later the *Daily Express* saw fit to describe England as world champions, with no need for inverted commas, after a victory over Germany in a politically charged game, overshadowed by the threat of war.

For Aberdeen fans it would have been enough to be Scottish champions. Throughout the decade, the Dons improved their standing until, in season 1936–37, they were runners-up to Rangers in the league, albeit seven points adrift. But the vain pursuit of the Ibrox side was forgotten as they reached their first-ever cup final, against Celtic, by way of Inverness Thistle, Third Lanark, Hamilton Accies and Morton. In the three weeks between the semi-final victory over Morton and the final itself, excitement mounted steadily.

In the week leading up to the big match, the *Press and Journal* reported a Nationalist threat to British ships as a consequence of the Spanish civil war, but these were far-off events. Of more immediate interest was the 'rush for 400 Hampden enclosure tickets', with 'young man's vigil in early morning' and 'woman's four-mile walk' the human cost of obtaining the precious documents. On the Wednesday, ever alert to the great events of the day, the paper reported: 'Two young men went cycling up Union Street on the first stage of their journey to Glasgow. There was no need to ask if they were off to cheer the Dons. On their heads were black-and-gold berets, and strapped to the rear of their machines were all the paraphernalia for overnight stops under canvas.'

Jack Anthony was at the Tivoli with *Giggles and Girls* and Harry Gordon was, as ever, at the Pavilion, but they must have wondered if it was worth opening on Saturday as they saw Aberdeen leave *en masse* for Glasgow and glory. It is estimated that between 20,000 and 30,000 Aberdeen fans made the journey, an unprecedented number in an era when large travelling supports were very much the exception. They helped to swell the Hampden crowd to over 146,000, which remains a British record for a game between club sides. Perhaps the vast crowd put the Aberdeen side at a disadvantage against a Celtic team who were used to playing before large crowds, for the Dons failed to rise to the occasion and suffered an honourable defeat by the odd goal in three.

They had fought back courageously after losing an early goal to equalise almost immediately, but Buchan scored the decisive goal for Celtic with 20 minutes to go and ensured that the only silverware on the train back to Aberdeen would be in the hands of the waiters serving high-tea in the dining-car.

Wasn't it wonderful how they could pour the coffee and milk into the cup at the same time from a height of about seven feet while the train was shoogling round a bend and never spill a drop? It didn't make it taste any better – let's be honest, it usually tasted like it had come out of the engine – but the ceremony of the pouring was a real work of art. You don't criticise a painting because it doesn't taste nice. Nor would you have criticised the railway waiters or their coffee, for the very good reason that their deadly aim could just as easily be switched to your lap, with potentially devastating results. Credit where it's due; those waiters were artists, practitioners of an art form now sadly lost in the age of the Maxpax. We shall not see their like again.

Nor, in the days of all-seated stadiums, shall we see the like of that Hampden crowd again. To the Aberdeen section of it, the wonders of railway catering were deemed to be of minor importance. Too many of their heroes had failed to play to their full potential on the day, and Willie Mills in particular had been a star who had failed to shine.

On the Monday even the *Press and Journal* reported that Celtic were 'deserving of success'. Having predicted a Dons victory – how could it do otherwise? – it offered as the 'most feasible explanation' that the Aberdeen players were 'affected by nerves'. A reporter from a later period might have referred to a lack of self-belief, a common failing in provincial sides playing against Old Firm sides in Glasgow. Although Aberdeen were to win the cup ten years later, it would be more than 30 years before they could go to Glasgow believing they could beat an Old Firm side in a cup final, and another decade after that before they would go there *expecting* to win.

Of Cooper, the report said that he 'found Murphy an elusive opponent, and was sometimes disconcerted by the winger's speed, but worked hard throughout'. He never did any less. For those of us too young to have seen the final, it is captured by the photograph of Cooper in dogged pursuit of the great Celtic centre-forward, Jimmy McGrory, against a solid backdrop of spectators. It is a picture which somehow symbolises the game, the season and the whole decade for Aberdeen – always chasing, but never quite catching, the Old Firm.

The Aberdeen team that day was: Johnstone, Cooper, Temple; Dunlop, Falloon, Thomson; Benyon, MacKenzie, Armstrong, Mills, Lang. Cooper was the only survivor of the side in which he had made his début in 1928; it was a team which had started to take shape in 1932–33, when Falloon, Benyon, Armstrong and Mills had all played.

Broadcasting of football matches was commonplace by then. Television had been invented more than ten years previously, but had not made any impact on the public, and certainly not on the sporting public. If you wanted to see an event, you went to the stadium, which is what 146,000 souls had done that Saturday. How much they actually saw of the game was another matter. To judge by some of the letters to the press, not much.

It was later that same year that football was first broadcast on television. It was a programme about Arsenal – so often the innovators at that time – and their training, and it was soon to be followed by the televising of the 1938 FA Cup final. No one at the time could have guessed the impact that television would eventually have on the game. But, with a tiny television audience, that was still some time in the future.

Throughout the 1920s and 1930s football continued to be the main form of Saturday-afternoon entertainment, with Pittodrie crowds averaging between 12,000 and 14,000 over the period. In the successful

1936–37 season, they averaged 17,000. More remarkable to the modern fan, used to audiences restricted for safety reasons, are the huge crowds of over 30,000 who squeezed into the ground for the 'big' games against the Old Firm. Those huge 'gates' were a feature of the mid- to late-1930s.

To accommodate the fans, the wing stand at the Beach End was built on the site of the old pavilion in 1937. To provide a modicum of comfort for the standing spectator, a roof had been erected over the King Street End three years previously, but in general it was up to the fan to provide his own overhead protection from the elements in the form of the ubiquitous 'bunnet'. Crowd photographs of the period show a solid phalanx of bunnets, broken only by the occasional trilby, stretching upwards to a horizon clouded by cigarette smoke; the inescapable conclusion is that no one, save the very young, was admitted to the ground without some form of headgear and a packet of Woodbines.

According to Broonser's dad, such photographs were faked. He said that the crowd was packed together into a small section of the terracing, partly to make the picture look good, and partly to conceal the fact that the fans in the middle of the crowd weren't wearing any trousers. These were the fans who had to pawn their trousers to get into the game. So Broonser's dad said, but I always found it strange that they had pawned their trousers rather than their bunnets.

On the pitch, too, there were changes. Having played in black-and-gold strips since 1904, the club changed its colours to red and white in March 1939. Changing more than 30 years of tradition was never going to be greeted with unanimous approval, but by September of that year even the most obsessive Dons fan had something else to occupy his mind.

With the onset of war, Willie Cooper went back to his trade of marine engineer, and must have thought that his career as a full-time professional footballer was over. Seven years later, there was a hole in the ground where the Palace Hotel had stood in Union Street; in the east end of the city there were gaps like broken teeth in rows of tenements; but Cooper was still at right-back for the Dons. In fact he did not play at Pittodrie until 5 October in that first post-war season, against Motherwell in a League Cup qualifying game. But what a reassuring sight he must have been as he trotted to his usual position, as though he had never been away. Cooper was at right-back, and things were back to normal.

The League Cup was a competition in which Aberdeen were to do well that season, reaching the final only to fall at the last hurdle, this time against the other half of the Old Firm. Once again Cooper found himself on the losing side at Hampden. The real glory was to come in the Scottish Cup, but Cooper would be denied the ultimate success. It is an irony of a career notable for its longevity, consistency and a record number of con-secutive appearances that he is remembered more for one game he missed than the matches, all 373 of them, that he played.

When the Dons were drawn against 'B' Division Arbroath in the semi-final, hope grew into anticipation that this might at last be their year. On 12 April Scotland were playing England at Wembley, but for Aberdonians the semi-final venue of Dens Park was the centre of the universe. Those among them who had already booked their seats on the Glasgow train must have suffered a few anxious moments as their favourites made rather heavy weather of beating a spirited but undistinguished Arbroath side, eventually winning 2–0. The disappointment at failing to reach the final could have been borne, even the humiliation of losing to inferior opposition, but, oh, to waste the price of a train fare! Still, in the end it wasn't wasted. The Dons were there, with genuine hope of winning the cup. But not with Willie Cooper.

On the Monday before the final, the *Press and Journal* ran the headline: 'Fate Plays Willie Cooper a Scurvy Trick'. He had pulled a muscle in the closing stages of the semi-final and had to be regarded as 'a very doubtful starter against Hibs in the Scottish Cup final'. The paper described the injury as 'a tough break for a great-hearted player', and for the rest of the week ran medical bulletins on his progress as though reporting a royal birth.

On 15 April the Dons left for their training camp in Largs: 'Willie Cooper is included in the party, but is still suffering from a pulled muscle, and it is doubtful if he will be in the starting line-up.'

Meanwhile, looking towards the following season, a tribunal on footballers' wages met the players' claim in full by awarding a maximum of £12 per week in winter, with £10 per week in summer, and minimum wages of £7 and £5 respectively.

On 16 April, looking no further than the following Saturday, it reported 'no better news of Cooper'. It was finally announced two days later that he would not play. His only role in what should have been a great finale to his career was as a spectator.

Willie Waddell, who came into the Cup-final side in Cooper's absence promised him his medal if the Dons won, but his generous gesture was to prove unnecessary: in missing the final, Cooper gained the unique distinction of having a special medal struck in his honour. What may have mattered more to him was the opportunity it gave the supporters to show their affection and gratitude, for after the Cup had been won they insisted that Cooper come out to join the other players with the trophy.

He continued with Aberdeen for one more season, but did not play for the first team until December, and featured in only seven games before finishing his Aberdeen career in an away game against Falkirk on 31 January 1948. The press report was generally scathing about the Dons' performance: 'The Bairns frolicked while the Dons floundered in the mud.' As had happened so often before, however, there was something to praise in Cooper's performance: 'Cooper and Waddell struggled gamely and not altogether unsuccessfully against the clever Alison and Inglis respectively.'

Cooper had been with Aberdeen for over 20 years. He had joined them in the Jazz Age and had seen them through the years of depression and war to the era of post-war austerity; at the time of his last game, the government was in the middle of a currency crisis and Sir Stafford Cripps had pledged to defend the value of the pound. When Cooper had started playing professional football, broadcasting was in its infancy; by the time he finished, football was being shown live on television. He had helped the Dons to become challengers, and had seen them, finally, emerge as winners. In that time he had earned the respect and affection of the Aberdeen support. The club has never had a finer servant.

The Defenders

In any list of great Dons defenders, in any list of great Dons *players*, one name is inescapable. Willie Miller captained the club through its greatest period of success, success which could not have been achieved without him. For more than a decade he was undoubtedly the most dominant defender and arguably the most influential player in Scottish football. If he has to be one of the defenders, who is there to compare him with?

The most obvious, almost the only answer in terms of a direct comparison, is Martin Buchan, for Miller's position of sweeper hardly existed before Buchan assumed the role. There are enough similarities to make worthwhile comparisons: both captained the side early in their careers, and both achieved early success; both captained Scotland; Buchan had the unique distinction of skippering Scottish and FA Cup-winning teams; Miller's string of domestic and European successes represents a unique achievement within the Scottish game. There are enough differences in style to make the comparison interesting: Buchan the interceptor, Miller the tackler; Buchan the calming influence, Miller the driving force; Buchan the organiser, Miller the inspiration. Buchan achieved more widespread fame by moving to the most glamorous club in British football and displaying at Old Trafford the same qualities he had shown at Pittodrie. Miller, by staying in Scotland, was less widely recognised in Britain as one of the game's top defenders, but his performances in Europe earned him praise beyond these shores. Karl-Heinz Rummenigge, to name but one, was left in no doubt as to Miller's qualities. But Buchan played alongside Clark and Harper, and I wanted to look at other periods of the club's history; eventually, I found a defender who appears to have had many of Buchan's qualities as a shrewd and perceptive organiser, but who was remarkable for what he achieved in his footballing dotage rather than his youth.

There are other central defenders who would merit inclusion, none more than Miller's constant partner at the heart of the defence, Alex McLeish. Since Miller's retirement, his own inspirational qualities emerged more clearly, both for Aberdeen and Scotland. He may have looked like an old-fashioned centre-half, forever heading away a succession of high crosses, but he was always much more than that. He may occasionally have been caught out by small, nippy players, but not often.

The old-style pivot may have been content to clear his lines with a mighty kick aimed only at getting the ball over the halfway line and as deep into enemy territory as possible. McLeish could clear the ball as far as any of them, but his apprenticeship in midfield was not wasted, and his clearances were invariably delivered with accuracy as well as length. But in this chapter I want to cover different periods in Aberdeen's history and the McLeish story, glorious as it is, runs almost exactly alongside the Miller's tale.

There are other central defenders I remember, and some I don't, but have heard of. There was Alec Young, smaller than most centre-halves, who played in the championship-winning side of the 1950s, and was famous for his sliding tackles. He was followed by Jim Clunie, who had been converted from an inside-forward into a centre-half and still bore some of the marks of his conversion. He used to like dribbling along his own goal-line. To be honest, I don't know if he *liked* it, but he did it anyway, and it was fun to watch. I liked it, but not everybody did. The team did tend to lose a lot of goals at the time.

Clunie was succeeded by the uncompromising (euphemistic adjective used to describe homicidal member of your own team) George Kinnell, a cousin of Jim Baxter, and the lanky Doug Coutts, who looked rather like a cousin of Bambi on ice. As the Dons were losing to Ayr United to go out of the cup yet again to Second Division opponents, his unsuccessful attempts to make contact with the ball brought forth the despairing cry from a spectator: 'Coutts! Ye should hae yer boots on yer knees!' To be fair to big Doug, the messages had a long way to go from his head to his feet.

Before the war, at the other extreme, there was Eddie Falloon, outrageously small for a centre-half at only five foot five inches, but nevertheless a vital part of the side of the 1930s which came so close to achieving success. Timing made up for lack of inches and enabled him to defy the stereotype of the immovable object of the traditional centre-half defying the irresistible force of the opposing centre-forwards. Like Alec Young, he perfected the art of the sliding tackle as a means of dispossessing larger and more powerful opponents.

Another untypical defender was Vic Milne, who combined university studies with playing for Aberdeen in the early-1920s. He, too, liked to play football in areas which did no good for the blood pressure of management and fans. As a doctor, he was probably trying to drum up business.

But those were in the days before the number 5 jersey signified a specialist defender, the man who used to be known as the 'pivot'. Before Arsenal set the trend by withdrawing the centre-half to a centre-back position, he was considered part of the half-back line, and was not expected to confine himself solely to defensive duties. Goals from anyone other than a forward were relatively rare until the more fluid patterns of the modern game replaced the old battle order of backs, half-backs and forwards. Until the 1950s, when Jackie Allister and Archie Glen contributed a few goals from the wing-half positions, the half-back line rarely scored more than half a dozen goals in a season, and these were just as likely to be scored by the centre-half as either of the wing-halves. In the seasons before the First World War, for example, Jock Wyllie was a regular scorer from the centre-half position, while his wing-halves scored only one goal in the seasons from 1910–11 to 1913–14. By way of contrast, Alec Young scored a single goal in 226 competitive appearances, and that represented the only goal scored by the regular defensive trio of Caldwell, Young and Mitchell in their combined total of almost 600 appearances. It was one of the most prolific goalscoring periods in the club's history, but goals were strictly for the forwards; the defenders were there to stop them.

All this changed as foreign influences brought in new styles of play, and the old demarcation lines became blurred. As wingers dropped out of fashion, full-backs were given more freedom to join the attack. As more attention was paid to fitness, tall defenders were brought into the attack at corners and free-kicks, and were expected to be able to get back to defend if the attack broke down. Willie Young was one of the first to be used in this manner, and scored a respectable 14 goals from 187 appearances. In a later period, and in a similar manner, Doug Rougvie had a comparable scoring record with 21 goals from 308 appearances. These totals are not huge, but they do provide an indication of how the pattern of the game has changed over the years, and, when goals are scarce, the defender's strike can be highly significant: there was Miller's goal against Celtic in the game which clinched the 1984–85 championship; McLeish's equaliser in the 1982 Cup final; and, most famously, his equaliser against Bayern Munich.

It is a measure of the greatness of Miller and McLeish that they have been so hard to replace. Gary Smith came, went and has come back again, without ever being totally convincing in any of the positions in which he has played; part of the problem has been that he has been asked to play so many different roles. Tony Kombouare gave us a name to conjure with, but also gave too much to the opposition. Derek Whyte may yet prove to be the defender of character and reliability a team needs to be successful, but defenders' reputations are built over seasons rather than months.

Before choosing another defender fit to go alongside Miller, a word for Brian Irvine. Never as comfortable on the ball as his more illustrious colleagues, prone to the occasional unforced error (aren't we all?), his stiff-legged, upright gait made him look like Robocop, operated by remote control from the dugout. But, once into his stride, that gait covered the ground as quickly as anyone, and his physique, as well as making him a formidable defender, made him a considerable threat in the opposing penalty area at set-pieces. He had as fine a scoring record as any defender, and no player has ever given more for the cause. Add to that his determination to overcome illness, and you have a player worthy to stand alongside the likes of Willie Cooper and Willie Miller as one of Aberdeen's great club servants.

But I have passed over all of these central defenders in favour of another full-back. What, *another* full-back? Yes, another full-back, because in his style of play he seems to have played as much as a covering defender as an orthodox back, a kind of Edwardian sweeper. In this, as in so many other areas, he was ahead of his time. He had a profound influence on Aberdeen's fortunes over a period of more than 20 years, and in this regard stands comparison with Miller. Those 20 years cover the earliest period of Aberdeen's history, and he had much to do with the development of the club into a major force in Scottish football. His name was Donald Colman, and his is one of the most unusual stories in Scottish football. And if I want to write about another full-back, I'll write about another full-back. It's ma ba'.

Donald Colman

Donald Colman signed for Aberdeen in 1907, when professional football was in its infancy, and the path from junior to senior football was a less well-trodden one. Yet even by the standards of the day, his career was remarkable.

For a start, his name wasn't Colman. His real surname was Cunningham, but he adopted the name of Colman when he started playing junior football in order to conceal his activities from his disapproving father. Assumed names may be common in the acting or the literary worlds, but hardly in football, at least not in this country. The Spanish may christen players with appropriate names – 'The Butcher', 'The Vulture', and so on – but it is not a practice which has ever caught on here.

Despite success in the junior ranks, where he won international honours, Colman was considered, at five foot six inches, too small for senior football until Motherwell signed him at the advanced age of 27. Two unsuccessful seasons seemed to confirm the opinion that he would never make the grade as a senior, and Motherwell released him. Aberdeen signed him on the recommendation of one of their forwards, Jimmy Muir, who had played with Colman as a junior. He had travelled with Muir and another team-mate to Aberdeen, apparently at a bit of a loose end, and while he was in the city Muir had suggested to Jimmy Philip, the Aberdeen manager, that Colman would be worth a run. Such was the casual nature of football in those days, and thus Colman found himself resuming his football career at 29. At that age he must have been regarded as something of a stop-gap; a stop-gap which was to last for almost 14 years.

His first game for Aberdeen was on 21 September 1907, away to Dundee. His arrival was unheralded, but then few signings in those days were greeted with the fanfare which now greets the most ordinary player. Indeed, there was little reporting of football, at least in the local press, apart from the detailed match report on the Monday. With that out of the way, there was no news of injured players, no speculation about new signings – 'Diego Maradona has been seen looking at houses in the Bridge of Don area' – no behind-the-scenes stories from Pittodrie. On the Friday before Colman's début there was no preview of the game against Dundee. In the sports page of the *Aberdeen Journal* there were reports on racing, swimming, shooting, bowling, golf (Forres versus the Hydropathic Visitors), and billiards (C. Dawson versus W.A. Lovejoy). On football there was nothing.

Elsewhere in the paper, it was clear that the automobile age had arrived. Under 'Cycles and Motors', a 15 h.p. Humber was offered for £320, with a 30 h.p. Beeston Humber on sale for £640. Moving down the horse-power range, a Raleigh cycle could be had for eight shillings and nine-pence down and 17 monthly payments of the same amount. The 'live now, pay later' philosophy was not an invention of the 1950s or 1960s.

Nor was popular entertainment; the Palace of Varieties and Hippo-drome was offering Florrie Forde ('Britain's Premier Burlesque Actress'), while the splendid His Majesty's Theatre, not long opened, had George Alexander's Company in *His House in Order*. As in the 1950s, there was a strong musical influence from America; ragtime was all the rage. Those who deplore current standards of popular entertainment might note that Humber's Waxworks in George Street was advertising 'Beaute, The Continental Fasting Champion', who was fasting for 35 days and nights. The public were assured that a local doctor was in attendance. Those who wished to know the future could have had their palms read by Madame Stevenson (patronised by Royalty) or by 'Zillah', who appealed to the more advanced thinkers by offering 'scientific palmistry'.

It's doubtful if they offered the answers to any really important questions, such as 'Is Beaute, the Continental Fasting Champion going to die?' or 'What's going to win the 3.30 at Kempton Park?'. All the same, the punter seeking an answer to the latter question would have found the palmists just as reliable a guide as the sports pages of the *Aberdeen Journal*. The paper was at that time too canny to employ a tipster of its own, and instead reported a selection of tips from other newspapers. On the Saturday, the four anonymous tipsters from the *Morning Leader*, *Sporting Life*, *Daily Mail* and *Daily Express* were unanimous that Faskally would win the first race at Hurst Park. Turning to the *Aberdeen Journal* of 23

September, we find that Faskally did indeed win the first race, but at 7–4 would hardly have won the punter a fortune. The *Sporting Life's* tipster was the only one of the four to suggest another winner, apart from the last race, which was a walk-over for Burscough; the men from the *Morning Leader* and *Daily Mail* couldn't even get that one right. I find that remarkable, and, from a punter's point of view, utterly deplorable. Two supposed experts, writing in national newspapers, failed to predict the outcome of a one-horse race. Think about that next time you consult the racing page.

If there was no attempt at forecasting the result of the Aberdeen game, there was some compensation by way of a detailed report in Monday's paper. The *Journal* reported that 'Aberdeen introduced Coleman (Motherwell) at right-back'. It would be some time before the spelling of his name would settle down.

It would also be some time before the reporting of football would settle down, and at times the modern reader has the impression that the job of football correspondent had been handed out to whoever wasn't needed to report the fatstock prices at the Huntly mart. We are informed that 'right from the kick-off the game assumed an interesting aspect', and that it 'continued along brisk lines, and although the quality of the play at times left something to be desired, still the players never slackened their efforts'.

The report also reveals some idiosyncratic ideas on the laws of the game: 'Unfortunately for Aberdeen, Wilfred Low handled the ball in the penalty area. Dundee were awarded a free-kick, and Dean sent the ball flying past MacFarlane. This was distinctly hard luck on Aberdeen, who had up to this point played the better football, and Low's offence was a very mild one.' This sounds like someone who has been taken off crime reporting; compared to the theft and throat-cuttings which form the warp and weft of a crime reporter's working life, handling the ball in the penalty area probably does seem a fairly mild offence, unless the other hand was used to stab the referee. The modern reader, even the most rabid red-and-white fanatic, would find it difficult to see what other decision the referee could have given.

In the light of these views on handling, it is hardly surprising that the reporter's grasp of the offside law was less than perfect: 'A few minutes later Dainty banged the ball into the net, but the goal was disallowed owing to Welsh being offside and spoiling the goalkeeper's view.' In his summing up, Dundee were described as 'lucky in winning', thus establishing right from the start a good solid tradition of biased reporting. The crowd was reported at 8,000, contributing a total of £217, with £187 from the terracing and £30 from the stands. Never mind the game, what were the takings? Commercialism is no new phenomenon; it has simply adapted to the times.

To get back to the game, the Aberdeen team was: MacFarlane, Colman,

Hume; Davidson, Halkett, Low; Muir, Murray, Wilson, O'Hagan, Lennie. The newcomers in the side were Colman and Low, both of whom were praised by the reporter as being 'prominent for fine work'. Their presence, we are told, 'encouraged other members of the side'. More particularly, Colman was 'cheered for his clever tackling'.

He made his home début in the Monday holiday game on 23 September against Celtic. Aberdeen won 2–1, and followed up with two more home victories against Partick and Kilmarnock on the following Saturdays. The crowds for these games were between 7,000 and 8,000, about average for that pre-war period. Football had not quite established itself, at least in these parts, as the mass entertainment it was to become in later years, although Rangers attracted an exceptional crowd of 20,000 in 1912. Apart from that, the season's largest crowd was usually between 14,000 and 16,000 for the visits of Celtic, Rangers or Dundee.

The Pittodrie those crowds squeezed into would have seemed as strange to the modern spectator as the players in their collarless black-and-gold jerseys, with legs encased in long black shorts and feet in boots which looked as though they had been designed for kicking lumps of granite. A new stand and pavilion had been built in 1905, with the pavilion giving the stadium the appearance of a cricket ground. The terracing was relatively low, uncovered, and separated from the pitch by a fence rather than a wall.

It was over this fence that the Aberdeen fans had their first glimpse of Donald Colman in those games against Celtic, Partick Thistle and Kilmarnock. One assumes that the *Aberdeen Journal* reporter saw the games from the stand. Wherever he was, he had a good view of the goal against Partick: 'The ball was sent out to Lennie, who responded with one of his characteristic races down the field. He beat the halves, and ran round Lyon like a flash, and made obliquely for Massie's citadel, finishing with a fine drive which landed the sphere in the corner of the net . . . It was strong and clever work on the part of the winger, and its result was hailed with an outburst of enthusiastic cheering.'

In the reporting of matches of the period, there is, through all the descriptions of 'spheres', 'citadels' and so on, an impression of a game which relied more on individual effort than teamwork, of titanic duels between centre-half and centre-forward, winger and full-back. An impression also emerges of Colman's play, which does not entirely conform to the stereotyped image of the primitive full-back.

In the match against Partick Thistle, 'Coleman made a bad mistake when he miskicked and let Callander and Gray away, but the back effected a splendid recovery and kept the wing at bay till reinforcements came up and relieved the pressure.' Against Kilmarnock (when the reporter stated baldly, 'the strangers looked a big lot'), 'a foul dangerously near the Aberdeen penalty line looked like yielding the equaliser, but Coleman blocked the shot, and then cleared . . . Coleman was very prominent in the Pittodrie defence, and on not a few occasions his smart tactics were responsible for saving the side.' And in the next game, away to Falkirk, in which Colman and Hume were outstanding: 'Coleman fortunately stepped in at the right time and cleared.' The style shines through: Colman the interceptor, the calming influence, the organiser, the all-round defender.

With performances like these he established himself in the side and missed only one game in the remainder of that 1907–8 season; he was an ever-present throughout the following season, and missed only a handful of games between then and the outbreak of war in 1914.

The war was not regarded, initially at least, as a reason for curtailing the football season. When it started, in June of that year, it was the war that would be over by Christmas. War seems to have been regarded as something like professional sport, fought on battlefields by the professionals while the nation cheered on 'our boys'. Conscription was not introduced until 1916, and only gradually did it become apparent that the Great War was not the great game, but meant total war, something which would affect every facet of civilian life. In the local press, the classified advertisements were still on the front page, and inside the paper the war could be reported under a headline such as 'European War Crisis' – something that was happening somewhere south of Stonehaven.

These were the days before air travel took us to Europe and across the world, and before television took the world into our living-room. When the *Aberdeen Journal* correspondent explained the cause of the Balkan conflict, it must have seemed very remote, and altogether baffling: 'In the southern part of Austria-Hungary the Servian race predominates, and Servia is accused of stirring up the people against Austria with the idea of seizing the province of Bosnia at the earliest opportunity.' Eighty years on, and with the benefit of television, it may seem less remote, but is no less baffling.

The relatively new medium of the cinema could not explain, but it could bring some sense of immediacy, even if it could not yet offer news-reels. The La Scala Picture House offered a 'first-class varied programme' and announced that 'latest war news is communicated by special phone from the *Aberdeen Journal* and will be screened immediately on receipt'.

Whatever the news, there seemed to be no reason to stop the football season going ahead. The *Journal* was able to report 'Aberdeen's Great Opening Victory', although the war did impinge to some extent on the proceedings: 'The call to arms has made serious inroads upon the resources of the club and it was, under the circumstances, most gratifying to the supporters of the Aberdeen club that the team should have opened the season so auspiciously by ousting their great Dundee rivals at Dens Park by three goals to one.'

If the war report reveals that the Balkans have changed little in the course of the century, the football report says much the same of local derbies: 'As is usually the case, these inter-city matches are not productive of football of a high standard. The pace at which the game was contested, the very pronounced rivalry between the teams and the keen desire to excel at the outset, all tended to lower the standards in what was otherwise a fast and most interesting game.' The reporter found time to praise Colman's performance. He also found the team's performance particularly meritorious because they lacked the support 'usually available at the first of the northern "Derbies", there being no excursion train from Aberdeen'. We see here the first incursion of the war into civilian life with the disruption of public transport. We can also infer that it was already customary for a large number of supporters to travel to away matches, at least as far as Dundee, and this probably accounts for the fact that the Dundee games were at that time just as likely to attract large attendances as matches against the Old Firm.

The next game was against Rangers at Pittodrie. The crowd of 15,000, while slightly less than might have been expected under normal circumstances, was more satisfactory than the result (a 2–0 defeat) and, together with reports of good attendances elsewhere, prompted the *Aberdeen Journal* to comment that 'the attendance at Saturday's football matches in Scotland further justified the decision of the national association in proceeding with the season's programme'.

Of the game itself, it was reported that 'Colman on the Aberdeen side was outstanding for brilliant work'. His 'brilliant work' and consistency had by that time earned him the club captaincy and four international caps, the first of which was won in 1911 at the age of 33. He continued playing for Aberdeen through the early years of the war, until the league programme was finally abandoned at the end of the 1916–17 season. When football was resumed in 1919 he was still with the club, and, at the age of 42, played 11 games in season 1919–20.

In that first post-war season it was apparent that football had become a mass entertainment. As noted in the chapter on Jock Hutton, the average crowd had jumped from the 9,000 or so of pre-war years to 12,000, with a top crowd of 24,000 for the visit of Rangers on 20 March 1920. The manager of Aberdeen, Jimmy Philip, had been serving on a part-time basis during the war, and the directors had been too canny to reinstate him as full-time manager immediately on the resumption of the football programme. The question was raised at a meeting of the directors in April, however, but was deferred for a special meeting of the board 'to be held at an early date'.

It was not only professional football that was booming. On 5 April there was a public meeting to agitate for additional pitches. With 1,500 players in the junior grade in the city, the number of pitches fell very short of the demand. Nor was football the only sport increasing in popularity. The Aberdeen Coal and Shipping Company organised a 'marathon' for its employees (in fact a road race of seven and a half miles along the South Deeside road to the company's sheds at Albert Quay). It was won by a Mr G. Park, at the age of 50.

If Mr Park was able to show his younger colleagues a clean pair of heels, it seemed that time was at last catching up with the 42-year-old Colman. In the report of the Aberdeen game against Albion Rovers, which ended in a 1–1 draw, Colman and Hannah were described as 'too slow for the young Rovers'. Worse was to follow. On 10 April Aberdeen were defeated 5–0 by Celtic, although Colman received praise for his performance – 'seen to advantage'.

Aberdeen fans depressed by that result might have been cheered up by going to La Scala to see the cinema's latest offering, *Tommy Atkins in Berlin*: 'Mack Sennet's Greatest Triumph – Five Riotous Reels of Yells, Screams and Bathing Beauties'. Or then again, maybe not. If they were unmoved by Mack Sennet, there was always Charlie Chaplin the following week. '*A Day's Pleasure*,' cineastes were assured, 'will be greatly enjoyed by admirers of the great film comedian. It will provoke the most austere to laughter.' And if that were not enough, there was also a five-part story of the west, *Wild Life*, portraying 'many magnificent mountain scenes, daring feats of horsemanship and vivid glimpses of western dance-halls'. They must have been queuing round the block for that one.

While those films were showing to a Wednesday-afternoon audience on 21 April, Aberdeen were playing at Kilmarnock. The team was: Anderson, Colman, Hume; Wright, Wyllie, Hannah; Massie, McLaughlin, Connon, Wilson, Archibald. They won 3–0. The crowd was only 3,000, and it is unlikely that there were many Aberdeen fans among them to see Colman's last game for the club. He went out in the same quiet way he had come in, hardly mentioned in the match report, although the defence as a whole came through 'with flying colours'. Of the team with whom he had started his Aberdeen career in 1907, only his full-back partner, Jock Hume, remained, and he, too, was to depart at the end of the season. In the intervening years the world had changed utterly but some things remained constant. The *Aberdeen Journal* now quoted eight racing tipsters instead of four (why not? – they weren't paying them), but the punter would still have lost money following their selections. Between them, they could only muster one winner at Epsom, and at 4–7 it would hardly have funded the herd of losers. With an advertisement on the same page announcing 'New Hair for Bald Heads', there was plenty to appeal to the incurable optimist.

There must have been something of the optimist in Donald Colman to have embarked on a professional football career when he did, and at that point the most foolhardy punter would not have been tempted, whatever the odds, to bet that the player would become an international, and would still be playing in 1920. Yet even that was not the end of his football career, or of his association with Aberdeen.

When he left the club at the end of the 1919–20 season, he joined Dumbarton as player-manager, and did not finish playing until he was 47. During this period he spent the summer months coaching in Norway. He returned to Pittodrie as trainer in 1931, brought back by Paddy Travers, who had been a playing colleague of Colman's and had become manager in 1924. Colman's influence over the following years up to the outbreak of the war was immense, and had much to do with Aberdeen's rise to prominence in that period. He broke the mould of the 'bucket and sponge' trainer. He was a thinker and innovator, constantly working on tactics and training methods.

He is credited with inventing the dugout, from which he would make notes of each game for subsequent analysis. This methodical approach was to be adopted by European coaches, and was regarded as a novelty in Britain when Don Revie introduced it to his Leeds United side of the 1960s, but Colman had been there 30 years before him.

He died of tuberculosis in 1942, at the age of 64. He did not live to see Aberdeen win the trophies for which he had worked so hard, but he, more than anyone, had laid the foundations of the post-war success.

Willie Miller

Willie Miller signed for Aberdeen in June 1969, when he was 16. He was spotted by Bobby Calder, who had a reputation for discovering forwards rather than defenders, and it was as a striker that Miller was signed from Glasgow juvenile club Eastercraigs. Long after he had forsaken his striking role (if not his goal-scoring ambitions), the *Green Final* described him as 'the Eastercraigs youngster', which made him sound like a western gunslinger – 'the Hogsbreath Kid', or some such soubriquet – and it was not until his youth was well behind him that the tag was dropped.

He had in fact started as a goalkeeper with his school football team, but Glasgow schools football is played on blaize pitches, and to remain in that position for more than half a dozen games on such pitches requires an excess of courage or a deficiency of brain cells. Some boys never learn that the excruciating pain they feel after diving on that surface is caused by the contact between the particles of grit, of which the pitch is composed, and their skin. They continue to dive to prevent goals, and suffer pain each Saturday, first as the grit goes in, and again as it is scrubbed out. Such boys are jewels beyond price, and they go on to become professional goal-keepers, war heroes or PE teachers. Miller never lacked courage, but he never lacked sense either, and soon moved to an outfield position.

When he was called up by Aberdeen in 1971, he was 'farmed out' to Peterhead. He must have wondered what he had done to deserve that, but he responded by scoring 23 goals in a reasonably successful first season in senior football. It was not until December 1972 that he first played as a central defender, in a reserve game against Rangers. His progress from then on was good enough for him to gain a place on the substitutes' bench at the end of the 1972–73 season, an away game against Morton on 28 April. His experience in both defensive and attacking positions had possibly been a factor in his selection, and he came on in the second half as a substitute for Arthur Graham.

Cappielow is a strange ground; dilapidated, as most of the minor West of Scotland grounds are, it is the sort of place which is the soul of Scottish football, and, half-empty, makes you wonder if it is a soul worth saving. It is set amid industrial (or, worse, post-industrial) squalor, with great cliffs of blackened tenements rising up behind it. And yet, standing on the terracing, you can look over the roof of the stand to the most glorious view of the Firth of Clyde, a vista of sparkling blue water and distant hills. On a clear spring day, with a gentle breeze from the right direction, you can almost hear Kenneth McKellar singing, '*The River Clyde, the wonderful Clyde . . .*'

So it was that day, and, yes, you could almost hear the voice of Kenneth McKellar. It was emerging, barely audible, from the typically inefficient public-address system. '*The name of it thrills me, and fills me with pride . . .*' Yes, I was there when Willie Miller made his début for Aberdeen. Did the small band of Dons fans chant 'Here is a veritable titan who will lead us to unprecedented domestic success and eventual triumph in Europe'? A *Sunday Times* reporter might have said so, but it hardly trips off the tongue, does it? Did we chant 'One Willie Miller, there's only one Willie Miller'? More plausible, but no; he was an unfamiliar figure, and you can hardly expect a crowd of fans to have that sort of collective prescience. Ah, but did I, the discerning spectator, have the individual foresight to say to myself, 'Here is a veritable titan, etc'? No, I did not. To be honest, it was only when researching this chapter that I realised I had seen Miller's début, and all I can remember is the view over the Clyde and the sort of game which, if it could be bottled, would make a most effective anaesthetic. If I said anything at all, it was probably along the lines of 'What's Bonthrone playing at, putting this bozo on for Bumper?' Messrs Ladbroke and Hill will testify, with a degree of satisfaction, to my powers of prediction in footballing matters.

Like their predecessors of Donald Colman's day, they could also look unperturbed at the efforts of the racing tipsters. By this time, the *Press and Journal* was employing its own experts, and, to be fair to them, they did no worse than the efforts of the combined force of newspaper expertise half a century earlier. Between them, 'Oliver Chisolm' and 'The Colonel' managed to tip two winners out of a possible 13 at Kempton Park and Hamilton, and they even both managed to tip Hulita to win the 4.30 at Hamilton. At 11–8, with the other winner at 15–8, however, they were hardly likely to make up for the losses on all the others, and Mr Hill would have been able to pay his grocery bills for another week.

Alastair Macdonald, writing in the *Press and Journal,* agreed with my view of the game: 'The result was the only Greenock bright spot.' The result was an important one for Aberdeen, in that it secured a place in the UEFA Cup the following season. No one could have guessed that the most significant event of the afternoon had been the introduction of the man who was going to become the most influential and successful Aberdeen player of them all. The report stated: 'Willie Miller, making his first-team competitive début, when he replaced Arthur Graham shortly after the interval, did not have much chance to shine, but the reserve-team centre-half did enough to demonstrate his versatility by playing among the front-runners without looking out of place.'

As one career with Aberdeen was starting, another, from Aberdeen, was finishing. Denis Law was given a free transfer by Manchester United, and so ended a career which had taken him from Powis School to clubs in Huddersfield, Manchester and Turin, and all over the world for Scotland. Well, not quite ended, but the rest of that story is another chapter.

Elsewhere in the football world, English teams were making good progress, with Derby County, Leeds United, Tottenham and Liverpool all through to the semi-finals of the various European competitions. Leeds and Liverpool went through to their finals, which would have been bearable if it hadn't been for Jimmy Hill telling us how good it was for English football.

It was a time of platform soles and flares, and even footballers had long hair. The music of the 1960s hadn't died, but it was dangerously ill after being almost kicked to death by the likes of Gary Glitter and the Bay City Rollers. The cinemas were certainly dying, one by one. By 1973 we were down to the Capitol, ABC, Cosmo, Majestic and Odeon in Aberdeen.

It was at the start of the 1973–74 season that Miller played his first game in the number 6 jersey he was to make his own. The position of sweeper had never really been filled convincingly since the departure of Martin Buchan in 1972. Tommy Wilson had been converted from promising midfield player to apprentice sweeper, but Buchan was a hard act to follow, and in the first game of 1973–74 the position had been taken by Henning Boel. When he was injured, Miller was called up, starting with a game against Dundee United at Tannadice on 15 August. The report said of him: 'Willie Miller can be reasonably satisfied with his performance as deputy for Henning Boel as the Dons' sweeper . . . he did all that was asked of him with great coolness.' As he started, so he continued. The number 6 jersey was his for virtually the whole of the rest of that season, and for every season after that. He scored his first goal against Hearts in November of that year, but of more significance to the team was the run of eight games without conceding a goal. This established the kind of defensive meanness which was to be the foundation of the club's success in later years.

Not that Miller's first season was without blemish; there were mis-judged pass-backs, misguided clearances, and the occasional rash tackle in and around the penalty area which led to the loss of goals. Gradually, the mistakes were eliminated, and the 'goals against' column was filled with blanks. In that first season as sweeper, the defence which it was his responsibility to marshal conceded an average of only 0.76 goals per game. Miller had established his authority.

I had seen it develop largely from a western perspective, as a small band of exiles followed the Dons around the football grounds of faraway places with strange-sounding names. Places like Broomfield, with its quaint pavilion, giving it the air of some English county cricket ground. You'd swear you could hear the sound of leather on willow, until you remember you're in the middle of Airdrie, and realise that it's someone being hit over the head with a baseball bat.

Then there was Firhill, friendliest of football grounds. You got used to the hostility at Paradise and the other place ('Orange bassterts' one week, 'Fenian bassterts' the next) but no Partick Thistle fan goes to Firhill expecting his team to win – supporting the Jags is eccentric, expecting them to win is certifiable – so any success, however fleeting, is a huge bonus, and defeat is just the way of the world. Visiting fans are welcome to join the party. The only serious threat came from the hulking youths hanging around outside the ground with the plea: 'Gie's a lift ower, Mister?' You were never sure whether the greater threat to your well-being lay in agreeing or refusing. They were certainly big enough to beat you up for refusing, but if you agreed you risked serious injury trying to lift them over the turnstile to gain them the free entry they were looking for. The trick was to walk just behind an inoffensive-looking wee man they were sure to accost, and accelerate smartly away as they stopped him – a tech-nique learned from a lifetime of avoiding tappers. Once inside, you felt perfectly safe, as long as you avoided the pies.

South of the Clyde there was Shawfield, which, along with the corner pubs, was practically all that was left on that stretch of the river, as old Glasgow fell to the hammer. The Gorbals had almost disappeared, but we just managed to find Malarkeys Bar, like an archaeological fragment. It was a small, very ordinary bar, with no kind of distinction other than the fact that it was one of the last of its kind. That, and its customers and John, the barman. On Tuesday night they came from all parts of the city to the pub that had been their local, to talk of old times and listen to John, the banjo player (as far as I could make out, everybody was called John, except Solly), and sing along. He played whatever they wanted, but it was mainly the songs of the 1920s and 1930s, Al Jolson numbers and the like, along with some Scottish music-hall songs. There was just one rule – no Rangers, Celtic, Orange or Rebel songs. Apart from that, it depended on whether John the Banjo knew them. Solly sang 'Hello Solly', which was as about as recent as it got; Blind Docherty (another one who wasn't called John – I forgot about him) sang 'My Big Kilmarnock Bunnet', with a break in the middle for a couple of jokes, the same two jokes every week, which never failed to raise a laugh. Most surprising was one old boy who looked as though he was held together with string, and didn't seem to have the wit or the strength to sing along. One night he broke into a soft shoe shuffle, all elegance and timing, and was transformed from old mac and bunnet to top-hat, white tie and tails – well, sharp suit, shiny shoes and brilliantine. It was another fragment of the 1930s, preserved in a few dance-hall steps. The second-last song was usually 'We're no awa' to bide awa', but for some reason I could never fathom, the last one was always 'North to Alaska', from a John Wayne film of the 1950s. '*North to Alas-ka, we're goin' north, the rush is on!*' The last chorus would ring out, and John the Banjo would solemnly intone, 'Well, folks, the clock has beaten us again,' and John the Barman would yell out, 'Time, gentlemen, please!' and all the John the Drinkers would drink up and be gone. So it was every Tuesday. But John the Banjo was ill, and getting weaker. For the last few weeks he played with the banjo propped up on the bar, then the clock beat him for the last time, and another piece of Glasgow was gone.

Shawfield has gone too, now, but then it was still impressive, not for the architecture (half football ground, half greyhound stadium, wholly nuclear waste disposal site) nor for the catering (pies like mortar shells) but for the empties. The traditional 'screwtap' was on the way out by then, replaced by the can, but the serious drinker still relied on the sort of drink that only comes in bottles – fortified wines like Lanliq ('Feel That Kick'), Four Crown ('For Men of Spirit') and Eldorado (when the only word that rhymes with your product is 'desperado', you have a marketing problem). There was a fair number of those empties scattered around the terracing as we made our way out after a 1–1 draw, and understandably so; it had been a raw January afternoon, with a good drying wind to induce the need for a refreshment both warming and thirst-quenching. Amid the usual debris, however, there was an empty Harvey's Bristol Cream. That was a touch of real class, and illustrates what a loss Clyde and Shawfield have been to the top flight. It was in places like these that Miller learned his trade, and established his authority over his opponents, team-mates and referees.

This authority was recognised officially (not by the referees) in December 1975, when he captained Aberdeen for the first time, in a 1–0 victory over Rangers. It was not an easy time to take over the leadership on the field, for the Dons were going through one of their less successful seasons, and it was only on goal difference that they avoided relegation from the Premier League in its first season. Not for the first time, Aberdeen found themselves having to win their last game to be sure of avoiding relegation, and did so, beating Hibs 3–0 at Easter Road. If it was not a successful season, it did set a pattern of winning the really important games.

Miller's club performances had already been recognised by Scotland, with his first full international cap in June 1975 against Romania. He played in the number 8 jersey, in what was ostensibly a defensive midfield role in a difficult away game. According to Alastair MacDonald: 'Miller turned in a typically wholehearted performance, although it was only in the second half that he could be spared from duty as an extra defender to fulfil the constructive midfield role assigned to him.' This may have had something to do with the fact that Scotland needed an equaliser. They got it, and returned with a very creditable 1–1 draw.

The next significant début was in 1978, but it wasn't one of Miller's. It was on 2 January 1978, when Alex McLeish played his first game for the team, against Dundee United, and began the partnership which was to dominate opposing attacks for the next decade. Miller and McLeish; it's like Morecambe and Wise, or Fred Astaire and Ginger Rogers, partnerships which were greater than the sum of their parts, with the individuals seemingly made for each other. I suppose, with his red hair, Alex McLeish would have to be Ginger to Miller's Fred Astaire, but don't tell him I said so. They are undoubtedly the greatest defensive partnership Aberdeen have ever had, or are ever likely to have, and if there has ever been a better one in Scotland, I can't think of it.

McLeish did not become fully established in the side until the second half of the 1978–79 season, and even then played for some time in midfield, but once he had taken a long-term lease on the number 5 jersey the goals conceded fell to an average of less than a goal per game, and stayed that way as long as the partnership remained. Apart from their complementary abilities and intuitive understanding, they each had a fiercely competitive nature which would never contemplate defeat, and would only admit it when they saw the *Green Final* score confirmed in the Sunday papers.

They played as a central defensive pairing on several occasions in 1978–79. The following season McLeish established himself in the team, but in the first half of the season was used more frequently in midfield. They finally established the partnership in March 1980, when a series of indifferent results had left the Dons hopelessly adrift of leaders Celtic. Or so it appeared. We all know the rest, but, like a child with a fairy-tale, we never tire of hearing it. They did not lose again in their 14 remaining games. As Aberdeen gathered momentum, Celtic began to falter. The impossible dream was beginning to look as though it could come true. Saturday, 19 April, was a turning point. Miller conceded a penalty against Kilmarnock at Rugby Park. He was injured, but refused to come off, and the Dons won 3–1. Meanwhile, Celtic were losing 5–1 at Dens Park. Just as important as Aberdeen's belief that they could win the title was Celtic's belief that they could lose it, and this result must have done more than anything to convince them that they would. If it was down to self-belief against self-doubt, there could only be one winner, and that was the side with Willie Miller.

On 3 May the Dons went to Easter Road needing a win, just as they had done four years earlier, but this time for a very different reason. Again they won when they had to, this time triumphantly, 5–0, and the league title was theirs. In those last 14 games they had conceded just ten goals, and from then on an Aberdeen side without Miller and McLeish was unthinkable.

They did, of course, have help from the rest of the team, most notably from Cooper and Simpson in front of them, but they were the solid rock on which all the success of the 1980s was built. As well as their defensive qualities, there was always the annual goal-scoring contest. McLeish usually had the edge here, thanks mainly to his heading ability at set pieces, but Miller could usually be relied upon for a few goals a season, his most notable effort being the header against Celtic which virtually secured the 1984–85 league title.

The goal which McLeish will always be remembered for is his header against Bayern Munich, but Miller's defensive contribution to that game must not be forgotten, particularly his second-half tackle on Karl-Heinz Rummenigge, when the German seemed certain to score. And, though less dramatic, it was a brilliant defensive performance in Munich, almost totally stifling one of Europe's finest attacks, which had made the Pittodrie result possible.

If it was the self-belief emanating from Miller and spreading through the rest of the team which did so much to make that result (and all the other European results) possible, it was the same attitude which enabled them to take on and beat Rangers and Celtic, home or away, and thus ensure domestic success. Under Miller's leadership, the Dons came to regard themselves as the equals of the Old Firm, and ultimately proved themselves better. They are the only provincial club ever to have gone to Glasgow not only thinking that they *could* win, but that they *would* win, the only club to have come away from Ibrox or Parkhead disappointed with a draw, the only club to have beaten the Old Firm pair regularly on their own turf.

In the years between the wars, Aberdeen won only twice at Ibrox and three times at Parkhead. They did rather better at Pittodrie, beating Rangers four times and Celtic nine times, but overall a draw against either of the Old Firm teams was regarded as a good result, and out of a possible 80 points they only gained 24 from Rangers and 33 from Celtic. The better performance against Celtic was mainly due to a remarkable run from 1926–27 right through to the war, when Celtic failed to win at Pittodrie.

After the war, there was some improvement in the away record, with four victories over each of the Old Firm in the period from 1946–47 to 1965–66. Results at Pittodrie were fairly similar, leaving Aberdeen in an improved but still markedly inferior position, with 30 points out of a possible 80 from Rangers and 34 from Celtic. In contrast, during the period from 1975–76 to 1984–85, with the same number of points at stake, the Dons took 50 from Rangers and 46 from Celtic. During that period Rangers recorded one solitary win at Pittodrie. It makes you feel sorry for the poor man clad in blue, making the long journey north in the certain knowledge that his team was going to be beaten, and making the long, weary journey back south, with his worst fears confirmed. Who am I kidding? It was wonderful.

Prejudice and gloating aside, the lesson for any team aspiring to win the Scottish League is clear: you must beat Rangers and Celtic yourself, because no one else is going to do it for you. Perhaps it helped that Ferguson, Miller and McLeish were all Glasgow boys, so that the place held no terrors for them; you could sense that Ferguson, in particular, delighted in putting one over on his former employers. But I think it had more to do with character than provenance. Aberdeen happened to have, as well as talented players, a bunch of totally indomitable characters, from Miller and McLeish to Cooper and Simpson, and through to Strachan and McGhee; not the dirty dozen, but what might have been described in the westerns as a bunch of 'ornery critturs'. Perhaps it was good management. Perhaps it was providence. But it worked, and we can only be grateful.

There were attempts to lure Miller away from Pittodrie, most notably by John Greig when he was manager of Rangers, but Miller stayed for the duration. Greig, who knew a thing or two about defending, described the player as the best penalty-box defender in the country. There are few who would have disagreed with that assessment, and with his performances in

Europe and for Scotland he established a reputation as one of the best anywhere. When Aberdeen played Hamburg in the UEFA Cup in 1981, he did not suffer in comparison with his opposite number, the great Franz Beckenbauer. The Kaiser was admittedly nearing the end of his career, while Miller was in his prime, and Miller could never claim to have the creative skills of Beckenbauer, but then there were few in the world who could. On the other hand, there were few who could tackle as well as Miller, and tackling is as much a skill as any other facet of the game. The effectiveness of the Miller–McLeish partnership, and the team as a whole, also owed much to the accuracy of their distribution; when the ball was cleared it seldom came straight back.

His international career, having begun in 1975, did not really get going for another three or four years, but by 1980 he had established himself in the Scotland team, and by that time he had McLeish alongside him. He played in the World Cup finals in 1982, and the following year captained Scotland for the first time. In 1980 he had even managed to score the only goal of the game to beat Wales, which put him one ahead of McLeish as an international goalscorer, a position he retains to this day.

It was an injury suffered when playing for Scotland against Northern Ireland in November 1989 that effectively ended Miller's career. He had already had knee problems, and on this occasion was unable to return to the first team until nearly the end of the season.

On 2 May Aberdeen were due to play Celtic in what was to be a rehearsal for the Cup final. Miller was selected, for match practice was essential if he was to have any chance of playing in the final. The weather was unseasonally hot. (On May Day, Lossiemouth had recorded a temperature of 27° Celsius, the hottest May temperature on record, only to be beaten the following day by Glenlivet, with 27.9°.)

It was a time of departures, or possible departures. Kenny Dalglish came on as a substitute for Liverpool in their game against Derby County, with the league title already won, 'to show gratitude to the fans, and sometimes you find it difficult to express the way you feel in words'. We had noticed, Kenny, and thanks for the memories. He did add that it 'may not be the last time'. Predictably, Liverpool won 1–0. The widow of Bill Shankly collapsed while opening a playing field in memory of the man who had done so much for Liverpool. Like Dalglish, Shankly had always appreciated the fans who were so much a part of the Liverpool legend. Unlike Dalglish, he was able to express his feelings in words: 'Eh, Liverrrpool fans are the grrreatest in the world. That is why they deserrrve the best team in the worrrld. Eh, and that is what they get.' Not a man of many words, but he made every one count. Dalglish's former Celtic colleague, Lou Macari, was also in the news; in his case, the Inland Revenue had been doing some counting and had held him pending their investigations into the running of Swindon FC while he was manager.

The press report on the Dons' game against Celtic on 2 May was all about arrivals rather than departures: 'Young Lions Roar For Dons'. Aberdeen won 3–1 with: Snelders, McKimmie, D. Robertson, Graham Watson (sub. Gregg Watson), Irvine, Miller, C. Robertson, Simpson, Booth, Jess, Cameron, a side which included several young players. Jess (2) and Graham Watson scored the goals. Like so many departures, Miller's went unheralded. The report simply stated: 'Old hands Neil Simpson, Willie Miller and Theo Snelders did their bit when required.' Miller survived an appeal for handball inside the penalty area, and a collision with former colleague Billy Stark on the edge of the area. Many years of cultivating a friendly relationship with referees had no doubt paid off. The result gave the Dons confidence for the forthcoming Cup final against Celtic. Miller had come through the game intact, and was hopeful of a place in the final. On 11 May the *Press and Journal* reported: 'Skipper Willie Miller watches and waits to see if he is in the frame for a Hampden spot', rather in the manner of the bulletins on Willie Cooper which had preceded the 1947 final.

The following day it was reported that he was in the squad of 18, but might have to settle for a place on the bench. In the event, he did not even get that. Meanwhile, his old mentor, Alex Ferguson was leading out Manchester United against Crystal Palace in an FA Cup final he would eventually win in a replay. After the game Miller said he would be back, and manager Smith echoed this confidence, but it turned out to be misplaced. On medical advice, Miller announced his retirement before the beginning of the following season. It was the end of the most distinguished playing career ever seen at Pittodrie, but not the end of his connection with the club. Like Colman before him, Miller continued to have an influence behind the scenes, as a coach and as the man in charge of the reserves. His name was linked with several managerial vacancies, but he stayed where he was; Alex Smith suffered a series of bad results, and when he went only one name was mentioned in connection with the post. He was the fans' choice as manager. But he was to suffer the fate of so many players stepping up from the changing-room to the manager's office – John Greig is an obvious example – and the fate of all the Aberdeen managers who have followed Ferguson. Second to Rangers in his first two full seasons in charge was by no means a bad performance, but to an Aberdeen public who had become used to winning or had grown up with success, it was not quite good enough. And when a collapse in form the following season saw the club leading the way towards the First Division, the fans' choice for manager became the fans' choice to go.

When Miller joined the club, the stadium was substantially as it had been after the war. He had seen it become the first all-seated stadium in the country. By the end of the 1992–93 season the new Beach End had risen from the mound which had been there, and a Pittodrie had taken shape which would have seemed like some futuristic dream to Donald Colman. Likewise, the success of the 1980s which Miller had done so much to bring about would have been unimaginable to the Donald Colman (*né* Cunningham) who had joined, late in his career, the struggling northern club.

Some things don't change, though. Talent has to be tied to application to bring success. And don't rely on the racing tipsters; on the day Miller played his last game, they only had two winners out of 12, although to be fair Pat Archer did tip Teamster in the 2.30 at Ascot at 7–2. Well done, Pat.

The Midfielders

The midfield is the creative heart of the team, and any successful team usually has at least one dominant player in that area. It is also the place where footballers can express themselves most freely, yet be continually involved in the game. Consequently there is no shortage of players who deserve to be included as someone's favourite player.

Yet the term 'midfield' hardly existed before the 1960s. We had wing-halves and inside-forwards, who would now be categorised, roughly, as ball-winners and ball-players. That isn't quite true, because some wing-halves were cultured players – Jim 'Three Livers' Baxter to name but one in his early 'Slim Jim' playing days, and two at the end of his career. Also, some inside-forwards were really strikers rather than midfield players – Harry Yorston, for example.

Looking back at the pre-war players who would fit the modern category of midfielder, one stands out: Willie Mills. His is the name which is probably recalled with most affection by Aberdeen fans old enough to remember the 1930s. He was the player who brought genuine midfield play to Pittodrie, with a mixture of close control and sweeping passes, the kind of football which Alex James played to establish Arsenal as the dominant force in the English game of the 1930s.

His career paralleled that of Charlie Cooke in a later era, playing for only one season in junior football before joining Aberdeen, and going almost straight into the first team at 17. He was certainly superior to Cooke as a goalscorer, forming a prolific partnership with Matt Armstrong and emerging as top scorer in season 1933–34, with 28 goals to his credit. He scored 114 times in 210 games for Aberdeen, an excellent record when it is remembered that he was primarily a creator rather than a taker of chances; it puts him ahead of most centre-forwards or strikers in terms of goals per game. It is the misfortune of one on whom so much depends that he is blamed when things go wrong. When Aberdeen lost to Celtic in the 1937 Cup final, Mills, possibly overawed by the occasion, had a quiet game. It was a case of 'Aberdeen expects', and when Aberdeen was disappointed it was Mills who was blamed for failing in his duty. Nevertheless he is a player who is remembered with something approaching reverence by all who saw him.

Before Mills, there was Alex Cheyne, part of the forward line I learned like a catechism: 'Love, Cheyne, Yorston, McDermid and Smith'. He is best remembered for scoring direct from a corner against England at Hampden, the incident that is credited with begetting the 'Hampden Roar'. It was his shrewd and accurate service from the inside-right position which created many of the opportunities for Benny Yorston.

After the war, Jackie Allister and Archie Glen were the the wing-halves who provided the driving force of the 1954–55 league champions. Bobby Wishart was a stylish inside-forward in that side, with a powerful shot, but hardly the dominating or flamboyant type of player who finds favour with the crowds. One of his fiercest critics was a certain Charlie Leslie, a tailor to trade, but a sportsman at heart. He had a great shock of unkempt hair, a few blackened teeth scattered at random around his gums and, in the days before designer stubble, contrived to have a permanent three-day growth of beard. He showed his contempt for the vanity of his customers by wearing an ancient, ill-fitting jacket over a semmit, without the intervention of a shirt, far less the tie which was more or less mandatory everyday wear in the 1950s. He showed his contempt for the shortcomings of footballers in rather more direct and voluble fashion, and was holding forth on the subject with my father in the street when he saw Wishart approach. He accosted the player: 'Heymin!'

'Yes, Charlie.'

'Fit aboot Setterday?'

Wishart, sensing some impending criticism, asked him to be more specific, whereupon Charlie delivered his opinions of his most recent performance in the most forthright and colourful language, commenting specifically on a lack of physical involvement on Wishart's part. By now all of Union Street, and a good part of the suburbs from Woodside to Torry, were aware of Charlie's opinions, for Charlie's voice was not low, neither was it gentle, but Wishart took it in good part, and replied that he preferred to walk off the pitch at the end of the game, rather than be carried off.

It was an exchange which says much about the Scottish game at the time. The fans appreciated the fearless, physical type of player who was constantly involved in the action. They were less likely to appreciate the type of player who did good by stealth, and that is just as true now as it was then. Billy Stark, for all the vital goals he scored from his midfield beat, was always a likely scapegoat for the team's shortcomings.

The exchange also illustrates the closeness of the fans to the players; they all knew Charlie. That has changed, for Charlie has long since gone, and there are none to replace him, and players did not go straight from school to the football club cocoon. These were the days before sponsored cars, when players actually went to work on the bus, just like the rest of us. Wishart was going to Pittodrie on the bus that day. By the end of the 1950s he was taking the bus to Dens Park, where he won another league championship medal with Dundee, playing at wing-half, and went on to reach the semi-final of the European Cup in their splendid run of the following season.

The early-1960s had Charlie Cooke and Dave Smith in the side, and with two such talented players it is difficult, at this distance, to believe that the team did so badly. If you had seen them you would have believed it. Dave Smith was an elegant wing-half, an excellent long passer and crosser of the ball, who committed the ultimate sin of leaving Aberdeen for Rangers. Does that sound biased? Damn right it's biased. He was signed by the Forces of Darkness to replace Jim Baxter, and of course nobody could, but he finished up playing as sweeper in the side that won the 1972 Cup-winners' Cup, and a very good one he was. It was just a pity about the colour of the jersey.

Another of the Smith clan, Jimmy of that ilk, had his fans in the late-1960s, but I wasn't one of them. Certainly he had great ball control, could beat a man, and was a good passer, but he always gave me the impression that he only played when he wanted to, and that wasn't often enough. He reminded me of the amateur players who would have a couple of drags on a fag before the game and put the fag-end behind their ear for the half-time refreshment. I always thought that Smith grew his hair over his ears to hide the half-time fag, but perhaps I do him a disservice.

Tommy Craig, who played only 62 games for Aberdeen, was immensely impressive when he came into the side as a teenager, and might have developed into one of the Pittodrie 'greats' had he stayed longer.

Another midfield player who deserves to be remembered as one of the most effective is Steve Murray, who beat a path for Gordon Strachan by coming to Aberdeen from Dundee, where he had been captain, and adding a vital ingredient to the side. In Murray's case it was energy rather than flair, but his running was always purposeful. Always available, never dwelling on the ball, at times it seemed that every other pass was made by or to Murray. He transformed a side which had been a trifle fortunate to win the cup into a side which was unlucky not to win the league the following season.

During Murray's relatively brief time at the club Zoltan Varga arrived. Now there was a name to conjure with. It is a measure of the impact he made that children were named after him. There are those who consider him the most skilful player ever to wear an Aberdeen jersey. He probably had the widest range of skills of any Dons player I have seen, for in addition to ball control which was probably as good as Cooke's (not better – I'll never suggest that) he had shooting power which Cooke never had and scored some spectacular long-range goals. He was Hungarian, and had been banned from playing in the German Bundesliga for taking bribes, all of which added to the aura surrounding him and made him something of a cult figure. There is nothing like a good old-fashioned betting and bribery scandal to bring a touch of colour to professional sport. It brings the game back to its roots. But Varga's influence was fleeting, lasting only a single season before he went back to the continent to play for Ajax.

Neil Simpson was one of the driving forces of the great team of the 1980s. In many ways he was an old-fashioned wing-half, never out of the action. His contribution to the team was epitomised in the Cup-Winners' Cup semi-final against Waterschei when, after Dougie Bell's corkscrew run had laid on the first goal for Black, he demonstrated the other way of going through a defence by running straight through a series of tackles to score the second. Together with Neale Cooper, he provided the bite in midfield that any team needs to be successful.

As that side broke up with the departure of Strachan and McGhee, Alex Ferguson appeared to secure the continuation of Aberdeen's dominance by signing Jim Bett. He announced his arrival in 1985 with a spectacular goal against Hibs, but on the whole his play tended to be subtle rather than showy, and he was never the crowd-pleaser that Strachan had been. As a result he tended to be underestimated, especially when Aberdeen lost their dominant position after the departure of Ferguson. But, as Joni Mitchell said, 'You don't know what you've got till it's gone'; it was the season after Bett left that the Dons finished in ninth position and narrowly avoided relegation. In the previous nine seasons he had done much to keep the club near the top of the league as the most consistent challenger to Rangers.

Of the midfield players who have come and, in most cases, gone in the 1990s, only Lee Richardson had the blend of skill, commitment and personality to make any real impact on the fans. Unfortunately, his impact on opponents was considered rather excessive by a few of our referees, and he departed after a couple of entertaining seasons and a few spectacular goals. Eoin Jess, in his second coming, may yet prove to be the midfield player to lead the Dons out of the wilderness, but, for all his undoubted skill, he is not the type of dominating player who can inspire a team single-handed. He will need more consistent support if he is finally to realise his full potential in an Aberdeen jersey; and, if he does, it appears to be more likely that it will be as a striker rather than a midfield player.

I hesitate to name any of the younger players as the potential successors to Cheyne, Mills, Smith, 'Simmie' or Bett, since, with my record in fore-casting, they would surely then be condemned to a career in the Highland League – the player I thought would be Strachan's successor was Steve Gray.

Whatever the merits of any of these players, only two were seriously considered for inclusion. One had to be Gordon Strachan, because he achieved glory for himself and for the team, and the other had to be Charlie Cooke, because he was Charlie Cooke, and he was my hero. The Aberdeen team he played in achieved nothing, but every time he got the ball was a little piece of glory in itself. There are also a couple of 'guests', who are completely unknown, but will be familiar to anyone who has pulled on his school team jersey with pride, and dreamed of glory.

Charlie Cooke

In the days before global warming, the seasons followed a predictable pattern. It was cold at Christmas; it was cold at Easter; it rained on the July holiday.

The football season started in August with the 'trial'; not a trial of those responsible for the failures of the previous season, although that would usually have been deserved; not a trial for the spectators, although it usually was; but a trial match, pitting the reserves against their supposed superiors in the first team. It was not intended to be a serious test of ability. It was an opportunity for the seasoned professionals to stretch their muscles before the more searching examinations to come, for ambitious youngsters to make their mark, and for the long-suffering punter to hand over a few more coppers before the inevitable mid-season disillusionment set in. At least on this occasion it was guaranteed that Aberdeen could not lose.

The trial of 1960 was different. It heralded the arrival of a phenomenon, and its name was Charlie Cooke. Here was a teenager, in his first appearance for the reserves, daring not only to take on and beat established first-team players, but to take them on two and three at a time. Not only that, but he did it with a style all of his own, with a flair which marked him out then and was to remain a hallmark to the end of his career.

Most young players on their first public appearance are intent on not making mistakes. They tend to concentrate on making safe, simple passes. Not Charlie. Right from the kick-off he wanted the ball, and when he got it, did not want to give it away; not to the opposition, not to his own team-mates, not to anybody. Time after time he would venture into a thicket of defenders, where escape seemed impossible, only to emerge, after a series of bewildering, unpredictable changes of direction, with the ball at his feet. He had a natural, swaying movement of the upper body when he ran, his shoulders always dipping one way or the other, and he could move with equal facility in either direction. He also had a distinctive, wide-legged gait which allowed him to run with the ball between his feet as though, in those days when footballs still had laces, it were tied to his boots.

It has to be said that the changes of direction were no more predictable to his own team than to his opponents, nor was his ultimate direction always towards the opposition goal. But what did that matter? Here was an alchemist who had turned the dross of the pre-season trial into pure gold. Here was entertainment. As the crowd left the ground, in rather better mood than they had entered it, the talk was of one name only. Who was he? Where had he come from?

Charlie Cooke had been signed from Renfrew Juniors by Bobby Calder, who sent so many talented youngsters from the West of Scotland to Aberdeen. Of them all, however – Jimmy Smith, Tommy Craig, Arthur Graham, and many others – Cooke was his favourite. Such was his brilliance, his potential could not be missed. The problem lay in signing him ahead of all the other clubs on his trail, but this was a problem which Calder, with his uniquely persuasive abilities, was adept at solving. As he had done so often before, he signed a promising player for Aberdeen while the Old Firm wondered how they had let another player on their doorstep slip away.

So Cooke arrived at Pittodrie, just one of many hopeful young players starting their careers, all of them dreaming of fame and glory, most of them just thinking in the first instance of getting a game for the reserves. Not Charlie. After that trial game, there was only one place for him, and his first game for Aberdeen, his first game in senior football, was in the first team. The opposition was Ayr United, the competition was the League Cup, and the Aberdeen team lined up as follows: Harker, Kinnell, Hogg; Burns, Coutts, Brownlee; Herron, Little, Davidson, Cooke, Mulhall. The Dons won 4–3, and Cooke had arrived in Scottish football.

After the trial, Norman McDonald had written in the *Press and Journal* of his performance: 'The brightest prospect . . . was undoubtedly Cooke . . . a natural ball player with good ball control and an intelligent sense of position. Such was his confidence and cleverness that he quickly won the admiration of the 8,000 crowd.' After the Ayr United game, he commented: 'The former Renfrew Juniors inside-forward confirmed the bright impression he created in the public trial.' If this seems scant praise for a genius arrived among us, the remarks must be judged in the context of place and time. The post-war period may have been over, but in the North-East austerity still prevailed, and 'nae bad' was regarded as a superlative.

He was all we talked about that autumn, Broonser and I. We tried to copy him, too, with varying degrees of success. I couldn't control the ball and Broonser couldn't control his legs. He fell over the ball, and broke his two front teeth on the kerb. Such were the hazards of street football, along with wifies and buses. It was supposed to have given us the grand masters of the past, the Gallachers and the Mortons. It didn't do much for us, but it did give us a link with the past.

For Aberdeen Football Club the final links with the post-war period and its league and cup successes had disappeared, following the departure of Archie Glen, Jackie Hather and Fred Martin. Tommy Pearson had taken over as manager after the brief and unsuccessful reign of Davie Shaw, but, with no money available to purchase replacements for the departed stars, he was forced to rely on youngsters. It must also be said that at no time did Pearson show the talent for management that he had displayed to such dazzling effect as a player. He presided over a period of decline which coincided with Cooke's Aberdeen career.

In case it should be thought that this was no coincidence, it must be pointed out that the failings were largely defensive. Even in those more carefree and profligate days, no team could succeed by conceding four, five or even six goals with the regularity achieved by the Dons. Not that Cooke was regarded as entirely blameless. There were those who thought that he concentrated on his own play to the detriment of the team: 'Delighted the crowd with his ball juggling, but . . . was inclined to overdo it at times,' wrote Norman McDonald. Covering a friendly against Bahia, a Brazilian team, in September 1960, he wrote that Cooke was 'as much of a ball artist as any of the Brazilians, but would have been twice as effective if he had been prepared to release the ball more quickly'. Again we hear the complaint – 'still too much of an individualist'.

The fact is that for most of his time at Pittodrie Cooke had few players worth passing to. Although he is best remembered for his dribbling skills – and rightly so – he was also a superb passer, who could thread a ball through a defence with devastating accuracy when the opportunity presented itself. What he was not, however, was a finisher. It is odd that a player who could hit such perfectly weighted passes over 30 or 40 yards to land on a colleague's bootlace should find such difficulty in hitting a target measuring eight yards by eight feet. His definitive moment came in a Scottish Cup tie in February 1961 against the Highland League side Deveronvale. The match report ran thus: 'Cooke's outstanding memory of the game must surely be the golden opportunity he missed in the first half, after a brilliant individual run. He beat five 'Vale players, including keeper Morrison, and then did the seemingly impossible by hoisting the ball over the empty goal.' It was my outstanding memory of the game too, and, I'm sure, for everyone else who was there. It was pure Charlie, pure entertainment, pure 'tanner ba''.

Gordon Strachan, of whom more anon, has been described as the last of the tanner ba' players, but he was always too mindful of the end result to qualify as the genuine article. Tanner ba' was not only about skill, it was about a belief in the expression of that skill as an end in itself. I don't suppose tanner ba' players ever thought of it in quite those terms; they just liked playing with the ball; they liked beating defenders, turning round, and beating them again. For the supporters it was about entertainment, exhilaration and, in no small measure, frustration, as yet another golden opportunity was wasted by some piece of Baroque elaboration. 'Hey Jimmy! Cut oot the Baroque elaboration!' was a cry frequently heard from the terraces. No, it wasn't really, but it is true that supporters often had an ambivalent attitude towards players who were just as likely to waste opportunities as create them. Opposing supporters would love them for their entertainment value, and delight in their downfall. Like many a prophet, they were honoured more away than at home.

Tanner ba', like so many Scottish phrases and the country's most famous product, can only be absorbed by the English after so much dilution as to rob it of its true flavour and essential character. 'Ball juggling' conveys nothing of the background: the back green, the playground and street games which gave the tanner ba' player his character, his loving of playing the game for its own sake. Possibly the decline of tanner ba' can be traced to post-war inflation, when the price of a ba' rose beyond the magic tanner. A one-and-ninepence ba' player somehow wasn't quite the same. Certainly the kind of street and playground ball changed, with the old rubber ball replaced by the larger, lighter, red plastic Frido ball. It was more indestructible than the rubber one, but it couldn't break a window as well.

My outstanding memory of street football is the time Skeneser lashed a drive past Broonser, and just inside the lamp-post, through the imaginary net, and on through the very real net curtains of a ground-floor flat, by way of the window. The amazing thing was the way that the window didn't shatter; the ball left a perfectly round hole, as though it had been cut just to let the ball through. We stopped to admire it for a moment, but only for a moment. When I came to read Tam O' Shanter, I immediately understood the line 'And in an instant all was dark'. In an instant the street was clear, as we did our speedy utmosts to reach our respective sanctuaries. To no avail; the only other person on the street at the time was old Mrs Wilson, who was too short-sighted to identify us, but, equally, was an extremely unlikely suspect. Quite apart from the problem of motive – why should an old lady suddenly take it into her head to belt a ball across the street? – there was the problem of her arthritis, which would have rendered her incapable, even if she'd wanted to. So we were fingered, and paid our shares of the damage, or rather our parents did, and shots from the wing were banned. We could live with that, because the result didn't matter as much as having a game.

By the time Cooke came along, results were starting to matter too much – not that a Dons supporter would have noticed – and there was less room for the pure entertainer. Charlie, along with Jimmy Johnstone, represented the last, late flowering of tanner ba'.

When he arrived at Pittodrie, the 1950s had gone, but the 1960s had not yet arrived. They would not get under way properly until 1963, but there was a harbinger of the decade in the report of the 'obscenity test of noted novel' – *Lady Chatterley's Lover*, available in Penguin for three shillings and sixpence. For the first and only time, Wyllie's bookshop in Justice Street (Dirty Wyllie's) had a window display consisting only of a Penguin book in its plain orange-and-white cover. Teenage boys would gaze at this display and try to imagine what unimaginable wickedness these innocent-looking covers, adorned only with a black-and-white drawing of a phoenix rising from the ashes, might contain. I'm still wondering.

In the Rome Olympics, a young American light-heavyweight boxer by the strange name of Cassius Clay, born in 1942, the same year as Cooke, had also laid down a marker for the coming decade by winning a gold medal in a style no one had seen before. He totally bemused his stolid, orthodox East European opponent by dancing round the ring with his hands hanging loosely at his sides, swaying out of reach of the other man's jabs, and flicking his stinging replies like a ringmaster cracking a whip. It would be a couple of years before we would notice him again, and learn that he floated like a butterfly and stung like a bee, and really was the greatest.

With the departure of the 1950s went the successful post-war period, not only of Aberdeen, but of the game as a whole. Crowds had started to dwindle as fans found, or were persuaded, that there were other things to do on a Saturday afternoon. The pubs were shut, there was *Grandstand* on the telly, there was gardening, there was home decorating, there was shopping. It must be admitted that much of the fare on offer at Pittodrie at that time made an afternoon in C&A and Woolies seem attractive. The more affluent Saturday shopper could have bought a radiogram from Bruce Millers for £147 6s. 0d. and on delivery could have played the latest hit from Cliff Richard ('Please Don't Tease'), the Shadows ('Apache'), or even Cliff Richard and the Shadows. These were exciting times. For Saturday evening entertainment there was a choice of 12 cinemas, and Sandy West was playing traditional jazz at the Beach Ballroom. Elvis was out of the army, but it was trad, dad, and rock'n'roll had had its day, and everybody had known it wasn't going to last.

On the football park the traditional team pattern, with the old certainties of half-back lines and forward lines, was beginning to give way to new formations. In truth, the half-back line had hardly existed since Arsenal had introduced the 'third back' game in the 1930s, but that basic pattern had remained the standard one for British football until the mid-

1950s. New formations had been introduced by foreign teams such as Hungary, with their deep-lying centre-forward, Hidegkuti. They failed to win the 1954 World Cup, but they captured the imagination of football fans everywhere, and gave us our first glimpse of the Real Game. Only a glimpse, because we just caught snatches of it on newsreels. But by 1958 we could see the Real Game live on TV, when Brazil won the World Cup, playing a 4-2-4 formation, with Didi, the Black Prince, supplying Garrincha, the Little Bird with the question-mark legs, and the young Pele. The latter would come to dominate his sport in the 1960s, much as Clay would do in his, and, like him, would become an instantly recognisable icon throughout the world, in a way that no footballer had done before.

Perhaps it was the visit by Bahia that influenced the Dons. In Charlie Cooke they had a player with Brazilian standards of skill. With a leaky defence they adapted the Brazilian philosophy of 'You score four, we'll score five' to 'No, no, *you* score five, *we'll* score four'. And in 1961–62 they adopted the 4-2-4 formation. This was the start of the 'numbers' game, with 4-2-4 becoming 4-3-3, 4-4-2, and so on. What would now seem a recklessly adventurous formation was then seen as a move towards defensive football. In the long run it was, but, in Scotland at least, the average number of goals per game remained around the four mark until the mid-1960s.

But the game has always been about players rather than numbers. Cooke now had the benefit of a full season behind him, and, with the introduction of Dave Smith into the left-half position, in what the sportswriters were beginning to call the midfield, the Dons practised the new formation with a degree of initial success.

It was during this period that Cooke played some of his best football for Aberdeen. Most notably, they achieved a win against Celtic at Parkhead and were denied a victory over Dundee only in the last minute. That may seem a very minor achievement now, but this was a Dundee side fresh from the most stunning début in European football, an 8–1 defeat of Cologne, the German champions. Perhaps the Dens Park men were suffering some reaction from their midweek performance, but Aberdeen matched them in every respect, and Cooke capped a fine performance by scoring one of his rare goals with what the *Press and Journal* reporter described as 'an exquisite lob'.

The early-season promise disappeared along with the autumn leaves, as the team's defensive frailties became ever more apparent. This was to be the story of Cooke's Pittodrie career. All too often the brilliance of his own play failed to bring any response from his colleagues. And if success was achieved at the opponent's end, it was all too often nullified by an ever-open invitation to score at the other.

Against this background of collective failure, Cooke achieved a degree of personal success by winning three under-23 caps, and was clearly marked as a player with an international future. Just as clearly, that future was not going to be with the Aberdeen team of that period. By the autumn of 1964 he had made it clear that he wanted to leave Pittodrie, and his name was being linked with clubs such as Blackpool, Wolves and Celtic.

It is intriguing to think what he – and Celtic – might have achieved had he gone to Parkhead to become part of what was, in any case, the greatest Scottish club side of all time. Managers do not always produce teams in their own image. It was Tommy Pearson, the ball artist, who failed with Charlie Cooke; it was Jock Stein, the workaday centre-half, who nourished and cherished and ultimately succeeded so brilliantly with the unpredictable talent of Jimmy Johnstone. He extracted nuggets of talent from the other members of that side and blended them into a durable alloy with a cutting edge, but Johnstone he allowed to glitter in his own way. What else could he, or anyone else, have done with such a unique and wayward talent, but who else could have deployed it so effectively? Perhaps one genius was enough, and perhaps Cooke would have upset the balance of the side; perhaps that alloy had enough precious metal with Johnstone. But wouldn't it have been beautiful to watch?

All of which is what-might-have-been. What *did* happen was that in December Dundee sold Alan Gilzean to Spurs. The headlines of that period have a familiar ring. On 11 December a City (London, not Brechin) bank crashed. On the 12th a new high in mortgage rates was announced – a whopping 6.75 per cent. A Labour government was in power.

With all these banks crashing, why not take your money out while it was still there and blow it on having a good time? You could try the Tivoli, which was showing *A Toast to the Tartan*. For those with more cosmopolitan tastes, there was His Majesty's Theatre, with Jimmy Logan starring in *Swing o' the Kilt*. There again, you might have had more fun keeping your money in the bank and watching it crash. From a choice of a dozen cinemas, the discerning film buff might have chosen *The Young Ones* at the Capitol, starring the man who was to become the eternal young one, Cliff Richard. Those who preferred home entertainment could buy a Phillips 19-inch TV (with 625 lines, ready for BBC2) for 67 guineas from Bruce Millers. And from the same shop could be had the number-one record, 'I Feel Fine' by the Beatles, who also had the best-selling LP, *Beatles for Sale*. The Rolling Stones had also had their share of hits, and the Who were about to release their first single, 'I Can't Explain'. Rock'n'roll was back, the times were a-changing, and if any further explanation was required, a young man called Bob Dylan was there to provide it. The 1960s were most definitely under way.

On the world stage, Mia Farrow and Frank Sinatra were 'just good friends'. The modest young man who had won a gold medal in Rome had become the world heavyweight champion by beating Sonny Liston and become 'The Louisville Lip' by telling everyone how great he was. BBC radio announcers still had impeccable diction, and I can remember the distasteful shudder in his voice as the newsreader reported Clay's words after the fight: 'I whipped that big ugly bear and I whipped him [disapproving pause] good.' Almost immediately he became Muhammad Ali and began to transcend sport in a way no sportsman had done before. Locally, Dr McQueen collected 'bouquets and brickbats' in the report on the typhoid outbreak which had made Aberdeen the 'beleaguered city' of the previous year.

Meanwhile, Charlie Cooke played his last game for Aberdeen on 12 December, against Hearts at Tynecastle. In a game which typified much of his time with the Dons, the result was a 6–3 defeat. He signed off with that increasingly rare occurrence, a goal, only his second of the season. The Aberdeen team that day was: Ogston, Shewan, Hogg, Burns, Coutts, Smith, Lister, Cooke, Morrison, Kerrigan, Kerr. Of the players in the team when he had made his début in 1960, only Hogg, Burns and Coutts remained. The comments in the *Press and Journal* on his final game for the Dons retained much of their 1960 content: 'Cooke always looks a stylish player on the ball. Although he was prominent at Tynecastle, he too often ran into trouble to earn star rating.'

'We don't want to sell Cooke,' declared Tommy Pearson at the beginning of the following week. Within two days the player was transferred to Dundee for £40,000. The fee was a record for a transfer between Scottish clubs, but it represented a better deal for Dundee than Aberdeen. Just how much better can be measured by the £72,000 fee which Dundee collected from Chelsea for Cooke just two years later.

Cooke's form improved at Dundee. He benefited, as so many players have done, by a temporary move back to wing-half, and by playing in a better side, albeit one which was past its peak. His next move took him to London and the swinging sixties, and a Chelsea side with the kind of talent which was able to respond to his promptings. A Chelsea historian described him as 'an expert dribbler, often leaving a string of bemused opponents in his wake'. Sounds a fair, if inadequate, description. The dominant personality in that side was Peter Osgood, with the emerging talent of Alan Hudson in midfield, and Cooke was asked to perform a more peripheral role than he might have liked in order to conform to the demands of the team. It was his passes, however, which were decisive in winning the FA Cup for Chelsea in 1970 and the European Cup-winners' Cup the following year. After the European win, Osgood, the scorer of the winning goal, acknowledged Cooke's contribution and his superior skill.

During this period Cooke also contributed to Scotland's cause on occasion – less often than his skill merited, but it was a period when Scotland had an unusually plentiful supply of individual talent in midfield and attack, with players such as Law, Baxter, Mackay and Murdoch. Their talent, unfortunately, was not matched by achievement. The Scottish press considered that their 1967 defeat of England (in which Cooke did not play) made them world champions. It was not an opinion shared by the rest of the world. The following year Cooke was in the team against England. It was a curious game, played for some reason in February instead of the usual April or May (possibly because it doubled as a qualifying match for the European Championship), and it had been in doubt because of snow. The lines were marked with sawdust to make them visible, which gave one of the big occasions of the year the look of a challenge match between rival branches of the Co-opie. Scotland needed to win to qualify for the European Championship, but could only draw 1–1, despite, or possibly because of, some great dribbles from Charlie. Scotland also had big John Hughes, 'Yogi', 'Ra Berr' in the side, and he was another player who could be a little reluctant to release the ball. It was Hughes who scored the equaliser but Cooke who earned the praise for his display: 'With his powerful runs and accurate passing he repeatedly worried the defence.' A pitch with uncertain footing was an ideal surface for Charlie, and the *Green Final* match report is full of his 'mesmerising runs' to set up chances for others. If his experience in England had improved his team play, the story of his finishing was a familiar one to those of us who had first seen him in that pre-season trial: after a series of inch-perfect passes which failed to find a suitable response from his teammates, 'Cooke gets the ball on the edge of the penalty area and tries a shot, but is well wide.' On a grey February day, his performance was the one bright spot in what journalist James Forbes described as a 'shoddy international'. Nor was the praise confined to the local press, which tended to take a paternal interest in Dons 'old boys'. *The Times* was, if anything, more extravagant: after going behind and being outplayed, 'Scotland were offered a chance of reprieve. It was their man of the hour, little Cooke, who all but seized it. Cooke is a brilliant dribbler and for that explosive period he dazzled England, left them breathless, hanging on the ropes and grateful for the interval.'

I only saw him play on one other occasion, a league game for Chelsea against Derby in 1971–72, when the latter became unexpected league champions. It was a dull game, with Derby grinding out a narrow win on their way to the title, but lit up by one glorious pass from Charlie, threaded through a space that no one else saw. It was a bit like those early days at Pittodrie, when it looked as though no one else knew what Charlie was on about. At Chelsea, it looked as though they knew, but couldn't be bothered. It hadn't always been like that. He had played an important, if not dominant, role in winning the FA Cup in 1970 against an apparently invincible Leeds side.

Chelsea's opponents in the European Cup-Winners' Cup final of the following season was the even more formidable Real Madrid. They were no longer the imperious team of the 1950s, though, and the fact that they had a member of that side, Gento, still playing at 39, was an indication of their current fallibility as much as a reminder of their former greatness. Nevertheless, their record was a daunting one, and the sight of the famous all-white strip was enough to inspire terror in opponents. And enough to inspire Charlie. The chance to play the Real Game against Real Madrid must have been what he'd been waiting for all his life. His team-mates seemed overawed by Real until, according to Geoffrey Green's report in *The Times*, 'Cooke took up the running. With swaying footwork and fine control he inspired some of his colleagues to finally show what they had in them.' He did so to such effect that they looked like winning the game until Real equalised in the last minute to take the game to a replay. A replay, rather than penalties, sounds like a quaint concept now. According to Green, 'only Cooke's footwork and balance could vie with these Spaniards, Amancia, Zoco, Pirri, Jose Luis and Velasquez', who seemed unlikely to give Chelsea a second chance. But, as they had done the previous year, Chelsea triumphed against the odds, and, as Green reported, 'Chelsea's hero again was Cooke, always hungry, always running eagerly, full of zestful control, as he became the midfield commander-in-chief, driving his men on and matching it all with a boldness of thought in his distribution.' If Green, for some unfathomable reason, had been reporting an Aberdeen match ten years previously, he could have written the same things, apart from the bit about distribution, for then he had been inclined to pass the ball only when he'd run out of defenders to beat.

Chelsea sold him to Crystal Palace in 1972, but bought him back in 1974 to help guide a young team which included a youthful Ray Wilkins. It was the same year that Ali astonished the world yet again by regaining the world heavyweight championship from George Foreman, who was about the size of a half-back line. With that fight, and his series of epic struggles against Joe Frazier, and the sheer size of his personality, Ali was to dominate the 1970s as much as he had done the 1960s. Eventually, and sadly, he was worn down by the years and the cumulative effect of all the punishment he had absorbed, and his career petered out with a couple of stumbling defeats.

In rather better circumstances, Charlie Cooke also finished his playing career in the USA, as did so many footballers in that period. He chose to stay, but do not mourn his loss to the game. He continues to coach under the auspices of the Coerver Coaching School, which preaches the doctrine and development of pure skill, a message which he is uniquely qualified to convey.

On a recent visit to Scotland to spread the word, he demonstrated that he had lost none of his skill, nor any of his enthusiasm. In demonstrating his various moves – and he had a bewildering variety: the Matthews, the Puskas, the Cruyff, the Maradona – his balance was uncanny, his footwork dazzling, his ball control magnetic. In talking about the game and his coaching principles, he said that his skills had not improved from the time he had entered the professional game. For those of us who had seen him in the trial game of 1960, it was hard to imagine how his skills *could* have been improved, but the point was well taken. In all the work on fitness and tactics, basic skills get squeezed out. However good you are, there is always room for improvement. Genius is talent plus practice.

He also felt that by playing the all-action 'method' game of the English league in the 1960s his skills had been blunted; energy spent in chasing back to cover when the other team had possession had taken the edge off his own attacking game, depriving him of the acceleration he needed to exploit his skills to the full. As he spoke, I remembered that, during his time with Crystal Palace, he had remarked that Don Rogers, newly arrived from Third Division Swindon, had retained a sense of adventure and individualism, something he felt he had lost through too much exposure to the realities of the First Division. There was a sense of regret that he had not been truer to his principles of how the game should be played. Well, Charlie, we all have to earn a living, and what you did was good enough for me.

More than anything, he still impressed me with his enthusiasm for the game, the same enthusiasm he had shown as a teenager, the same enthusiasm we all had as teenagers, only he could play and we couldn't. It was the feeling that he was there because he loved it, not because he was being paid, and wasn't life great, here I am, being paid for playing football, gimme the ball and let me play. In quiet periods (and there were plenty of those when he played for Aberdeen), you would hear his voice when someone else had the ball and didn't know what to do with it: 'Here I'm! Here I'm!' It was probably that self-same voice his team-mates heard at Hampden, and at Wembley, and that night in Athens when he beat Real Madrid, only we couldn't hear it for the noise.

He was always there, aways eager, always looking for the ball. And when the final whistle blew, he gave the impression that he wanted to carry on, like a small boy playing in the November dusk by the light of a lamp-post, going for the world record in keepie-ups (ten) and pretending not to hear his mother calling him in for his tea.

Gordon Strachan

As the first of our midfield men's career was drawing to a close, the second's Aberdeen career was just beginning. Gordon Strachan had signed for Dundee in October 1971, straight from school – by that time the almost universal pattern for promising young players. Cooke had been one of the last of the greats to have emerged from the Junior ranks.

Dundee were a struggling side and in 1976 achieved the unenviable distinction of being the first team to be relegated from the Premier League to the First Division. It is worth reminding any Dons fan convinced of his team's intrinsic superiority that it was a fate only narrowly avoided by Aberdeen. Be that as it may, it was the Dons who stayed up and Dundee who went down. In August 1977 Dundee were still in the First Division. In a side of moderate ability Strachan had quickly established himself as an inventive and influential player and, at only 20 years of age, had been appointed club captain. Elvis died.

In October, Charlie Cooke, very much alive, showed he could still spark off a *P&J* headline – 'Chelsea call up Charlie Cooke' – which reported that the 35-year-old had been 'buzzing in his new role as a striker'. His failings in front of goal have already been documented, and one can only assume that whoever saw him as a striker was also reporting sightings of Elvis.

As October gave way to November, Billy McNeill, the new Aberdeen manager, reported on the state of his side: 'In some ways we are lacking in flair at the moment and it is a player, or players with this quality – the ability to do the unpredictable thing – that I would like to add to the staff.' The following day the *Press and Journal* reported the possible signing of a new player from the Scottish First Division. On 3 November it was more specific – 'Strachan could be a Don today' – confirming the move the next day: 'Gordon Strachan, who began the season as captain of Dundee FC, yesterday became an Aberdeen player in exchange for Jim Shirra, and a fee believed to be about £40,000.'

If Dundee had stolen Cooke for £40,000 in 1964, then after 13 years of inflation the same fee plus the relatively modest abilities of Jim Shirra surely represented grand larceny. And if Tommy Gemmell failed to see what he was losing, his old captain did not: 'This may not be the biggest signing Aberdeen have ever made, but in my opinion it could well become the best. After all, Gordon is only 20 years old and the club can expect another ten years from him. It's a great signing for the future and I'm sure the Pittodrie fans will come to realise his great ability.' Prophetic words, but even McNeill could not have envisaged just how successful the signing would prove to be. The club did not quite get ten years from Strachan, but the seven they did get included the most glorious years in its history and when he went in 1984 the £600,000 fee comfortably beat the inflation on the £40,000 of 1977.

When Strachan signed, you could have bought a 1976 Mini for £1,575. Vacancies for fitters were advertised at a salary of £4,000. The Tivoli had long since closed as a theatre to become a bingo hall, but His Majesty's Theatre was still open. Tastes in popular entertainment had moved on since Cooke's day. In 1977 it was showing *The New 1977 Jim Macleod Show*, presumably a great advance on the old one.

If you preferred a film, your choice had been severely restricted, with only five cinemas still operating. The Capitol was showing *The Outlaw Josey Wales*, starring (and directed by) Clint Eastwood, who in Cooke's day had been Rowdy Yates in *Rawhide*. Recent concerts at the Capitol had featured Elkie Brooks, David Essex and Showaddywaddy. And somewhere, sometime, Sandy West and His Jazzmen were surely playing, just as they had been in Cooke's day.

If you preferred to listen to music at home, you could throw out the old radiogram you had bought when Cooke was playing for Aberdeen and replace it with a Ferguson Music Centre for £129.95 – less than the cost of the old radiogram. A band called called Baccara were top of the charts with 'Yes Sir I Can Boogie'.

There were demands for devolution. Labour were in power, and there was a 'Tory call for new Scots super-stadium'. Alex Fletcher, the Conservative spokesman on Scottish affairs, stated that the Government could divert funds from North Sea oil to build a completely new football stadium. The oil is still flowing, and we are still waiting for the stadium.

On Saturday, 5 November, BBC1 was showing *Doctor Who* at 6.10, followed by *Bruce Forsyth and the Generation Game*. Grampian, ever anxious to raise standards, was showing *Sale of the Century* at 7.30.

Those Dons fans who had rushed back from Dundee in time for such compulsive viewing had seen Gordon Strachan make his début against Dundee United, before a crowd of 10,000. It was Willie Miller who shone brightest in a 1–0 Aberdeen victory. Alistair McDonald in the *Press and Journal* rated his display as 'the best individual performance by an Aberdeen player I can recall in the years I have been covering the Dons' games regularly'. Such superlatives, rarely seen in the normally austere pages of the local journal, were put back in the vaults for Strachan, but he received praise nonetheless: 'After a quiet opening spell, Strachan improved as the game progressed, his confidence increasing in step with his understanding of his team-mates' play.' The Aberdeen team that day was Clark, Kennedy, McClelland, Smith, Garner, Miller, Robb, Jarvie (Campbell), Harper, Fleming, Strachan.

In his next game, a goalless draw with Ayr United at Pittodrie, Strachan's contribution was not deemed worthy of mention in the match report. On the same page it was reported that the Aberdeen Secondary Schools select had reached the third round of the national competition, and that four of the team had been chosen to play in an international trial, including a Hilton schoolboy by the name of John Hewitt.

Strachan scored his first goal for the Dons on 3 December, against Motherwell. It was his only goal in 16 appearances that season. His tally in the following season was only a modest six from 46 appearances, but from then on he became a regular scorer from midfield, hitting an impressive 20 goals in each of seasons 1981–82 and 1982–83. Not only did he score in quantity, he scored goals of quality. The range varied from 30-yard drives to the two-yard tap-in of the 1982 Scottish Cup final. There was, uniquely, a diving header from a John Hewitt cross against Dundee. But most typically Strachan were the cheeky ones: a shot curled in from a highly improbable angle against Hibs, and, best of all, a ball passed through a corridor of Dundee United defenders to find the corner of the net, a ploy that had Hamish McAlpine beating the ground in sheer frustration. One remembers, too, the sheer delight when one of these tricks came off, not the stereotyped ritual indulged in by so many players, but a sheer boyish exuberance to match the mood of the moment. This enthusiasm he shared with Cooke; the eye for goal was Strachan's alone.

If both players are noted, above all, for their dribbling skills, they also shared the ability to switch play tellingly with one sweeping cross-field pass. Strachan did this most memorably in the UEFA cup-tie against Ipswich when, in a match which was not otherwise one of his best, he twice picked up the ball from deep in his own half to find Peter Weir on the left wing; twice Weir cut in past a bemused Mick Mills to place the ball in the far corner of the net. The fact that the goals had been scored against one of England's top clubs did nothing to diminish the Dons fans' pleasure in the victory; the South Stand echoed to the sound of 'Cheerio, cheerio, cheerio!' God was, after all, a Scotsman.

Whatever nationality God was, he looked younger than Bobby Robson. Later that evening, as they settled down to enjoy the Bannockburn action replay, the Dons fans who had sent him homeward to think again would gain the first glimpse of that crumpled expression which he was later to adopt so frequently as England manager. With the insight that only comes after many years in the professional game, he explained that, when the score was 1–1, the game was even, and that if Ipswich had scored instead of Aberdeen they would have won. This might have been described as a statement of the obvious, but clearly it must have impressed someone in the FA; it was to serve as the script for many an England post-match conference.

In some ways it was the night the Dons found their feet in Europe. They had eliminated the UEFA Cup-holders. In the next round they further enhanced their European reputation by scoring three goals against Hamburg – a tally which could easily have been doubled – only to throw away their chances in the return leg by conceding two of the silliest goals ever lost in the Ferguson era.

Strachan was establishing his own European reputation and in the 1982 World Cup he arrived on the world stage, proving himself a player capable of taking on the best of defences. His red hair made him instantly recognisable, and the Spanish fans, always keen on nicknames, christened him 'Little Orange'. I wasn't there, but Broonser was. He enjoyed it immensely, and came back with a sombrero but with no memory of a single incident after the second goal against New Zealand. By his own admittedly modest standards, this made it a hugely successful expedition. By Scottish standards, it was a reasonably successful World Cup – a win against the minnows, a draw against the USSR, and a great goal against the Brazilians from David Narey.

It was the following season that the Dons and Strachan, having established their reputations, found real international stature. The season may have reached its climax in the Ullevi Stadium, but before that there was Pittodrie's greatest-ever night, when the Dons defeated Bayern Munich 3–2.

It was the greatest night before a ball had been kicked. Here were the Dons, Aberdeen FC, on the brink of beating one of European football's greatest names to go into the semi-final. Pittodrie was packed well before kick-off, and buzzing with that intensity peculiar to floodlit matches. From the Beach End, I gazed down on the pitch I had looked on from behind the goal, scarcely able to believe that this was the same place that had housed so many drab, scuffling affairs on grey afternoons. I looked round at the crowd, scarcely able to believe that this was the same crowd that had moaned its way through those drab, scuffling affairs, until, despairing of excitement or goals, had sought only the merciful release of the final whistle. Here was a crowd united by a common purpose, anticipating action and glory. And as I looked round I saw Victor, with whom I had travelled on that vain quest for the league title all those years before. He saw me, and, too far apart to speak, together we raised our fists in a gesture that spoke of old, lost campaigns as well as the present struggle.

The teams came out, side by side, and our mute gesture was lost in a roar the like of which I had never heard at Pittodrie. The hairs rose on the back of my neck. This was a crowd willing a team to victory. On to glory. *Here we go, here we go, here we go.*

It didn't look that way after ten minutes, when Augenthaler's shot from

Breitner's free-kick veered wickedly away from Leighton into the top right-hand corner of the net. I was perfectly placed to see that one going in all the way, and wished I hadn't been. At other times a setback like that would have turned the crowd against the team, but not this time, and when Simpson was first to a rebound it seemed that it was the crowd as much as the player forcing the ball over the line. All square at half-time. I looked around for Victor just before the start of the second half, and we raised our fists again. This time glory. *Here we go, here we go, here we go.*

But not yet. Bayern showed their class with a superbly taken goal by Pfugler, and defiance turned to despair. *There we went.* The Dons, trailing 2–1, seemed to be on the way out when they won a free-kick on the right of the penalty area. Strachan and McMaster lined up to take it, and there was almost an audible groan from the crowd as they recognised the prelude to the familiar 'bungled' free-kick routine: 'They're not going to try that one again,' seemed to be the pessimistic consensus at the Beach End. But, if the groan was audible, the Germans failed to recognise its significance, and if the ploy was by then familiar in the Premier League, it was unknown in the Bundesliga. Strachan and McMaster pretended to collide, as the fans knew they would; Strachan, in the middle of remonstrating with McMaster, wheeled round to float the ball into the penalty area, as the fans knew he would; McLeish went for it, as the fans knew he would, and soared above a static Bayern defence to head the equaliser, as the fans never believed he could. 'It worked! It worked!' Pandemonium. And still more pandemonium when John Hewitt completed the *Boys' Own* story by scoring a winner which I suspect most of the still-celebrating crowd never saw.

Aberdeen, with Strachan at the hub of most of their moves, went on to win the European trophy by beating Waterschei easily, and Real Madrid gloriously; the Scottish Cup was won by beating Rangers, rather fortunately.

Success continued the following season as Aberdeen dominated the league championship, reached the semi-final of the European Cup-Winners' Cup, and won the Scottish Cup for the third successive year. It was a sequence of success unparalleled by a Scottish provincial club, but long before the season ended it was clear that it would be Strachan's last with Aberdeen. Whatever the Dons might offer by way of winning trophies, reaching cup finals and enjoying forays into Europe, there remained the grind of a Premier League programme which entailed twice-yearly visits to half-empty grounds. As Strachan said, he'd met all the tea ladies, tasted all the pies – his courage was never in doubt – and it was time to move on.

Moving on was to prove less than simple, but after some confusion over a contract with FC Cologne, Strachan signed for Manchester United on 9 May 1984. He completed his Aberdeen career in the finest possible manner, by helping to beat Celtic in the Scottish Cup final. The Aberdeen side which took the field at Hampden on 19 May was: Leighton, McKimmie, Rougvie, Cooper, McLeish, Miller, Strachan, Simpson, McGhee, Black, Weir. It was by that time a reassuringly familiar line-up to the Dons fans, which seemed to have been there forever, but, of the players with whom Strachan had made his début in 1977, only Willie Miller remained.

Since then inflation had continued apace. Grampian Region was advertising a vacancy for a secretary at a salary of £5,640. A Porsche was for sale at £14,250, but if your cheque book didn't run to that, your wallet might have coped with a 1978 Datsun at only £425. New houses were for sale at the Bridge of Don which, according to the advertiser, offered 'suburban purity' at prices ranging from £27,250 to £74,900. Aberdeen was in the middle of an oil boom which everyone thought would go on forever.

Those fans wishing to soothe their nerves before the final could have watched *The Beechgrove Garden* on BBC1. After the final they could have wound down with *The Price is Right*. If that wasn't good enough, the choice of entertainment outside the home was more limited. Aberdeen was down to three cinemas – the Capitol, the ABC and the Odeon. The Capitol had been showing a Clint Eastwood film in 1977, and was showing another in 1984 – *Sudden Impact*. Not, alas, a Western; the genre had not been seen for many moons, and was rumoured to have gone to Boot Hill along with Josey Wales. Elvis, meantime, had gone in the opposite direction; he had a death certificate, but was seen more often than before he had obtained the paper qualification. If there was nothing you fancied at the cinema, and there probably wasn't, there was always the video, an unheard-of device in 1977, but commonplace by 1984. The Dons fan who went to Hampden could now return home to gloat over his recording of yet another Aberdeen triumph.

In the event, it was a triumph laced with some controversy, involving as it did an opening goal for Aberdeen which to many seemed offside, and the dismissal of Roy Aitken for a foul on Mark McGhee. Strachan was involved on the margins of that incident but, more crucially, was part of both Aberdeen goals. The first came from a Strachan corner, and the second from a cut-back to McGhee, which gave him the opportunity to score with almost his last kick as an Aberdeen player.

Strachan then bade farewell to the club and the fans: 'The fact that it was my last match in front of the Aberdeen fans made it special and memorable for me. It will be a wrench leaving so many great friends at the club and in Aberdeen itself, for I have really been very happy with the Dons.'

Alex Ferguson was philosophical about losing Strachan and McGhee, two of his best players: 'One thing about football is that it keeps throwing up new players and it could be that the vacancies which are occurring now are just what is needed to create opportunities for youngsters on the staff.' He must have known that players like Strachan, or McGhee for that matter, do not come along very often. The great midfielder was not replaced, and never has been. Even with a much-diminished side, Ferguson kept Aberdeen on a winning course, but the vacancy which occurred two years later was the Manchester United job, and he once again found himself managing Gordon Strachan.

By this time the player had established himself as a favourite at Old Trafford and had won a Cup-winner's medal. He continued his success at both club and international level, scoring Scotland's only goal (whisper it, off a German deflection) in the 1986 World Cup finals in Mexico. Broonser went there, too, with the 1982 Spanish sombrero for good luck. It had to be discarded after an unfortunate incident on the plane, but the purchase of a replacement in Mexico should not have been too difficult, even for one of Broonser's limited commercial skills. He could only afford the single fare, and was relying on a bet on Scotland to win the World Cup for the fare home. He felt that it was the least he could do for Scotland.

By 1989 Ferguson considered that Strachan had done all he could for Manchester United, and transferred him for a second time, on this occasion to Second Division Leeds United. It was a decision which was to give him some cause for regret. Far from playing out his career in the lower division, Strachan inspired Leeds to win promotion and, within two seasons, win the First Division title at the expense of his old club. To old Leeds fans it must have seemed like the second coming, for it was another diminutive Scottish midfielder, Bobby Collins, who had found an Indian summer at Elland Road and inspired their earlier success under Don Revie.

His international career was also revived; after being omitted from the 1990 World Cup finals, he was recalled by Andy Roxburgh to help Scotland qualify for the 1992 European Championship. In the course of that qualifying campaign he captained Scotland in the match against San Marino, and gained his fiftieth cap.

Injury problems prevented him from taking part in the finals, but Scotland's hideous new strip had given him the opportunity to prove that a 35-year-old could not only keep running for the whole 90 minutes, but could do so wearing shorts made out of barrage balloons. (After decades of steadily diminishing shorts, from the all-enveloping garments of the previous century to the athletic brevity of the 1960s and beyond, fashion had decreed a return to the baggy bloomers of the 1930s.) I can't help feeling that the fact that he captained Scotland in the away strip may be a source of regret in the years to come. 'Tell us about the time you led out Scotland in the dark blue, Grandad.' 'Well, actually, son, it wisnae dark blue. It was white wi' wee purpley bits, but . . .' At least he had plenty of appearances in dark blue to fall back on.

He attributed his continuing stamina to a diet of porridge and bananas. Certainly he looked after himself well, and his career can be contrasted with those of equally talented players who would consume bananas only after the fruit had been fermented and distilled, and who were effectively finished before they were 30.

But there was more to his sporting longevity than diet. He used his experience well, conserving his energy for when it mattered. He popped up all over the pitch, but his ubiquity was not the product of incessant, mindless running. Timing was all; when the vital opportunity arrived, he was there, and thus conveyed the impression of non-stop involvement. Nor was everything done at top speed, though when the sudden burst of acceleration was required, it was there; a vital yard was gained, and made to count.

Most important of all was the enthusiasm which he showed as a teenager and never lost. It is this enthusiasm which allied him to Charlie Cooke; that, and the ability to convey his love of the game to the crowd. The schoolchild watching Cooke could see in him the boyish enthusiasm that he felt for the game, and a source of inspiration for what it was possible to achieve. The adult watching Strachan could see in him the boyish enthusiasm he once had for the game, and revive it. For the adult, he would also serve as a reminder of those possibilities first revealed by Cooke; the possibilities of the daring and unexpected, as well as excite- ment. And for the schoolboys in the crowd, there would be the same inspiration that Cooke had provided in an earlier era, and perhaps one of them would have the ability and determination to achieve the possibilities which players like Cooke and Strachan can reveal. When they played, we had a chance to see the Real Game.

Both players will perhaps be best remembered for their dribbling skills, but in contrasting styles. Strachan never had the close dribbling skills or repertoire of moves that Cooke had. The ball was pushed in front of him rather than held close to him, in the manner of Cooke. He invited the tackle, rather than defying it. He would not be able to retain the ball as long as Cooke, but then he wouldn't want to. For him, movement was all, but not for its own sake; it had to be a telling movement. His instinct was for the effective rather than the decorative. He always entertained – well, usually – but always with the end result in mind. He had the ability to find a way through a crowded penalty area, but it was with a burst of speed and an eye for unconsidered space, rather than the intricate control of a Cooke or a Johnstone.

With his red hair, and its proximity to the ground, comparisons with Johnstone were inevitable, and indeed their careers overlapped briefly at Dundee. If Johnstone influenced the young Strachan's style on the park, his influence off it was not always for the better, according to Strachan's autobiography. Certainly Strachan had the winger's instinct to head for the bye-line and cut the ball back. In an earlier era, his style and stature may well have confined him to the stereotyped winger's role, forever going round the full-back and crossing the ball for his centre-forward to head home. But Strachan's vision was always wider than Johnstone's, who often gave the impression that the defensive confusion he created was at least matched by his own. When Stein tried him at inside-right, he tended to dribble in ever-decreasing circles, like a rowing-boat with only one oar, a situation with which he was not unfamiliar.

The more fluid tactics of the modern era allowed Strachan to develop the full range of his skills as a midfield player, and superior training, allied to his own dedication, allowed him to exert his influence in every area of the pitch. He was a player very much of his own time, whereas Cooke may have been happier in an earlier, more indulgent age as an old-fashioned inside-forward.

There is no doubt that Strachan was the more effective, and the more successful player. Not that Cooke was without his successes – 16 international caps, and FA Cup and European medals with Chelsea. But these achievements were dwarfed by Strachan's 50 caps, his full set of domestic honours and the European medal with Aberdeen, followed by FA Cup success with Manchester United and the culminating glory of skippering and inspiring Leeds United to the league championship. If it was his good fortune to play in great sides, it must be acknowledged that in each case his contribution was a crucial factor in making those sides what they were. It is too early to say if he will be as successful as a manager, but, at 39, he came back as a player to fill a vital role in keeping Coventry in the Premiership. Since then, the club has continued to progress under his direction.

But the choice of hero is not a matter of logic. In many species there is a period in the development of the young when they learn certain responses and the recognition of what will be important to them – their parents, their own kind, food. This period in development is known as the critical period. In the young male of the human species this critical period for the choice of football hero is somewhere between boyhood and adolescence, when he knows enough about football to recognise a great footballer but is still young enough to believe that heroes can walk upon the earth. The heroes of our youth, whatever their true stature, will always dwarf the stars we see in maturity. As a Dons player, Gordon was great, by any rational assessment the best I have seen. But, for me, Charlie will always be the greatest.

ABOVE: 'Keeper's ba'!' Fred Martin makes a
fine save at a packed Ibrox in November
1956, thereby attaining honorary status as a
Fenian b*****d while silencing the singing of
'The Sash'. Aberdeen centre-half Alex Young
ducks just in time, while wing-half Jackie
Allister looks on, blissfully unaware that he is
in the flight path of the robust Sammy Baird
of Rangers. On the far right, Rangers' South
African left-winger, Johnny Hubbard, is
hanging around waiting for a penalty, as usual.
Note Martin's woolly gloves ('Jist the job,
Maw.' 'You see an' wear them, son') and
Allister's old-fashioned boots, covering the
ankle and wrapped with yards of lacing.
(© Scottish Media Newspapers Ltd)

LEFT: 'Keeper's ba'!' Bobby Clark cuts out a
Partick Thistle cross in typical style at
Pittodrie. Need he have bothered? Yes;
Aberdeen's record against the Jags in the 1970s
was deplorable. It's about 20 years on from the
Martin photograph, but the gear is still very
simple – no gloves, no padded shorts, no garish top. In just a few years' time, a
father's relief at producing a son rather than a daughter would be tempered by the
thought that he might have produced a goalkeeper, whose kit would cost twice as
much as the average wedding. (© Aberdeen Journals Ltd)

RIGHT: Jock Hutton: Aberdeen's fearsome full-back of the 1920s, before he went on to play Hoss Cartwright in *Rawhide*. (© Aberdeen Journals Ltd)

BELOW: 'Aye, the two turnstiles'll be enough. An' min' – naebody gets in withoot a bunnet!' A typical crowd picture of the 1930s: Merkland Road East packed with fans, newly poured out of the pubs and off the trams, before a match with Celtic in 1937. (© Aberdeen Journals Ltd)

ABOVE: The picture that symbolises the 1930s for Aberdeen: Willie Cooper chasing Jimmy McGrory; the Dons always chasing, never quite catching the Old Firm, against a backdrop of huge crowds. On this occasion, the Cup final of 1937, the attendance was 146,433, the highest ever for a club game in the UK. (© Aberdeen Journals Ltd)

RIGHT: Donald Colman: one of Aberdeen's most distinguished defenders, and one of the game's great innovators, whose playing career spanned the first two decades of the club's history. (© Aberdeen Journals Ltd)

RIGHT: November 1960; a young and somewhat pimply Charlie Cooke in his early days at Pittodrie, with a then-fashionable Perry Como haircut. (© Scottish Media Newspapers Ltd)

BELOW: Willie Miller celebrates the goal against Celtic which virtually clinched the league title in 1985, with two matches to spare. Alex McLeish's joy is tempered by the realisation that Willie has just gone two up in their annual scoring contest. (© Aberdeen Journals Ltd)

LEFT: Joe Harper as he will always be remembered, celebrating one of his 199 Aberdeen goals in typical fashion.

RIGHT: A rare picture of Gordon Strachan releasing the ball – it must be a free-kick. His accuracy and ingenuity from free-kicks and corners were valuable attacking weapons in the all-conquering Aberdeen side of the 1980s. (© Aberdeen Journals Ltd)

ABOVE: 'I told yer to stand on his foot, man!' A frustrated Jackie Charlton can only look on as Denis Law soars above a sporting but earthbound Bobby Moore to score the finest headed goal ever seen at Hampden, Scotland's third in a 4–3 defeat in April 1966. The author can be seen in the fourth row of the North Stand, just behind one of the pillars. (© Scottish Media Newspapers Ltd)

LEFT: Still immaculate in the classic all-white strip of Real Madrid, Ferenc Puskas (the fat one) and Alfredo di Stefano (the bald one) embrace to the acclaim of a huge crowd at the end of the 1960 European Cup final, having just scored seven goals between them in Hampden's greatest-ever game.
(© Scottish Media Newspapers Ltd)

ABOVE: Always on the lookout for a shooting chance, Graham Leggat gets a shot on target past Airdrie defenders Quigley (centre) and Baillie, in October 1956. Mid-1950s pointers: the substantial crowd, although attendances had passed their post-war peak; Graham Leggat's quiff; Airdrie's 'continental' V-neck jerseys; the unpainted ball (the white ball, introduced for floodlit games, was still a couple of years off). It is unclear whether 'man mountain' Doug Baillie's pained expression is a result of failing to stop Leggat's shot, or not getting close enough to kick him, or a bit of both. Whatever the reason, he bears testimony to P.G. Wodehouse's assertion: 'It is never difficult to distinguish between a Scotsman with a grievance and a ray of sunshine.' (© Aberdeen Journals Ltd)

Blacklaw

No, I don't remember his first name. He was in Mr Wright's class, where the boys were known only by their surnames, although the girls were known by their first names. Like much that Mr Wright did, this policy could not be justified by any kind of logic, far less any notion of political correctness – he was a staunch proponent, and an occasional but fiercely effective exponent, of corporal punishment – but it worked. So Blacklaw remained plain Blacklaw, the single name enough to identify him, like an Italian Renaissance painter.

It was the only way he could have been likened to Michelangelo or Leonardo, for he wasn't very good at art. Let's be honest; he was hopeless. And art was his best subject, apart from football. As far as anyone in the educational system had been able to discover, football was the only approved activity at which he was any good, and the time had come to exploit this single and singular talent for the good of the school. He was to be the team's inspiration, its mastermind, the fulcrum of its operation. You may consider that this weight of expectation was a heavy burden to place upon 11-year-old shoulders, and you would have been right, if Blacklaw had had shoulders, but between his neck and the top of his arms there wasn't enough room to carry a schoolbag strap. Not that this was any great disadvantage to him in his school career, since all he really needed to carry to school were a couple of fags stuffed in a pocket. Matches he usually cadged. Nor was the rest of him any more impressive: a shuffling, knock-kneed gait; a concave chest; a battery of facial tics; straggly hair that flopped over his eyes at the front, and suffered the ravages of alopecia at the back.

His appearance was our secret weapon. He had great ball control, just enough pace to get past defenders, and an uncanny knack of arriving in the penalty area at the right time. When the opposition saw that they were being beaten by someone who looked like he did, they would be totally demoralised. That, at least, was the theory.

Not that we were totally relying on Blacklaw. At the back we had Wilson and Dawson. Wilson was the goalkeeper, picked for his height, handling and intense stupidity. The problems of goalkeeping on Glasgow school pitches and the painful transfer of grit to skin have already been explained in the chapter on Willie Miller. Goalkeepers maybe dived once, but not again. Wilson's great gift was not so much that he didn't feel pain, but that he never did make the connection between the diving and the pain. I know we should have told him; it was our duty to him as a child and pupil. But he was more than that. He was a goalkeeper.

Dawson was different. He had brains, which certainly made him different in that school, and marked him out as captaincy material. Let's be honest; it marked him out as a potential headmaster, but captain of the school team was as far as we could promote him until he was tall enough to wield the belt. He wasn't very tall, but he could tackle, was cool under pressure, and could organise the defence, so in he went at centre-half. Christ, the kids did as he told them. How did he do it? Winters was big and ugly, no brains, no skill, so he went in at full-back.

The only other player of any note was Walsh. He had stood out immediately in the trial game, even before it had started. He was tall and strong, barrel-chested, with legs like, well, legs; bone and muscle, stuff like that, compared to the hinged corner flags that most of our waifs used to connect their shorts to their boots. He stood out even more when the ball came to him; control it on the thigh, left foot, flick it past one player, past another, and let fly with a screamer from 30 yards that went just past the post and took the goalkeeper five minutes to retrieve. It was the first time I had seen Walsh, and my jaw dropped. Never mind the school team, would he make the Scotland team? My colleagues just smiled and nodded. They had seen him before. 'Just you wait,' said big McRitchie.

'You mean there's more?' I said.

'More of the same,' he said.

And that's exactly what there was. The ball came to him again: instant control with the left foot, flick past one player, past another, one more pace and let fly. This time he was pointing in a different direction, and the shot finished up nowhere near the goal. The next time, he flicked the ball past players that weren't even there, and failed to hit the penalty area. I got the message: one foot, one move, one brain cell. All you could do was keep him on the wing, and hope that every now and again he was pointing the right way when he shot. Apart from that, his great hulking menace kept up morale, and was liable to scare the opposition shitless.

Picking a football team in a large school is the closest most of us will ever get to being Cecil B. DeMille. From a cast of thousands, swirling this way and that, order must be created, and you don't even have a megaphone, just a whistle and your own voice, already badly worn after a solid day of shouting at the little bastards. It doesn't take long for the stars and the no-hopers to emerge, however. The stars are retained, along with the 20 or so who have some reasonable chance of being able to kick the ball at least once in every three attempts, and the no-hopers are sent home with their shattered dreams. You trust your judgement and hope that you're never mentioned in some ghost-written autobiography – *Kenny: The Road to Stardom*; *Willie: The Smell of the Liniment, The Roar of the Crowd*; or *Jimmy: Girls, Goals and Glory* – as the useless sod of a blind, self-important, know-all schoolteacher who failed to recognise the greatest footballing genius that Scotland had produced in a generation.

But who knows? Maybe that teacher did me a favour. 'Cause if he hadn't sent me home that day maybe I wouldn't have been so determined to succeed. Maybe I wouldn't have practised so hard if I'd gotten into that team. Maybe I'd have been just another schoolboy star who never made it to the big time.

But that day, as I trudged home with the boots weighing heavy in my bag, those boots my mother had made so many sacrifices to buy, and the tears streaming down my cheeks, I made up my mind. I'd make it all right. I'd play for Albion Rangers. I'd score all their goals. We'd win the cup, and the league. I'd play for Scotland. And of course it all came true. The cup and league double. Top goalscorer. Captain of Scotland.

But even I hadn't foreseen the rest. The transfer to Manchester United. More goals. Another cup and league double.

The dream move to Milan. More goals. More league titles. The European Cup. And finally leading Scotland to World Cup glory. Not bad for the wee boy whose teacher said couldn't play.

Not bad for the wee boy who couldn't get into his school team. The school team that won nothing. So all I've got to say, Mr Addison, Sir, is thanks. Thanks for throwing me out. Thanks for not giving me the chance. It was you who made up my mind for me. It was you who gave me the guts and determination to make it to the big time. And why? Just to prove you wrong, that's why.

So I hope you were watching when I lifted the World Cup. And I hope you remembered. And I hope you thought of all the other boys you sent home. The ones who might have made it, but thought they couldn't play because you said so. Sir.

Just one more thing, Sir. You were a lousy teacher too. In all those years you never learned me nothing. I never dreamed of Manchester or Milan because I'd never heard of them. So whose fault was that? Yours. I'd never even heard of France, never mind Milan. When I got there it was like being in a foreign country. Your fault, Sir. May you rot in hell. Sir.

Actually, it's never happened. Believe me, all the boys I sent home really were hopeless, although I do occasionally wake up in a cold sweat at the thought of being pilloried as the man who missed Scotland's football genius, like the man from Decca who sent the Beatles home.

However improbably, a side emerged from the primordial soup we had started off with, and not a bad side at that. Like every football manager at the start of the season we were 'quietly confident'.

It was August 1973. The England cricket team had just been thrashed by the West Indies, leaving English cricket despondent, especially as they were due to tour the West Indies that winter. The response to the crisis was the usual one: pick a new captain. Mike Denness, the Scottish captain of Kent, was the choice. He was reported as being 'very pleasantly surprised and obviously thrilled'. Now perhaps I'm missing something, but it's not at all obvious to me why he should have been thrilled at the prospect of leading a side to certain defeat, being pilloried in the press, and having missiles hurled at his head from about 20 yards away. Still, at that stage I suppose a few weeks in the Caribbean didn't sound too bad a way of spending the winter, and, with the West Indies fast bowlers a few months rather than a few yards away, it wasn't too difficult to sound confident.

In golf, great things were predicted of the 20-year-old Sam Torrance. He had every right to feel confident. He lived in an age when moustaches were fashionable. Gary Glitter was top of the pops with 'I'm the Leader of the Gang', and sounded somewhat brashly confident.

George Miller, the manager of newly promoted Dunfermline, was quietly confident. Previewing the match with Celtic, who, by that time, had been champions forever, he declared his commitment to attacking football, whatever the opposition. Celtic were not only the eternal champions; they had already beaten Dunfermline 6–1 in the League Cup. This was an opportunity for Mr Miller to display a manager's greatest gift: not coaching expertise, not tactical acumen, not the power of inspiration, but the ability to explain away resounding defeats. 'The score at Parkhead really flattered Celtic. We hit their bar twice and missed at least three great chances.' So, in a couple of sentences, a 6–1 defeat had been converted into a hypothetical 6–6 draw. Brilliant. And it confirmed, more than any statement of intent, Miller's belief in attacking football. Most managers would have tried to explain away some of the Celtic goals – blatant offside, blind referee, cruel luck, bad bounce, last goal deflected in by aliens – to get the PUG score down to a plausible 1–1. Not Miller: 'You score six on the park, we'll score six in our dreams.' That's my kind of manager. But he also revealed his weakness, and possibly the reason why he never made the big time. He settled for the hypothetical draw, rather than go for the moral victory.

PUG, by the way, stands for Parallel Universe Game. Every game consists of at least three games: the real one, played on the pitch, and at least two others, watched in parallel universes by the respective managers and supporters, in which all the refereeing decisions and twists of fate go against their side. The best example I ever saw of the disparity between a PUG and the real game was in the *Irvine Valley News*, a long defunct

Ayrshire journal. The local heroes, Darvel Juniors, had been beaten 12–8. Now in some parts of the country, a defeat of these proportions might be a cause for some light-hearted banter. But this was Ayrshire Junior football, where the game is played with all the seriousness and most of the viciousness of a civil war, and poking fun at the local football team is as ill-advised as poking a mafioso's sister. The reporter managed to spirit away all 12 of the opposition's goals with the usual mixture of bad bounces, bad decisions, bad weather and downright wickedness, while praising all eight of the home side's goals as gems of the footballing art, and lamenting the bad bounces, bad decisions, etc, which had prevented them from adding to their total. A 12–8 defeat was thus converted into a moral victory in double figures.

The *Irvine Valley News* reporter liked to use the phrases employed by journalists on the national press, or, rather, the phrases which had been used a couple of decades previously: 'the leather sphere'; 'the custodian'; 'the rigging'. Presumably this was intended to raise the status of the local games. I am convinced that, somewhere in this report, there occurred the old, old phrase 'defences were well on top' but I cannot prove it.

Well, our school team was going to have no need of those managerial or reporting skills. The skills were in our players. We had no need of clichés. We were quietly confident. We had some good lads. On the Friday before the big game they were sent up to Mr Wright's room to get The Lesson. This was their induction into The Great Mystery Of Life, the urban equivalent of The Horseman's Word, the rite of passage, the secret without which no boy can pass into manhood. The girls were ushered out of his class and dispersed to other rooms, while Mr Wright delivered the first great mystery: the offside law. He told them of referees, and rules, first half and second half, right-half and left-half, centre-half and centre-forward. They went in boys and came out men. More than men. They were right-back, or left-half or whatever. They had the school jersey, dark- and light-blue quarters, with buttons and a collar, long after they had disappeared from the rest of the football world, and long before the retro look brought them back. (In footballing, as in educational matters, Mr Wright was immune to the winds of change and the vagaries of fashion.) They were ready to face the world.

What they faced was, in fact, Barlanark Primary School, a distinctly more daunting prospect. It didn't help that they were at home, on the other side of the Stirling Road. The houses were identical, part of the great sprawl of post-war council housing on the east side of Glasgow, but as far as our kids were concerned, it may as well have been the other side of the world.

It could just as easily have been any other side of the city, Castlemilk to the south or Drumchapel to the west. Glasgow had passed its post-war era of reconstruction, and was struggling to cope with the mistakes it had made. Most of the city slums had been pulled down, and replaced by suburban ones. It retained its reputation as a hard city, the old street gangs overtaken by a network of younger, more violent gangs whose territories were proclaimed on tenement walls – TONGS YA BASS, FLEET, YY CUMBIE. The City of Culture was still some way off. The houses may have been identical, but the gang slogans were different, and the natives were definitely hostile. It didn't help, either, that the place's nickname, the Bar-L, recalled simultaneously the wild west and Glasgow's other Bar-L, the Big Hoose, Barlinnie Prison. One way and another, it felt like bandit territory, and the boys on our side who walked tall on their home turf suddenly shrank and looked like the wee boys they really were. To tell the truth, I wasn't walking too tall myself, and I found that I wasn't anticipating victory quite as eagerly as I had been. An armoured car with the engine running would have been useful. What we had was an uncertain bus service.

I needn't have worried. Blacklaw had started twitching uncontrollably the minute we had crossed the Edinburgh Road. He could have coped with that, but Mr Wright's lesson had been too much for him. He managed to get to the inside-left position for the kick-off, but stayed there the whole game. Whether he really thought that was what playing in position meant, or whether he was simply too scared to move out of the centre circle, I never found out. He did have a legitimate excuse for staying where he was, in that it saved time at the kick-offs and, with the Bar-L scoring nine goals, it meant he was within touching distance of the ball ten times, which was more than most of his team-mates.

Walsh received the ball twice. Control, flick it past one player, past another, hammer it with the left foot. The first time the ball went screaming into the top corner of the goal, an equaliser which gave us some hope and no little anxiety. We needn't have worried. The next time Walsh got the ball, he found himself facing the wrong way when the time came to shoot, and the ball went screaming into the top corner of a downstairs school window. By that time we were 4–1 down and sinking, so everyone except the Barlanark jannie was happy. Dawson tried valiantly to hold the defence together, but he couldn't hold together what wasn't there.

Winters was a disaster at right-back. He was completely unable to judge the bounce of the ball, and couldn't decide whether to kick it or head it. He tried to compromise by raising a foot and lowering his head at the same time. This was not a successful solution to his dilemma, and he found himself kicking thin air most of the time, which was at least better than kicking the opposition, especially with their supporters all round the pitch. Never sure of the distinction between arse and elbow at the best of times, he entered the second half in a state of hopeless confusion; by the end it was as much as we could do to keep him facing in the right direction.

Wilson did his best, let two through his legs, made half a dozen improbable saves, and did well to keep the score in single figures. This could be reckoned an honourable defeat, which was the best way to get out of Barlanark. Failing that, any defeat would do. Any other result, and there was no way out of the Bar-L. As it was, we were able to leave with our limbs intact, and skin (apart from Wilson's knees) unbroken. Sod the result; at times of physical danger, your hide is more important than your pride. A disgraceful attitude for the offspring of a warrior race, I know. Yes, if all Scots had been like me, there would have been no Bannockburn. But we'd have missed Flodden and Culloden too, wouldn't we?

Back in the real world, Dunfermline didn't do too badly that Saturday; they were only beaten 3–2, a score which had them edging towards victory in George Miller's PUG. The most remarkable senior game was Hearts' 3–2 defeat of Morton, with all three of Hearts' goals coming from penalties converted by Donald Ford.

On the way back from the match, we convened a management meeting in the Horseshoe Bar, which was at that time one of Glasgow's more splendid institutions. We agreed that Winters' physique was one of our main assets, but that he had been worse than useless at right-back. Shifting him to the middle of defence was unthinkable, but where else could we put him? If he couldn't kick a ball coming towards him, could he run after the ball and kick it? How would you feel if you were an 11-year-old defender and saw Winters bearing down on you? What would you do? You'd get out of the way, that's what you'd do. With opponents scattering out of his way like Hollywood extras before King Kong, would it matter if he didn't kick the ball too often? If you cared about football, yes, but this was the Glasgow East Primary Schools League, and results were what really mattered.

So Winters started the next game at centre-forward. I haven't been right too often in football but this time I was. Winters with the ball running in front of him was a totally different animal from the lumbering dinosaur we had seen the previous week. The first time the ball was played over the defence, he elbowed the centre-half aside, ran onto the ball and blasted it straight at the keeper.

A goalkeeper needs three things: anticipation, reflexes and courage. Their goalkeeper had only two of these attributes. He anticipated the shot well enough, and was quick enough to move; but he showed a certain lack of appetite for the fray by ensuring that his movement took him out of the way, and in the few milliseconds that it took Skinner's shot to reach the goal, the goalkeeper was no longer there. With experience, he would have learned to make it look like he had anticipated the shot wrongly – the outstretched hand groping vainly for the ball he had no intention of touching, the dramatic mid-air twist. This time, it just looked like he was getting out of the way. Who knows, with a few more games, he might even have had the chance to acquire a bit more courage. Judging from the comments of his teacher, however, it was a chance he was unlikely to get. His goalkeeping career was going to end abruptly on the final whistle, and, if he should be so unwise as to turn up for school on Monday, there was little point in bringing a playtime piece, as his life expectancy seemed unlikely to be prolonged beyond the morning interval.

That was his concern. All I had to worry about was not cheering before I blew the whistle to signal the goal, for, as the home side, we had to supply the referee, and I was that soldier. The more fastidious readers, who were a trifle disconcerted by the fact that Winters had scored after using his elbow to remove the obstacle of the centre-half, will no doubt jump to the conclusion that he was only allowed to proceed, and the goal to stand, by virtue of a biased refereeing decision. Nothing could be further from the truth. The refereeing in that game, and throughout the season, was scrupulously fair whenever we played at home; it was only in the away games that the decisions invariably favoured the home side. No, the phrase 'elbowed the centre-half aside' was just a shorthand way of saying 'applied a legitimate shoulder charge within playing distance of the ball in order to obtain and retain possession'. The goal stood, and rightly so.

Winters, thus encouraged, proceeded to play out of his skin. After being dumped on his arse a couple of times, their centre-half didn't want to know, and gave Winters the run of the park. From another ten chances, he managed to score three. Walsh managed to get one of his thunderbolts on target; the defence stood firm and tackled resolutely whenever the opposition ventured into our half, and we finished up by winning 5–0. After the tribulations of the previous week, this was a most satisfactory result. Phrases like 'dumped on his arse' and 'tackled resolutely' can be interpreted along similar lines to 'elbowed aside'; it's a physical game, and nowhere more so than on the banks and braes of the Edinburgh Road.

The boys dispersed to their nearby homes with the glow of victory shining through the week's accumulated grime. John Wright and I repaired again to the Horseshoe, this time in celebration rather than despair. The journey back into town was on the top of the number 53, from which the smoke never cleared. This was no bad thing for a bus which traversed the pre- and post-war housing estates to the east of the city. It shut out reality, and gave you the opportunity to imagine that you were on the Orient Express, and damn! had forgotten to close the window before going through the Simplon Tunnel. 'Dashed nuisance, these steam trains.' If the fug cleared enough to enable you to see out of the window, the illusion of travelling through the Southern Alps was dispelled fairly rapidly, to be replaced by the reality of travelling through South Carntyne; this was more reality than anyone should be expected to bear.

There were, in truth, very few points of similarity between the no.53 and the Orient Express, apart from the fact that you were quite likely to find a body on the 53, and even this, I suspect, was more legend than fact, part of the violent myth that Glasgow liked to wrap around itself. The passengers on every route prided themselves on travelling on the roughest, toughest, hardest-drinking route in town: 'Fight'n? Boadies? They wis three deep last Setterday, so they wis. Blood runnin' doon ra sterrs.' I didn't believe any of it myself, but then I never travelled the route on a Saturday night, and had no intention of doing so.

This time, in the glow of victory and a couple of 'hauf an' haufs' we could afford to congratulate ourselves on our tactical acumen and the shrewdness of our team selection. Dawson had been a rock at centre-half, Wilson impassable in goal, and Winters a revelation at centre-forward. There was just one niggle: Blacklaw. Once again he'd looked totally lost. Dawson was a real winner as captain, but the man we had looked to as our navigator looked as though he didn't know what a map was for; which, in his case, was literally true.

Big McRitchie went some way towards explaining the enigma of Blacklaw when we presented our match report in the staff room on the Monday morning. 'The boy is under severe psychological pressure,' he intoned in his gravest *basso profundo*. 'He's learning to read.' This was an alarming, but not uncommon, state of affairs for a child in the latter stages of his primary-school career. The educational theory was that you got all the learning stuff, the reading, writing and the rest, out of the way in the early years, leaving the boys free to concentrate on their football later on. But this was Glasgow in the early-1970s, an era of teacher shortages, with new methods coming in and, in many cases, adherence to the old standards going out the window. Not that we always had windows. What came in the window was usually stones. If you were lucky they came in when you were out of the classroom.

When the windows were intact, Mr Wright and I would go up to the first-floor landing and watch the lunchtime games to see if there was any talent we had missed. There was one outstanding player – tall, strongly built, good timing, well balanced – with just one crucial disadvantage: she was a girl. The rules have changed now, but at that time girls were not allowed to play for their school team under SFA rules, and as far as Mr Wright was concerned, rules were rules. Besides, she refused to have a haircut, so we had no option but to soldier on with what we had, and hope for some timely conversions from the local Catholic school. (The extent of religious segregation in the west of Scotland is always a bit of a shock to someone from an area where orange is only a fruit or a colour; at that time, the Catholic and 'non-denominational' [i.e. Proddie] schools played in separate leagues. Whether this was to prevent open warfare or friendship, I was never quite sure.)

The team settled down after the Barlanark débâcle (a much misused word, seldom seen outside the sports pages, meaning 'an utter defeat or failure', which summed up our experience pretty fairly). Wilson retained his courage while improving his positional sense and all-round play to such an extent that we put his name forward for the Glasgow primary schools select team. He didn't get into the team, because he couldn't find the park where the trials were being played. Another lost Scotland goalkeeper, which, considering our record, is maybe no great loss, but it would have made an interesting twist on the periodic Wembley débâcle (sudden collapse; confused rush or rout): rather than 'Martin Loses Seven' or 'It's Nine past Haffey' or 'Kennedy Loses Way At Wembley', we could have had 'Wilson Loses Way To Wembley', or 'Whaur's Wembley, Jimmy?'.

The defence, with Winters out of it, settled down, and the attack, with Winters in it, scored a fair number of goals. Dawson held the team together from the centre-half position, and generally played immaculately, apart from one extraordinary incident when he caught the ball in the middle of the penalty area. I didn't blow for a penalty immediately, partly because I couldn't quite believe what had happened, and partly because I was desperately thinking of some way of not giving a penalty. It was a bit difficult to justify waving play on with a shout of 'Accidental!' and an elaborate gesture indicating that the ball had struck him, when he was standing on the penalty spot with the ball clutched firmly to his chest. A penalty, reluctantly, it had to be.

Mr Wright would occasionally retreat to the first-floor landing during our home matches, the better to see the overall pattern of play and consider tactical changes. Certainly the landing afforded a splendid view of the pitch, but the significance of the altered perspective was never obvious to me, as our tactics never changed. What did alter, as the season wore on, was the weather, and it was noticeable that the need for the improved perspective increased as the weather grew more inclement.

The climate was getting distinctly chillier around the White House, as the Watergate investigation rolled on. In October Spiro Agnew had resigned as Vice-President after admitting tax evasion; by November there were calls for Nixon to resign. In Britain, even the most diehard republican could not have failed to notice that Princess Anne was getting married on 14 November. As it meant a day off school, we were all royalists that day.

*In Europe, it had been a sad day for Dons fans, as Zoltan Varga, who had lit up Pittodrie for one brief season, signed for Ajax. It was as though the King over the water was announcing that he'd no' come back again, if you were of a particularly sentimental disposition. It appeared that he had only been on loan to Aberdeen, which was how it felt after such a short time to appreciate his skill. The Dons had won nothing during that period, so that the only traces left of him were in the memories of the supporters, recalling their own favourite moments of Varga magic, and in the Christian name of a child called Zoltan, whose middle names were those of the rest of the Dons' first team.

By December, there were shortages of just about everything, even water; we were advised to 'flush only when necessary'. The fuel crisis, with coal and oil stocks perilously low, even affected football – it was that bad – with a ban on floodlights.

Football was further restricted when blizzards hit the Scottish cities. But not in Glasgow's east end. The blizzards hit us that Saturday morning all right, but the wind was blowing so hard that the snow was being driven horizontally, rather than falling on the pitch, so that the lines were still visible on the blaize surface. Mr Wright left the decision up to me, as referee, but made it clear that the team had played in worse conditions before, and a wee bit of exposure to the elements would do the boys no harm. 'Great day for a game. Test their inner fortitude.' It was certainly a great day for watching from the comfort of the first-floor landing.

It was the only game to go ahead in Glasgow that day. Conditions dictated that it had to be a game of two halves, with play confined to one end. The driving snow obscured most of the play and most of my memories of the game, apart from a few fleeting images of two sets of players in vain pursuit of a ball that was being blown faster than they were. Winters thrived in these conditions; Blacklaw shivered and shrank as his jersey sagged, and was utterly useless. Wilson, at the far end from the second-half action, didn't hear the whistle and couldn't see the rest of us going off. It was only when we wanted to congratulate him on his first-half saves that we realised he was still out there, and fetched him in. A warm and dry Mr Wright enthused about the quality of the game.

Blacklaw started the New Year by missing a couple of easy chances in the first game. In both cases the timing of the run into the box was perfect; in both cases the cross from Walsh was perfect, dropping right onto his moulting head as he arrived on the six-yard line; in both cases, with the impeccable timing of the natural ball-player, he ducked. 'The ba' looked hard, sur,' he explained, when berated by Mr Wright for gross cowardice and lack of moral fibre. This was actually an encouraging sign, as it was the first sign of a glimmering of intelligence, hitherto unknown in Blacklaw. The ball was a Mitre Mouldmaster. It *was* hard. I know. I had blown it up, and you certainly wouldn't have caught me heading it.

But, as winter stopped howlin' and crocuses started to appear, so did some hair on Blacklaw's bald patches. He had got over the shock of learning to read, and he was twitching less. Whatever demons still pursued him seemed to be running out of puff. We began to see the player we had hoped for at the beginning, but it was not until the last game of the season that he finally came good.

In the first half he found Walsh on the left with a 30-yard pass and, knowing the precise moment at which Walsh would belt the ball into the middle after beating his customary two opponents, real or imagined, he arrived on the six-yard line to meet the howitzer from the left. It usually went out for a throw on the far side without bouncing, but this time Blacklaw met it with a glancing header and it flew into the corner of the net, except that there wasn't a net. Whether he had meant to head it, or whether he hadn't had time to duck, I don't know, but that goal was the making of him. A few minutes later he chipped one in from the edge of the penalty area. In the second half, having seen half a dozen chances scorned by Winters, he went solo. He gathered the ball in the centre circle, shimmied his way through the middle of the defence, rounded the keeper, and was already celebrating his hat-trick as he slid the ball over the line.

The celebrations were still continuing on the Monday morning, as Blacklaw stood at the front of his class line, the glow of triumph still on his face. It would be exaggerating to say that he stuck out his chest, but it was less concave than usual. Mr Wright was so pleased that he didn't belt anyone that morning.

Colin

It was many years before I got involved with a school football team again, and a lot had changed. In 1973 Margaret Thatcher had been the milk-snatching Education Secretary. In 1988 she had been Prime Minister for what seemed like forever. The Glasgow school football of the 1970s had been something I could recognise – getting there by bus, well-worn strips, forward lines, tiny wingers, big scorelines. Aberdeen school football of the 1980s was all sponsored strips in hideous colours, lifts in the car, back fours, front threes and 11-year-olds built like the Incredible Hulk, who thought they were doing you a favour by turning up for a game.

Getting a game for the school team had been the overweening ambition of my own primary-school career. It was a case of many being called to the trial, but few chosen. Like so many of life's sweetest moments, anticipation was the greatest part of the pleasure, the proudest moment being when Skeneser, the team captain, came round to the class on the Friday after-noon with the team jersey. The best moment was just before he came round, and you imagined the knock on the door, and you knew who it would be, and Skeneser would take the jersey to the teacher, and she'd call your name, and you'd go out to the front to collect it, and you'd imagine everyone looking on admiringly, although the truth was that they didn't give a stuff.

The jerseys were officially blue, but had long since faded to a bluish grey, with the remains of some blue round the edges. They were real jerseys, of heavy knitted cotton, which absorbed every drop of moisture from the atmosphere, and on wet days tripled in weight. They also stretched with washing, so that you had to roll up the sleeves just to see your hands, and to roll them up to elbow level would have been like applying a tourniquet. The elongated body provided an extra layer of insulation under your shorts, which was useful on cold days, but in the case of Cliffie, our three-foot-high centre-forward, the jersey continued on past his shorts and down below his knees, lapping gently over the tops of his stockings. This gave him a unique, layered look, somewhat like a Bedouin Arab, which could be relied on to distract, and possibly even bemuse, the opposition defence for a while. It usually proved a short-lived advantage, however, and it was hard to think of any other reason for picking him.

The team was chosen by Mr Gordon, the deputy head. His initial choice for the trial match was on the basis of self-selection. 'Right, what do you boys play?' was his opening gambit to the clamouring horde. 'Please sir, please sir, I play football,' said Fraser, bouncing about at the front of the throng. This particular piece of lese-majesty was countered with a left to the solar plexus and a right to the side of the head, which left Fraser prostrate and the rest of us replying quietly and sensibly. Those were the great days of teaching. When it came to the team for the first game, my dad's advice to practise with the left foot paid off, and I was in the team at left-half. I'd always thought of myself as a flying winger, but I certainly wasn't going to query Mr Gordon's wisdom. Not at any time, and certainly not after what he'd done to Fraser. Maybe he thought that, because I knew my tables and alphabet, and what Robert Bruce said to the spider, and when the Battle of Bannockburn was, all that kind of stuff, I had the kind of brains he wanted in midfield. It didn't work out that way. I thought I knew where left-half was; it was where Archie Glen played. It looked different from the middle, however, and I might as well have been at Bannockburn with the battle raging around me, for all I knew of what was going on. So I was switched to the wing, and there I stayed, flying or not. The trouble with being on the wing was that you waited for ages to get a kick, and when you did, it was usually from the full-back.

While the positions, tactics and jerseys were strictly pre-war, some post-war developments had filtered through to school football. Millets boots were no longer the standard footwear. These had iron-hard toecaps, with uppers of a thick, unyielding, undyed leather, which, until it had been dubbined, had all the flexibility of armour plating. Dubbin was a greasy substance which had to be applied liberally and left overnight to soften the leather uppers. Once you'd put the dubbin on, and put the precious footwear under the bed, your bedroom reeked like a tanning factory, which you imagined was the smell of the Pittodrie changing-room. Waiting for the morning, and the magical transformation of the ten-bob boots into some kind of sporting magic slippers, was a bit like the way waiting for Santa had felt, when you still believed. And in the morning, all that had happened was that they were a bit easier to get into, but, with the rigid leather still in the process of absorbing the grease, it was a bit like walking in a pair of chip pans. There was a strap over the instep, the function of which I never did discover, apart from making it harder to lace the boots, and adding another layer of ritual to the Ceremony of the Boot. The laces were yards long, and had to be wrapped round the foot and ankle in yet another mysterious rite before they could be tied and the boots were finally on. That's when the blisters started, and the nails securing the studs to the soles began to make their presence felt.

These boots were still around, but there were a few newer designs based on the 'continental' boots, as worn by the magical Magyars or the brilliant Brazilians. They weren't a lot different; the mysterious strap had been done away with, and they only just covered the ankle rather than half the lower leg, but they still had rock-hard toecaps and studs nailed to the sole. But they were black, with white bits, and established the principle that has governed the design of sports footwear for the last 40 years: above all else, look flash. In the professional game, the painting of the ball for floodlit games had given it a waterproof surface which prevented it getting progressively heavier in the wet, and this in turn had allowed the introduction of lighter boots. In school games, we also had a new type of ball, the Mitre Mouldmaster, a heavy-duty plastic ball which also retained its weight because of its non-absorbent properties. It was just unfortunate that its original weight was about a ton, and that its surface had all the yielding qualities of a brick.

Playing for the school team was a proper game, and it was something you looked forward to every week, but it still wasn't like the real thing, and the best bit remained getting the jersey, even if it was well past its best. Thirty years on, attitudes had changed. The kids expected to win. Aberdeen supporters of the late-1950s grew up expecting to win nothing, and usually got what they expected. Kids in Glasgow's 'non-denominational' schools in the early 1970s were in the middle of Celtic's nine-in-a-row, and had grown up with the idea of the Celtic supremacy. As long as Stein the Magician was at Parkhead, there seemed no end to it. The Aberdeen kids of the 1980s had grown up with the new magician, Fergie, in charge of their home club, and had got used to the idea of winning. More than that, they were addicted, and were highly indignant if they failed to get the expected result, either for the team they played for or the team they supported. I soon changed that. Not deliberately, and not specifically, but after the third or fourth successive double-figure defeat, it would have taken an exceptionally dim child to go on believing that winning games was the natural order of things. You might have thought that it would take a similarly dim supporter to go on believing that Aberdeen's supremacy was the natural order after the departure of Alex Ferguson from Pittodrie and the arrival of millions of pounds at Ibrox, but there were obviously a few such supporters around, and not all of them were under ten years old.

That was how old this lot were when I first saw them, and I didn't think they looked too bad. There was Hamish, with good balance and timing; Stig, tall and gangly, with an awkward dribbling style reminiscent of Tommy Hutchison, forever seeming to lose the ball, then retrieving it, time after time; big Fin, built like the proverbial brick shithouse (odd how a building long since departed from the average domestic scene has retained its place in the language). There was Adder in goal, on the small side for a goalkeeper, but with a great pair of gloves. They should have been, at the price. And, slotting in at the back of one of the teams, was wee Colin, younger than the others, but coping very well with everything that came his way.

The other half of the management team – co-manager, as was fashionable at the time – was another parent. We agreed on the team, got the juice, got the cups, and set off in optimistic mood to meet Forehill. It was an omen that we took the wrong turning on the way to the pitch. We lost the ball from the kick-off, and only got it back at goal-kicks and the other kick-offs, of which there were plenty. After a couple of near misses in the first few minutes, Forehill scored. It took them about another quarter of an hour to score the next two, then it was a case of '*après trois, le déluge*', and I stopped counting. They eased off towards the end, and the score was printed in the paper that night as 9–0. We were to be on the wrong end of a few 9–0 scorelines that year.

The next match brought a little ray of hope with a 5–1 defeat; bad enough, but still a recognisable football score, and one that could be explained away and converted into a Parallel Universe draw, or even a win by a manager sufficiently skilled in that most essential of managerial skills, self-deception. It was a false dawn. The next few games were lost by scores so large that the combined forces of George Miller and the *Irvine Valley News* could not have explained away.

The real dawning for me was that the boys should not be playing there at all. When we had played in the school team, it had been a reward for the hundreds of games we had played in the playground, in the street and on the links. These kids had hardly played at all. They should have been out on the nearest patch of grass, with no referee, no fancy strips, and jerseys for goalposts, playing games where it didn't matter if they lost goals in double figures, because they'd score that many themselves, and maybe more. Instead we had all the panoply of proper games on proper pitches, only they weren't games at all, because the boys didn't know how to play. Somehow the idea had become lodged in the popular imagination that a proper game needed proper strips, and pitches with goals and a referee, or it wasn't a real game.

The opposite is the truth. At that age, the Real Game is the one played in the playground or in the park or in the field and, whatever the surroundings, in the mind, where the jersey is a goalpost, the crowd is always roaring, and all things are possible. The proper game takes all that away, and confronts the children with a reality that destroys their imagination; the magic is lost, and the game becomes a match, to be won or lost. Whatever the result, the children lose.

We were certainly losing, week after week. When you don't score any goals, and you concede far too many, it is difficult to know if your main problems lie in defence or attack. There was also some hint of a weakness in midfield. Colin had been playing solidly in the middle of defence, while everything crumbled around him, so I was a bit reluctant to change his position when he asked if he could move further forward. Still, by that time it was clear that he knew more about the game than I did, so he moved into midfield. That left a gap in the middle of defence to be plugged. The largest available plug was Simon, Stig's friend. They were inseparable, and complemented each other perfectly. Stig never stopped talking, Simon never said a word. Stig was a long streak of nothing, Simon was short and perfectly spherical, so that when they stood together they looked like a letter 'd' or 'b', depending which way round they were. Simon had been struggling at full-back, where he was a little too slow on the turn. He moved into the middle, where he was just as slow, but he timed his tackles well, kicked the ball cleanly, and didn't do too badly. He couldn't jump, so we just conceded all the high balls. Every team has its weaknesses.

With Colin in the midfield, we started to play a little football, and actually got the ball into our opponent's half now and again. Stig got the chance to indulge in some of his unpredictable dribbles. We started to get the ball out to our supposedly flying winger, Dean, who had apparently lost his speed. He was to diagnose his problem as 'heavy boots', but Mercury's wings would not have speeded him up when there was a risk of contact with the opposition, and a change of footwear failed to effect any improvement. The solution to this problem was to play it through the middle. If Ramsey could win a World Cup without wingers, maybe we could win a game.

And we did. Just before the end of the season, we managed to scrape a 1–1 draw, and the following week won 4–1. Two games without defeat. We were on a run. We came back to earth the following week, but the results had given us hope for the following season. For the start of the new season we were reinforced by a couple of lads from the previous year's first team (we had been playing in a reserve league), and the lads were a year older. Alas, after a year's coaching, coaxing, pleading and cajoling, they were only a couple of weeks wiser, and they were playing in the main schools league. We started with a 12–2 defeat, but that was a result gained with early-season enthusiasm. We couldn't maintain it, and we had an awful lot of 9–0 results published in the *Green Final.*

There were some hopeful signs. Colin continued to improve, and managed to score a couple of goals 'against the run of play', as the match reports used to have it. Any goal that we scored was bound to be against the run of play, apart from the one we scored right at the start of one game, before any play had run. It was against the might of St Joseph's, who expected, quite rightly, to walk all over us. What's more, the goal was a beauty. Colin started the move in our own half, kept running, switched play, and after half a dozen passes, Warren, our beanpole striker, volleyed a cross past their helpless goalkeeper. I was stunned. St Joseph's were so stunned that they only just managed to reach double figures, and not before Warren had added another. By our standards, it was a cliffhanger.

Warren had arrived midway through the previous season, and, with his height, had seemed the answer to our problems. He would have been had we been playing basketball. As it was, a certain reluctance to tackle made him a somewhat suspect centre-half. I tried the old Winters trick of converting an ineffective defender into a devastating striker. His size usually made an impression on defenders, until they realised that he was as feart as they were. There remained his potential as an aerial weapon. The problem here was that our wingers couldn't cross the ball high enough, and Warren was left trying to chest the ball into the goal. As a training in futile enterprises, our team was second to none.

As for the others, Big Fin got bigger, Stig got taller, Adder got new and even more expensive gloves, and a glove bag, and new boots, and a boot bag, and a bag bag to keep all the bags in. The idea was to fill the goal with bags. Simon just got rounder. I saw him on his way into school one morning, forming the usual 'b' with Stig. He was carrying a huge sports bag over his shoulder, and I asked him if that was his lunch. He just grinned his usual shy grin, and shook his head. Indeed it was not his lunch, for the bag was only half-full. He followed me into the local corner shop to fill the bag with goodies his mum's kitchen had been too small to provide. After his visit the corner shop provided lean pickings until the next visit to the cash and carry.

It was around this time, towards the end of the season, when we were actually in the lead, that Colin gave away a goal by trying a casual flick on the edge of our own penalty area when he should have booted it into safety. I yelled at him, and at half-time asked him what he'd been playing at. He said he thought he'd just try a flick. Of course. It had looked great; he'd been perfectly balanced in mid-air, and if it had come off, it would have been a little piece of magic; it hadn't, and we had lost a goal. Even if it had worked, it would have been totally ineffective on the edge of our penalty area. But did that matter? We were going to lose anyway. And even if it had lost us the game, did that really matter? Not really. I resolved that I'd never criticise him, or any of the other players, for trying something special during a game. Later on, he'd have plenty of managers and coaches telling him to lay it off, play the simple ball, or just get rid of it. If he wanted to try something different, the time was now. It's a mistake to attribute the same motives to everyone doing the same thing, especially when they're doing it for nothing. Not everyone who runs a school football team is power-crazy; some are reliving their youth; some imagine they really are running Manchester United in a hazy world between fantasy and reality; some are just helping out and wish someone else would do it; and some think they look pretty damn stylish in an Umbro manager's coat. I enjoyed the training, when we had a wee game at the end and I could be the biggest boy in the team, a privilege denied me in my undersized youth. In games, I enjoyed seeing boys like Colin and Stig, and players in the opposition, perform in a way I could never have approached. That's why I let them hold the ball and try to beat defenders. If they didn't learn then, they never would, and I wanted the spirit of Charlie Cooke to live on. I wanted to see that little bit of magic. It's easy having high-minded principles when you're 6–0 up, or are resigned to defeat.

My feelings were different when we played Cornhill, our fellow strugglers in the basement of Aberdeen Primary Schools League Two. With published scores limited to nine, it was difficult to gauge our respective demerits. Certainly we had scored a similar number of goals, and neither of us had disturbed the pristine quality of our W, D and Pts columns in the league table. But did their 9–0 against Middleton Park mean 18 to our 14, or did it just mean 10? Whatever it meant, it didn't count on the day. With the score at 1–0 in the second half, all the good intentions about how we played the game were forgotten, and all that mattered was keeping that slender lead. For ten minutes I was the tight-lipped, ashen-faced manager of popular legend. Then we scored a couple in quick succession, and I became human again. We added a final goal for a 4–0 victory, and life was sweet the following week, recollecting all those emotions in tranquillity. What it must be like to manage a team when the results matter every week, I can't imagine. All that tension, all those highs and lows, and if you expect to win every game, then it's nothing but lows. No wonder the professional managers age at a faster rate than American presidents. It was the only time we won that season, but it was enough to give us hope for the following one.

There was an air of quiet confidence about the school playing-field as we gathered for pre-season training. One or two older lads had gone, but we had replaced them with a 'Kipper' and a 'Haggis'; with Hamish converted by some mysterious process of schoolboy logic to 'Hambone', we were well on the way to a full Scottish menu. The air of quiet confidence usually appears around the same time as the first morning dew of the autumn, and evaporates just as quickly. We had our tactics sorted out. All the boys who couldn't play – and they were still in a very substantial majority – had to get the ball and pass it to Colin, who would do the rest. Not a terribly sophisticated plan, but it had the merit of simplicity, and it worked well enough for the first couple of games, both of which we won.

Not that we were blind to our deficiencies. The defence still looked a little frail under pressure. The main problem was that, apart from Kipper, who had a mean expression and a crew-cut, they all looked like the nice, floppy-haired, middle-class boys they were. When Paul, one of our defenders, couldn't manage to play, it was because he had a speech and drama lesson. Other teams lost players to black-belt karate gradings. Their players came back able to offer the realistic threat of cutting their opponents in half. All Paul could do to an uppity winger was threaten to enunciate his vowels more clearly.

The first real test came against Middleton Park, our 14–0 conquerors of the previous season. They had a lad with a great left foot who had destroyed us in that game, and he was still there. They set up camp in our half, but this time we defended our territory more resolutely, and Adder, desperate to protect the ever-growing collection of bags in his goalmouth, put up the shutters. We sneaked into their half twice, and scored twice. The air of quiet confidence was getting a little louder. Then they got a penalty. The lad with the left foot took what we assumed was the formality of converting it. He blasted it straight over the keeper's head; Adder fisted it over the bar, and our lads defended with renewed vigour.

Eventually, the tide lapped over our defensive wall, and we went in at half-time all square. Actually, we didn't go in, we stayed out for the half-time juice and the team talk, but it seems a shame to disrupt the flow of sporting clichés. It's hard to be a manager outdoors. You really need the tiled walls to echo your rants and raves, and to smash real crockery against; the effect tends to be lost when your finest invective gets carried away in the wind, and throwing a disposable plastic cup with all the force you can muster just makes you look ridiculous. Of course, if you're already wearing an Umbro manager's coat, you don't mind about things like that.

What their manager said was clearly more effective than my 'we shall fight in midfield, we shall fight in the penalty area, we shall never surrender' message, for they scored another three in the second half to win comfortably. Still, we may have been beaten, but we had not surrendered. The air of quiet confidence may have been blown away, but we could look forward to a season of football rather than basketball scores. Nearly. We didn't win too many, but at least the scorelines didn't have to be doctored by a sympathetic sub-editor. We still managed some unlikely scores, a 6–5 defeat and an even more improbable 6–6 draw, the result of a second-half fightback from the abyss of a 6–1 half-time score.

So, if there wasn't any glory, there was plenty of entertainment: Stig's mazy dribbles, impossible misses and occasional goals; Simon, rolling around in defence, saying nothing, enjoying every minute; Big Fin, creating mayhem in midfield; and Colin, always running, aways looking for the ball, always trying to do something with it. Sometimes, after all the frustration of silly goals conceded and daft ones missed, there would be a little moment of magic: a few passes strung together, a little flick, a pass threaded and weighted perfectly, or a shuffling, weaving dribble from Colin that reminded me of Charlie Cooke, and it would seem worth while getting out of bed on a Saturday morning to get cold and wet and miserable.

But the best games were on the Saturday evening, in the summer, when a few of us would go to the park, and the jerseys would go down, and we had a pitch, and the old magic returned. Not the old speed and skill – the speed had long gone, and the skill was never there – but the magic that could create a field of dreams, and let us believe for an hour or so that we had a left foot like Puskas, or could head like Denis Law, or dribble like Charlie Cooke. And every now and then it would happen just the way it should when you're playing the Real Game. The passer-by would have seen a couple of men old enough to know better playing football in the park with a group of 11-year-old boys, and would have found it hard to understand the reason for the jubilation. But the ball had come at knee height, he had controlled it in mid-air and, in one perfect movement, had brought it down and slid it into the far corner, just inside the post. He had been trying to do something like that for about 40 years, and would never do it again, but for that brief moment he was up there with the Greats, playing the Real Game. If you've seen *Field of Dreams* you'll know what it was like, when Shoeless Jackson and all the others came onto the field, but to see them you had to believe. The passers-by certainly couldn't have seen them, but onto the field that night came the Greats: Law and Puskas and Graham Leggat and Charlie Cooke, and on too came all the old crowd, Lavvie and Broonser and Skeneser, and it was as though they'd never been away.

The Strikers

Strikers, centre-forwards, call them what you will, depending on your age, are the players who can be measured. No matter how good they might look on the ball, no matter how entertaining, they are ultimately judged on one thing only: how many did they score? On this criterion, two players stand out. Joe Harper is Aberdeen's top goalscorer, with 199 goals in 308 competitive matches, including substitute appearances. Benny Yorston's 125 goals place him in only sixth place on the all-time list, but, in scoring them in just 156 matches, he put himself way out in front of all the others in terms of goals per game. He achieved a strike rate of 0.80, well ahead of Matt Armstrong in second place on 0.72 (155 goals from 215 games).

Many fans of the 1930s would choose Armstrong as their favourite Dons centre-forward, for he was fast and stylish and, in tandem with Willie Mills, scored goals with a degree of flair, which is a different thing from having a flair for scoring goals. Frank McDougall, for example, scored many vital goals for Aberdeen, but they tended to be of the functional rather than the spectacular variety, and as a result he was never as popular with the fans as his scoring record deserved. It was only when his career was ended prematurely by injury that his contribution was appreciated.

There is perhaps a tendency to think back to a golden age of goal-scoring, if you are being nostalgic, or to a time when goals were easy to come by, if you are being critical. In the latter frame of mind there may be a tendency to dismiss the efforts of old-time goalscorers as the collection of so many free gifts from Santa Claus defences. This theory is not borne out by the facts. Although the great individual scoring records – Dixie Dean in England, Jimmy McGrory in Scotland, Benny Yorston at Aberdeen – were set in the late-1920s or early-1930s, the pattern of goal-scoring over the years suggests that it is only the presence of first-class goalscorers, individually or in combination, which has ensured a high number of goals.

Goals were at a premium in the years before and after the First World War, and it was not until the change in the offside law that the supply improved. It required the presence of Benny Yorston to push Aberdeen's average to more than two goals per game, however, this being achieved for the first time in season 1928–29. After his departure the average dipped, and did not rise to over two per game until Armstrong and Mills forged their successful partnership.

The post-war period is remembered by many as a time of large crowds and plenty goals. Large crowds, certainly, but, for Aberdeen fans at least, not all that many goals. It was not until the championship-winning side began to take shape in the early-1950s that the average again rose above two per game. One of the strengths of that side was that it did not rely on any one player for goals, and as a result was able to maintain an average of over two goals per game from 1950–51 through to 1957–58, by which time the defence had got hold of the same idea. During that period the goals came from the cultured George Hamilton (153 goals in 281 games), the dashing Paddy Buckley (92 in 152) and the irrepressible Harry Yorston (141 in 277) in the centre-forward or inside-forward positions; but a feature of the side when it was scoring most freely was the significant contribution made by the wingers, with Jack Hather scoring 104 goals in 351 games and Graham Leggat, of whom more later, achieving the remarkable total of 92 from only 151 games. All of these players would deserve a chapter to themselves, none more so than George Hamilton, one of the most popular players ever to appear for the Dons. He was unfortunate to have his career interrupted by the war at what would probably have been his peak; but even with his best years taken away, he still gave the fans full value over many years in terms of skill, goals and entertainment.

After the decline of the side of the 1950s, there were some flurries of goalscoring, inspired mainly by Charlie Cooke, with finishing by a number of players, among them the bustling Ernie Winchester and the skilful Billy Little. The latter was a schoolboy international who never quite fulfilled his early promise, lacking the strength and pace to take full advantage of his skill and perception. He had a powerful shot and a subtle touch which appealed to the more intelligent spectator (me). The other spectator preferred Winchester. He had also been a schoolboy international, a centre-half of immense strength who was converted into a battering-ram of a centre-forward, without the subtlety of that instrument.

It was around the time that crowds started chanting, rather than just roaring their heads off in an unco-ordinated and incoherent manner; they began to be incoherent in unison, and one of the early Pittodrie favourites was: 'Ernie, Ernie, score a goal!' Not exactly the 'Hallelujah Chorus', but it did share with that ditty an invocation of an almighty force and an expression of hope over experience.

Bobby Cummings also scored a fair number of goals in the early-1960s, almost all of them headers from Dave Smith crosses. Once the opposition had rumbled that ploy, that was more or less it. He did score a hat-trick against Rangers, though, in a memorable and totally unexpected 6–1 victory, and for that alone he must never be forgotten. It qualifies him to stand with Joe O'Neill (1953–54) and Frank McDougall (1984–85) in the Pittodrie hall of fame as scorers of hat-tricks against Rangers. McDougall had the added distinction of scoring four against Celtic, a feat he regarded as the highlight of his career.

It was not until Joe Harper arrived in 1969 that the Dons once again had a striker of real quality, and it took his presence to raise the striking rate to over two per game, this being achieved in 1970–71 and 1971–72. The danger of depending on a single goalscorer was illustrated by the sharp decline in the scoring rate following Harper's departure. It dropped to a low of 1.35 in 1973–74, the lowest since 1948–49, and did not recover until after his return in 1976–77. He was assisted in his second coming by Drew Jarvie and Steve Archibald. Jarvie scored most of his goals in the early part of his Aberdeen career, when he suffered from lack of support, and he was at his best as the supporting act to a main striker, such as Harper, or Drew Busby, his striking partner from his days at Airdrie. In an age when footballers had started to resemble rock stars, his Bobby Charlton haircut shone as a beacon for the old-fashioned virtues of skilful football and futile attempts to disguise baldness.

Steve Archibald was never the most elegant of players, nor did he have a particularly impressive scoring rate – 46 in 112 games – but he did have the knack of scoring important goals with whatever part of his anatomy the ball happened to hit; he probably scored as many with his shinpads as his boots, but, as the saying goes, 'They a' coont.' He went on to have a lucrative career with Spurs and Barcelona, and continued his Pittodrie form at the Nou Camp by putting Barcelona into the European Cup quarter-final with an attempted header at the far post which went into the net off his shoulder.

Despite the efforts of Harper and his cronies in the late-1970s, it took the great side of the 1980s to once again reach an average of over two goals per game, in the seasons from 1982–83 to 1984–85. They resembled the high-scoring side of the 1950s in that they relied on a number of strikers rather than a single outstanding goalscorer. Mark McGhee missed too many chances to be described as one of the great strikers, averaging a relatively modest 0.40 goals per game, but he created a tremendous number of chances for others with his close control and determined running in the penalty area.

His striking partner, Eric Black, revived the old 'spring-heeled' cliché with some spectacular headed goals, most notably in European games, but he was also a skilful player on the ground, and it is surprising that his scoring rate was only 0.33 per game. He might have gone on to greater things, but from Aberdeen he went to the relative obscurity of Metz, in the French league, and had the misfortune to have his career curtailed by injury.

The most notable feature of that side was the scoring contribution by players from all departments. Strachan was a regular scorer from midfield, Weir chipped in a few from the wing, and the defenders were never averse to having a go at goal, with the annual contest between Miller and McLeish helping to boost the total. In this respect the team differed from the 1950s' side; at that time scoring goals was the forwards' job, keeping them out the defenders'. The regular defensive trio of Caldwell, Mitchell and Young scored just a single goal in a collective total of 583 competitive appearances.

But no matter how good the team effort, every side needs at least one player with that indefinable, unteachable, unmistakable knack of scoring goals, and since the premature retirement of Frank McDougall it is something which the Dons have lacked. Charlie Nicholas was one of Aberdeen's most imaginative signings, but it was a distinctly chubby Nicholas who arrived at Pittodrie, and, although his scoring rate improved as he recovered fitness, he was never able to recapture 'that first, fine, careless rapture' of his early Celtic days. Nevertheless, he gave us some rare moments of virtuosity, most notably in a game against Motherwell, a volley from a cute back-heel from Davie Dodds, of all people, which screamed into the top corner. It gave us a reminder of his sensational goal on his international début, and a promise of more to come. Not too many more did. He finished that 1988–89 season with a respectable tally of 17 goals, but his scoring rate declined the following season and then he went back to Parkhead, where his heart always had been. Hans Gilhaus, with tremendous pace and athleticism, showed promise until he lost interest, and turned out to be a scorer of great goals, rather than a great goalscorer. He might have benefited from a longer partnership with Nicholas. He scored 11 goals from 23 appearances in the part of the 1989–90 season they did play together, and had the ability to take advantage of Nicholas's perceptive passing.

The young player who promised most was Eoin Jess. His 13 goals from 20 games in 1990–91 was an outstanding performance in his first full season, but it was the quality of the goals and his overall play which excited the fans. In particular, there were the four he scored at Dunfermline, including a solo effort, finished with a coolness and style that offered reminders of Graham Leggat. He went on to play some great games, and score some great goals, but lacked consistency. One of his problems was possibly that he was asked to perform so many different roles – winger, striker, midfielder – that he never really settled down in any of them. For all his undoubted skill, he never scored enough goals to be regarded as a true striker, and never dominated games sufficiently to be regarded as one of the great midfield players.

The 1992–93 season showed some signs of goals coming back into fashion, with hat-tricks scored by no fewer than four Aberdeen players. Duncan Shearer had the single-minded attitude of the natural goalscorer, and started with an impressive tally of 22 from 32 games in his first season to put himself up among the best of Aberdeen goalscorers. Strikers have to prove themselves men for all seasons, though, and his scoring rate declined over the following years. By the end of the 1995–96 season he had scored a useful, but not outstanding, 49 goals from 105 appearances. Scott Booth also made his mark in that season, with 13 from 21 appearances, but failed to reach double figures in any subsequent season. As a striker, he failed to register on the Richter Scale.

Billy Dodds was a player who impressed me when he played in a poor Dundee side. Unfortunately for him, he did not arrive at Pittodrie until Aberdeen were in decline, and he only narrowly avoided the unique but unenviable distinction of being relegated with three different clubs. Like so many others, he had a promising first season with 15 goals from 35 appearances, but, for all his effort, he failed to maintain this rate the following season. His 20 goals in the almost disastrous 1996–97 season gave a hint of what he might achieve in a settled and successful side.

Which brings us back to Eoin Jess. He returned to Pittodrie as a midfield player who had failed to make his mark in England, and it was not until he moved back into the attack that he started to recover his form and confidence. If he gets the chance to play in a side which is challenging for honours rather than fighting against relegation, he may yet prove to be one of Aberdeen's top strikers.

But there were really only two strikers who were ever seriously considered for inclusion in this book. Benny Yorston and Joe Harper stand out as centre-forwards who were always the focus of attention, always expected to score. They were both of short, stocky appearance, which made them unlikely sporting heroes. Yet, for their respective generations of Dons fans, that is what they were.

Two 'guests' are also included: Ferenc Puskas, who scored one of the most memorable goals in the game's history, and did more than anyone to change the British public's perception of the game in the post-war period; and Denis Law, who was the greatest player, bar none, to come from Aberdeen.

Benny Yorston

Benny Yorston started at Pittodrie, not as a player, but as an office boy. He had begun playing for Kittybrewster school, and continued with Muggiemoss Juniors while working in the Pittodrie office. He was given a few games in the Dons' third team, but was considered too small to have any chance of making further progress, and eventually made his entry into senior football with Montrose, after moving from Muggiemoss to Richmond Juniors and winning a junior cap.

Even when he attracted attention with his displays for Montrose, the Aberdeen management considered him too small to succeed at the top level, and took some persuading that he would be worth another try. There is a story of Paddy Travers, the Aberdeen manager, going to Montrose with one of the directors to watch him play. After the game they were discussing his performance on the way back to the train, when they saw Yorston, and Travers suggested that they take the opportunity to speak to him. 'No, too wee,' was the verdict of the director, and they passed by without acknowledging the man who would later become Aberdeen's top goalscorer. Eventually the haul of goals for Montrose outweighed his supposed physical shortcomings, and the directors were persuaded to part with £40 to secure his services. At that price, even the Aberdeen directors presumably thought that they were not risking too much in taking him on to the playing staff, and he made his début at the start of the 1927–28 season, in an away game against Raith Rovers on 20 August 1927.

The grouse season had also just got under way, while Morrison's Economic Stores were announcing an 'end-of-season clearance', although which season was ending was none too clear. Following Lindbergh's flight in *The Spirit of St Louis* fron New York to Paris, there was further news of 'Atlantic flights by bold aviators'.

Paddy Travers had been bold in his team selection for the Raith Rovers game. The *Press and Journal* made no mention of Yorston, but commented: 'With the selection, all will not agree, but it should not be condemned without having had a chance to make good.' The team he had picked was: McSevich, Jackson, Livingstone; Black, McHale, McLeod; Wilson, Cheyne, Yorston, McDermid, Smith.

In the match report, the 'smart forward play' was praised. 'All the forwards worked harmoniously throughout and the combination between Wilson, Cheyne, Yorston and McDermid was a feature of the game.' Yorston started as he would go on, by scoring: 'McLeod lobbed the ball in front of goal for Yorston to run in and hook it cleverly past Muir.' He also had a shot blocked, and just missed a rebound. The Dons won 3–2, and there was to be no dancing in the streets of Raith that night.

The performance was good enough to establish Yorston in the side, and he went on to score 17 goals in 28 appearances in that first season. The initial complaints in the local press of 'lack of height and weight' had given way to praise for his 'opportunism', and by the beginning of the next season he was a familiar figure of whom much was expected. Many young players, particularly goalscorers, find their second season difficult, as opposing defenders learn to anticipate the moves which took them by surprise the first time round, and the surprised delight of spectators turns to expectation, and from there to frustration, exasperation and finally to disappointment, like a 'Fry's Five Boys' in reverse. (Most of us learned our big words from that chocolate bar, just as we learned our French from HP Sauce bottles: '*Cette sauce de haute qualité . . .*')

Yorston, however, had a speed of thought and movement which defied anticipation, and a confidence, bordering on arrogance, which weighed at nothing the burden of expectation. He revelled in his local celebrity; footballers had become prominent personalities with the growth of the game's popularity, even if the days of televised interviews were a long way off. Tommy Muirhead, the Rangers wing-half, was possibly the first player to set a fashion in hairstyles: 'Show the black upon the white, gie's a Tammy Muirhead', would be the request to the barber, in a demand for a short-back-and-sides of the utmost severity. The days were also far off when they would demand to have it dyed blue and white, or whatever colour Gazza happened to wearing that week.

Yorston started his second season as he had finished his first, by scoring a goal. The opening fixture of the 1928–29 season was against Cowdenbeath on 11 August, a day of major significance in sporting history. Not because of the game against Cowdenbeath, which Aberdeen won 4–2; not because of the Olympics, which were taking place in Amsterdam, with the Americans winning their usual haul of medals; and not even because of the Stoneywood Paper Mill Sports, where paper mill athletes had been in 'keen rivalry'. This was the day of the first edition of the *Green Final* – 'The Football Express in its New Green Dress'. Saturday nights would never be the same again. It promised that 'by the use of wire and 'phone it will be possible to give results and descriptions of the day's matches hours before any other paper circulating in Aberdeen or the North of Scotland'. Not that telephones or telegrams were needed with Patsy Gallacher selling the papers at his stand outside the New Market. The great news would be broadcast far and wide: '*Sen-sa-tion-al de-feat of the might-y Ran-gers!*' As rare then, alas, as now. The paper's advertising had a sporting theme, with Horlicks promising 'Olympic fitness', declaring that 'the world's greatest athletes train on Horlicks', but those were the days before the Advertising Standards Authority, and the days before steroids.

Typically, Yorston scored the first Aberdeen goal reported in the first edition of the *Green Final*. He started the move on the left with a crossfield pass to Love, and was in position to score with a header from the winger's cross. He scored with another header in the second game of the season, against Queen's Park, and in that match showed that he could make goals as well as score them by providing the cross for Merrie to get Aberdeen's third. Merrie was wearing the number 9 jersey that day, with Yorston at number 10, but by November Yorston had taken over the centre-forward role, and from then on an Aberdeen side without him at number 9 was unthinkable.

He finished that season with 32 goals from 35 league and cup games. He was to improve on that remarkable scoring record the following season, with a goal a game from the 38 league matches, and eight from four cup games. It was undoubtedly a great advantage for him to have a settled forward line around him during that period. In that 1929–30 season he started with Love and Cheyne on his right and McDermid and Smith on his left, and so it remained for the first 11 games of the season. They played in 31 of the 42 games the club played, and on only one occasion was more than one of the quintet missing. Consistency in selection was rewarded by consistency in performance, with the side finishing in third position in the league, scoring 85 goals in the process. A further 17 in the cup brought the total to over a hundred for the season, almost half of them scored by Yorston.

In looking back at teams of the past, we tend to think of them as constant entities, with half-back lines and forward lines tripping off the tongue. In fact they used just as many players in the course of a season as modern sides, and seasons like 1929–30 were the exception rather than the rule. The Dons used 21 players in that season, as low a number as they had used since the war, but the league-winning side of 1954–55 and the side which so narrowly failed to win the championship in 1970–71 featured only 19 players. What is true is that the more successful sides have been relatively stable, and it is the more successful sides that we tend to remember. They stand out like beacons in the memory, the familiar names recited to serve as landmarks in retracing our steps back through the past: 'Smith, Cooper, McGill' – the 1930s; 'Leggat, Yorston, Buckley, Wishart and Hather' – the 1950s are evoked, just as though we had heard a snatch of an old, half-remembered song, or the coffee and cooked-meats smell of an old-fashioned grocer's shop. So it was that Yorston and his fellow attackers stamped their image on the collective memory of Dons fans as the 1920s turned to the 1930s.

The football tradition of the New Year 'derby' was by now well established alongside the other, more ancient, Hogmanay traditions. On 1

January 1930, as the Dons travelled to Dundee, the *Press and Journal* reported the success of a local runner, D. Brown, in the Powderhall sprint. He hadn't won, but he had qualified from the heats, and his local status was enough to earn him top billing as far as the editor was concerned. The paper also reported: 'Aberdeen and N.E. Welcomes 1930 – Gay Crowds Throng the Streets'. On the same page it reported on Aberdeen's falling birth rate – 'the lowest for ten years'. Untroubled by thoughts of the falling birth rate, or at least postponing doing anything about it for another day, over 2,000 Dons fans travelled to Dens Park in the football 'specials'.

They were probably more troubled by the report that Yorston was injured, but were promised that he would be in his usual place in the Dons line-up. Perhaps the report of Yorston's injury was an early example of the kind of pre-match gamesmanship which we have come to expect before any important match, for the report on the game spoke of a 'personal triumph for Yorston, who registered the hat-trick'. The first came from an opportunity created by Cheyne, when Yorston, 'with his usual nippiness', beat a Dundee defender to the ball and shot low into the net. Proctor, the Dundee defender, broke his leg in making the challenge. Yorston was also injured in the collision, but was able to resume playing after treatment. Dundee, a man short, played the 'one back game', and caught Aberdeen offside on several occasions. When they did break through the depleted Dundee defence, the Dons had 'various shots negatived by the home goalkeeper'.

Aberdeen made the decisive breakthrough in the second half when 'Love raced away and centred on the right of goal for Yorston to jump high and head past Marsh from a difficult angle'. After that, the supposedly injured Yorston, miraculously restored to full health, went chasing his hat-trick. Several times 'he went within an ace of scoring. Ultimately the little centre-forward was rewarded when he followed up a return to dart through between Brown and the advancing Marsh, and slip the ball into the net.' The report summed up: 'Yorston was the nippiest player on the field and all his goals were the outcome of brilliant efforts.' It was a game which encapsulated his Aberdeen career: heading ability, for all his lack of inches; speed of thought in seeing a scoring opportunity; speed of movement over those first few yards to convert a potential opportunity into a real one; the courage and determination to pursue it under the fiercest of challenges; and the coolness to convert the opportunity into a goal.

Not all his goals were spectacular, and almost all were scored from inside the penalty area. What he had was the striker's gift for always knowing where the goal was, and always, or nearly always, getting his shots or headers on target. Sounds simple, but it cannot be taught, and it is the rarest and most priceless gift in football. Wherever that gift came from, he undoubtedly had it, and the confidence to go with it. It was stated earlier that his confidence was bordering on arrogance, and from what I can gather his contemporaries would only have taken issue with the 'bordering on' element of that statement. 'Big-heided' or 'cocky wee bugger' might be more typical epithets applied at the time. When he came off the pitch at Pittodrie after the Dons had drawn a Scottish Cup-tie against Raith Rovers, a fan voiced his opinion of the performance in uncomplimentary terms and advised him of the arduous nature of the task confronting the team, which, in his opinion, rendered success improbable, or words to that effect: 'If ye canna beat 'em here, ye winna beat 'em doon there.' Yorston's precise words cannot be printed in a respectable publication, but he refuted the fan's opinion in no uncertain terms, expressed a degree of optimism as to the result, and ventured a forecast that he would score a hat-trick. That is precisely what he did, and the Dons won 7–0. But it was an attitude that made him admired for his skill and audacity, rather than loved in the same way that 'King Joey' would be 40 years later.

With his scoring record for Aberdeen, it is surprising that Yorston gained only one international cap, against Northern Ireland in 1931, but it was a time of great centre-forwards, and Hughie Gallacher was first choice; there may also have been an element of prejudice against players who were not from the Old Firm or a major English club, but even the Celtic scoring-machine, Jimmy McGrory, was restricted to seven international appearances during the period from 1928 to 1934.

The 1930–31 season was a less productive one for Yorston, with 22 goals from 33 appearances. The forward line was less settled that season, but the crucial factor must have been the absence of Alex Cheyne, who had been transferred to Chelsea in the close season. With him went the inspiration for so much of the Dons' attacking play, and the consistent service on which Yorston, like any other striker, depended.

The next season was to be his last for Aberdeen. He did not start as brightly as in previous years. He scored his customary goal in the opening game, against Cowdenbeath, and followed it with a goal against Airdrie in the next match. There then followed an unusually barren spell of six games without a goal, and by 14 November he had scored only seven goals from 17 matches. On that day he lined up against Kilmarnock at Pittodrie with the following team: Smith, Jackson, McGill; Black, McLaren, Hill; Warnock, Adam, Yorston, McDermid, McLean. Of the players with whom he had started his Aberdeen career, only Jackson, Black and McDermid remained.

An all-party National Government, led by Ramsay MacDonald, had been elected, with an overwhelming majority. In the book reviews in the *Press and Journal*, the question was asked, 'Was Shakespeare a woman?' and while you pondered that one you could chew on a Yeast-Vite tablet, or perhaps one of Dr Cassell's – 'thoroughly efficacious'. If Shakespeare, man or woman, was a little too heavy for your taste, there was always the latest Laurel and Hardy, *Jailbirds*, their first full-length feature film, at the Grand Central.

Monday's *Press and Journal* reported a somewhat fortunate draw for Aberdeen under the headline 'Dons Save Unbeaten Home Record'. The equaliser had come with only ten minutes to go, when 'Warnock carried the ball along, and McLean cutely deceived the defence to allow Yorston to slip in and score'. It sounds like a typical Yorston goal, and his overall performance was praised as 'elusive and clever'. The other forwards were criticised for 'too much tip-tapping', finally redeemed, as so often before, by Yorston's opportunism. It was to be the last time.

Elsewhere on the sports page, Steve Donoghue was reported as having ridden two 100/8 winners, which might have landed you a nice double, as long as you weren't relying on the *Press and Journal* tipsters.

It was a bet laid several weeks previously which was to end Yorston's Aberdeen career. On the Wednesday, under the headline 'Dons' Drastic Changes', the dropping of several star players was announced. 'Mr Travers declined to enter into the circumstances, but admitted that it was on account of some domestic trouble,' was the only explanation offered. On the following Saturday, Yorston played in the reserves along with McLaren and Hill. Black and Galloway were injured. None of them ever played in the first team again, and were transferred that season. The affair was known as 'The Great Mystery', and remained just that until the revised edition of Jack Webster's history of the club, when the story appeared in print for the first time. This confirmed the rumours which had long been known to the Aberdeen betting fraternity: Yorston, along with the other players, had been involved in an attempted betting coup, involving half-time draws and full-time wins. Such a result had occurred in the game against Dundee United some weeks previously. It can never be known if this was the result of deliberate contrivance, nor is it known if any bets were successful, but there was sufficient evidence of conspiracy for the Aberdeen management to get rid of the suspected players.

It was not the first time that professional football had been tainted by corruption, nor would it be the last. We tend to associate betting scandals with the early years of professional sport, picturing 'sportsmen' in bowler hats and high-buttoned waistcoats 'making arrangements' with fistfuls of notes in smoke-filled snugs, but betting and bribery scandals have persisted at all levels of the game right up to the present day. It has already been mentioned that one of the most skilful players ever to play at Pittodrie, Zoltan Varga, arrived on these shores because he had been barred from the Bundesliga following a bribery scandal. There was a major match-fixing case in the English First Division in the 1960s, and the European Cup was, for a period in the same decade, the most corrupt competition of all. Strangely, it was the one competition my dad's friend Shirran never queried. As a punter who had also worked behind the counter of a bookie's office, he had a profound distrust of his fellow man, especially if he was involved in any way with betting or professional sport. His verdict on the outcome of any sporting contest, especially if it had a surprise result, was invariably a 'fix' or a 'cut-up'. I don't know if he felt that way before the Yorston incident, but he certainly felt that way afterwards, especially if the match involved Aberdeen. The indications are that the club acted entirely honourably, at the expense of losing some of its best players, but it was a sad and premature end to one of the great Aberdeen careers.

Yorston moved to Sunderland, and then to Middlesbrough, but, like Harper, never quite recaptured the form he had shown at Pittodrie. For him, however, the circumstances of his departure made it certain that there would be no return for the prodigal.

Joe Harper

Trick question: against which team did Joe Harper score his first goal at Pittodrie? The answer, of course, is Aberdeen. He scored for Morton in their 6–3 defeat on 2 April 1969, a result which helped to secure the Dons' First Division status towards the end of another none-too-successful season. On this occasion his goal was no more than a consolation for Morton, but earlier in the season he had inflicted some damage by scoring the only goal of the game at Cappielow. The following season he failed to score in Morton's 2–2 draw on 13 September, but his free-kicks laid on both of his side's goals, and his performance convinced Eddie Turnbull that he was a man who would be better playing for the Dons than against them.

On 2 October the *Press and Journal* announced a 'record capture' for the Dons, at a price of £40,000. For their money, they were getting a player who had scored 27 goals in the previous season for Morton, and a free-kick specialist with the ability to bend the ball round defensive walls. He had already displayed these gifts against Aberdeen, and he was given his first opportunity to display them in a red jersey on 4 October, against Ayr United.

If it was a red-letter day for Harper, it was a black day for the city's 'doggy men', for it marked the closure of the dog-track. The rent money would never again ride on the dog in trap one, or the housekeeping on trap four. That Saturday evening the bookies shouted the odds and stashed away their winnings for the last time, and the punters, having lost the bus fare on the last race, plodded their weary way home without the consoling certainty that they would recover their losses the following week. For those concerned about the fate of the dogs, it was reported that the top dogs had been sold to other tracks, with homes being found for all the others. No concern was expressed about the fate of all the punters who had lost their spiritual home. What did they get in its place? Fine Fare. For those concerned about the results, the last race was won by Swanee, the 9/4 favourite, so at least some punters went home happy.

The Tories were worried, as usual, about 'scroungers'. 'Call the hippies up for useful work' ran the headline on the front page. On the back page, it was reported that Celtic had decided to call up one of their promising youngsters for what was to prove some very useful work, with the début of the 18-year-old Kenny Dalglish in what was still known as the half-back line.

Harper made his début for the Dons in the number 7 jersey against Ayr United. He helped the side to a 2–1 victory, and on the Monday the verdict was reasonably favourable: 'Newcomer Joe Harper didn't make a spectacular début, but his play was impressive enough to suggest that he will be a valuable acquisition on the right wing. Repeatedly he was to be found lurking in the middle and he provided the ball for Dave Robb's first goal.' The team that day was: McGarr, Boel, Hermiston, Murray, McMillan (McKay), Petersen, Harper, Robb, Forrest, Wilson, Hamilton.

Harper played most of his early games for Aberdeen on the right wing, switching later in the season to the number 11 jersey, and it was not until he was recalled to the side for the Cup final that he found his true position as a central striker. He established himself as a penalty-taker with a goal from the spot on his home début the following week against Partick Thistle, but for his first goal from open play we had to wait until 29 November, when he scored Aberdeen's second against Kilmarnock in a 2–0 victory. Playing on the wing, he combined with George Murray to score from the centre-forward position.

For his first hat-trick we had to wait until the new decade. The 1960s may have gone, but on 10 January Harper finally arrived with three goals against Raith Rovers in a 5–1 thrashing. The headline stated, 'Harper begins to repay fee', reflecting a feeling of slight disappointment with his contribution up to that point. According to the report, he played most of the game in the centre-forward position, although wearing number 11, and added to his earlier penalty goal with two smartly executed goals involving Robb and Willoughby.

He followed this up with two goals in the cup-tie against Clyde two weeks later, but these were to be the last he scored until the final game of the season. That, of course, was the game which made the whole season worth while, the game which set the seal on the revival of the Dons' fortunes under Eddie Turnbull, and the game which established Harper as one of the Pittodrie legends. Once again the Dons went to Hampden to play Celtic in the Cup final, as they had done in 1937, 1954 and 1967, but on this occasion they were to gain revenge for those earlier defeats with a 3–1 victory. Harper's goal came from a penalty, but before taking it he had to wait several minutes for the Celtic players' protests to subside, and, with nothing better to do in front of 108,000 spectators, filled the time playing keepie-up. When the moment came, he placed the ball on the spot and sent it exactly where he had intended, into the right-hand corner of Evan Williams's goal. The Harper legend was created.

Yet this was a match he might not have played in, for his form had been indifferent, and he had missed several league games. February and March had been months of goalscoring drought, relieved in April only by a return to the reserves. Nevertheless, his two goals against Hearts' reserves were enough for the *Press and Journal* to announce: 'Joe Harper shoots back into the Hampden picture'. While the next game failed to inspire the paper's reporter with any optimism – 'no hope of glory for Dons on this form' – it did convince him that, whatever the team's chances, Harper could only improve them: 'If there was ever any question about Joe Harper playing against Celtic at Hampden, it must have been dispelled after last night's game at Kilmarnock. Operating at inside-right, he was the mainspring of the Dons' attack and their most dangerous forward. Harper played a leading part in both goals.' It was to prove a timely return to form, and a profitable one for both Harper and the club.

The magnificent Hampden victory established the team as potential challengers to Celtic in the championship. The acquisition of Steve Murray from Dundee was the catalyst required to realise that potential, and by Christmas they were on top of the league, having climbed over Celtic by beating them at Parkhead on 12 December. The single goal which secured the points was scored, naturally, by Harper. Not only did he have the temerity to score against Celtic on their home patch, he had the effrontery, as the smallest man on the park, to do so with a header, nipping in front of Billy McNeill to send the ball past Fallon from close range. But by then we had come to expect this from Joey. It was his 20th goal of the season. The goalscoring machine which had been somewhat reluctant to start the previous season was now operating at peak efficiency. The surge to the top of the table may have owed much to a defence which was to achieve a record of 12 games without conceding a goal, and in particular to the outstanding form of Bobby Clark and Martin Buchan, but there was no doubt who the idol of the fans was.

He had started the new season as he had finished the old, scoring four against Airdrie in the League Cup, and starting the league campaign with another against the same side. After that, they just kept coming: left foot, right foot; inside the box, outside the box; headers, mazy dribbles; best of all, a mazy dribble through a 'bemused Rangers defence'. By the end of the year he had scored 22 goals, and after his brace against Airdrie on 26 December – how they must have hated him – the *Press and Journal* was moved to report: 'Harper may not be the best centre-forward that has ever worn Aberdeen's colours, but he is one of those highly regarded select band of players who score goals with priceless consistency.' A slightly grudging tribute, considering the skill he had shown in scoring some of those goals, but what did that matter? It seemed that he could not stop scoring, and until the New Year he couldn't. After Hogmanay he did.

The Dons survived the first three games of the New Year without a Harper goal, thanks to their watertight defence. They went to Easter Road on 16 January comfortably on top of the league, and looking for their 16th successive win. In January 1955 they had gone there in a similar position and had extended their lead at the top to six points by beating a formidable Hibs side. Paddy Buckley's solitary goal on that occasion was to prove as decisive as any in bringing the championship to Pittodrie at the end of the season. In 1971, as in 1955, Celtic were chasing. It had been Buckley's first goal for three games. If Harper could emulate Buckley – and it seemed inconceivable that he could go another game without scoring – then Aberdeen would go into February with an almost uncatchable lead.

But when Pat Stanton became the first player to beat Clark since what seemed like the beginning of time, the match, and the title, started to slip away. Harper, from being able to conjure goals out of nothing, found himself unable to score even when the goalkeeper was beaten; he rounded Baines and slid the ball towards the untenanted goalmouth, only for a defender to race back in time to clear off the line. Robb's goal near the end was not enough to prevent defeat after Joe Baker, returning to his old haunts, had extended Hibs' lead.

The following week brought Harper back onto the goal standard with two against his old club, Morton, but they were to be his last of the season. An arid February brought a defeat, two draws, and no goals for Harper. If his favourite reading was Chaucer, he would have known all about 'the droghte of Marche'. If it wasn't – and somehow I don't see Joey as a Chaucer man – the *Green Final* told the same story: no goals for Harper. It did, however, bring four straight wins for the Dons to keep them at the top of the league. The fluency of their play earlier in the season had gone, but they showed with a series of gritty displays that they were not going to concede the title. Their fighting spirit was never seen to better advantage than at Tynecastle, when they were fortunate to be only one goal down at the interval after a dreadful first-half display, with Hearts having missed a penalty.

We'd had a game that morning, Victor, Peter, Broonser and the rest.

We'd only meant to have a kick-around on the Meadows, maybe a gentle game of three-and-in, but when a bunch of 12-year-olds challenged us to a game, we couldn't resist. Edinburgh *v* Aberdeen. It was a kind of omen. We started off expressing our natural superiority, all flicks and feints, pretending to play the Real Game, and not trying too hard to get the ball back when we lost it, or to score when we had it. The trouble was, they were a bit better than we thought, and we had Victor in goal, and in no time we were three down and struggling. We reckoned that Victor would do less damage out than in, so in I went. With his first touch, ignoring my shout to leave it, he sent a looping header over my despairing fingers (I'm no believer in palmistry or any of that nonsense, but you really can tell a goalkeeper by his despairing fingers) and into the net. I say 'net', but I'd lost the ability to see posts and nets where none existed. What was beyond dispute was that it was a goal, of the 'own' variety. By the time the sprawling goalkeeper got up to look for him, Victor had decided that it was safer to be at the other end of the pitch, both for reasons of personal safety and defensive security. Nobody was arguing. Having failed to make our superior skill tell, for the very good reason that their skill was superior to ours, we set about the serious business of turning height and weight to advantage. Forget about playing the Real Game; this was a real game. It wasn't pretty, but it was effective. Gradually we pulled back, until, with the scores level, Peter found himself in front of goal. A tap-in would have been enough, but he was taking no chances; he blasted the ball so hard that it practically disappeared from view, and ensured the end of the game by giving their keeper no chance of retrieving the ball before lunchtime. What we had been unable to do with skill, we had achieved through grit, determination and making full use of our unfair advantage. Perhaps it was an omen after all. Would Turnbull be able to pull a similar stroke for the Dons?

Certainly it was a different side which came out for the second half. I don't know what Turnbull had said to them at half-time – presumably nothing too complimentary – but it was soon obvious what he had done tactically. Harper was withdrawn into midfield, and his blunted foil in attack was replaced by Dave Robb's sabre. With his head swathed in bandages after an aerial collision, Robb scored three goals to win the match and keep the Dons at the top of the league. He may have been the blood-stained hat-trick hero who had led the cavalry charge, but Harper had been the midfield general whose shrewd and accurate passing had created the breaches in the Hearts defence. That day he showed that, if he was not scoring goals, he could still play.

It was a happy band of Dons fans who left Tynecastle. Such is the power of football to make us forget our woes, for Broonser had just lost his job, and was back on the 'burroo'. His problem was that, like me, he had received most of his education at the Kingsway, our local cinema, rather than King Street, our local school. As a result, he had seen too many cowboys, too many gangsters, and too many paperboys delivering papers by throwing them up the front drive to land on the front porch of clapperboard houses where some horrible murder had been committed. What worked fine on film sets, and possibly even in the Californian suburbs, was rather less effective when applied to streets of Scottish tenements, and Broonser was not a success in his brief career as a paperboy. That had been some years previously. What had been an ineffective strategy for newspapers, however, was to prove disastrous for doorstep milk deliveries. At the end of his first round, his employers had been delighted at the speed with which he had completed it. They were rather less delighted when the complaints from irate customers came in, and they learned that he had effected the ultimate in non-stop delivery by lobbing the bottles onto the front doorsteps from his float as he cruised past the doors. He did not get a second chance to pilot a milk float. That's the way he told it, but with Broonser you could never be sure.

And so to Cowdenbeath. In the dark days, we had dreaded going there because it represented relegation, the sort of place that could only ever have a Second Division side. Now we dreaded it because it represented the sort of obstacle which the Dons were only too likely to trip over on the way to the title. When we got there we realised that there were reasons other than the sporting for avoiding the place. It is unlikely to figure highly on anyone's list of places to visit in Scotland. As my granny would have said, it is 'nae a bonny place'. Still, duty calls, and with the Dons in sight of the title, we had to be there. The pub nearest the ground is the Masonic Arms. When we went in there to calm our nerves, we knew that the boys were taking the championship seriously; half an hour before the kick-off, and not one of them, not even Joey, in the pub. We drank our pints with pride, and made for Central Park.

It had been almost two years since Armstrong had walked on the moon, but the pictures of man in that alien environment were still fresh in the memory. Where on earth could they have prepared for that? When we saw Central Park, Cowdenbeath, we knew. From certain angles, the resemblance was uncanny, and I'll swear we'd only had the one pint in the Masonic. Trained? They could have filmed the whole thing there. There are some conspiracy theorists who believe that the moon landings were faked. Before you dismiss the idea out of hand, have a look at Central Park.

When the game started, the players seemed intent on maintaining the illusion by making the ball defy gravity. On one of the fleeting occasions when it returned to earth, one of the Cowdenbeath defenders did us a favour by putting the ball past his own goalkeeper. We were on our way.

A few minutes later Henning Boel repaid the favour by doing the same thing at the other end. We were not on our way. But, with about 15 minutes to go, George Buchan headed one of the three goals he scored for the Dons. The news came through that Celtic had dropped a point. We were on our way after all. Joey had been saving his goals for the hat-trick he was going to score against Celtic, and the title would be ours. We left Cowdenbeath in good spirits. Who does not?

April is the cruellest month. It raised our hopes, only to dash them. Harper didn't score his hat-trick against Celtic; he didn't score at all. It was Alex Willoughby who equalised from Murray's precise chip over the Celtic wall, and Arthur Graham who missed the chance to win the league when Evan Williams managed to get a fingertip to the ball as Graham went round him. The challenge eventually petered out with a 1–0 defeat at Falkirk the following week, but that only confirmed in cold figures what we already knew in our hearts. The title was going to Parkhead, as it had done for the previous five seasons, and would for evermore. It was the natural order. As for the Dons, the season may have ended not with a bang, but with a whimper; but taking it all in all, it had been a glorious failure, and they are the best kind.

The following season it seemed that the natural order was to be over-turned, as Aberdeen raced to the top of the league and stayed there for the first few months of the season, with Harper restored to goalscoring form. Turnbull had gone, to be replaced by Jimmy Bonthrone, but with Harper in such irresistible form at centre-forward, the man in the dugout hardly seemed to matter. This time the goals did not dry up after Hogmanay, and Harper ended the season with 33 league goals, and 42 in all competitions. By any standards it was a remarkable performance, and even the most diehard old-time fan who still cherished memories of Benny Yorston would have to admit that Harper stood comparison with the great man.

The problem that season was at the other end, for after Martin Buchan had been transferred in February, the defence started shipping goals in what we recognised as true Aberdeen fashion. Celtic won the league at a canter; it was the natural order.

If there were any arguments that season over the best centre-forward to play at Pittodrie, they were settled on 17 November. Was it Yorston or Harper? Neither. It was Anastasi. Juventus had won 2–0 in the first leg of the second-round UEFA Cup tie in Turin, and nobody outwith the ranks of the seriously deranged thought that the Dons could overcome that sort of deficit against the mighty Juve – that would have been like beating Real Madrid in a cup final – but it was a privilege to see a team like that at Pittodrie, and gave us a taste of what European football could be: the floodlights, the atmosphere, the big names, the glamour. The Real Game.

Anastasi was a big name, and he scored a goal with a speed of thought and movement that left Buchan for dead, and a precision of finish that gave Clark no chance. Harper managed to squeeze in a header in a crowded penalty area near the end to prove that, even if he lacked the class of Anastasi, he could still score in the highest company.

It was a fact noted elsewhere, and when he scored on his Scotland début in a World Cup qualifier against Denmark in October 1972, transfer rumours intensified.

The following month, the SNP were warning that the newly discovered North Sea oil could be 'a bubble of disaster'. Harper was warning the Dons that 'they need success to keep me happy'. As had so often happened previously, a taste of the international scene had given a player a glimpse of the opportunities and rewards to be gained on the larger stage. Harper said that any move he made would be for financial reasons, and that he was 'deeply grateful' for the support from the Dons fans.

He won his second cap for Scotland against Denmark on 15 November. His only entry in the referee's notebook on that occasion was a caution, but Scotland won 2–0 to keep their World Cup hopes alive. It was becoming clearer that Harper's hopes were to be elsewhere. He scored against Kilmarnock with a typical 'gem of opportunism', and also against Celtic in the League Cup semi-final on 27 November, but when Aberdeen lost that game 3–2, and it seemed that Celtic were destined to win everything in Scotland forever, the official transfer request went in.

It was the era of 'glam rock'. Gary glittered. It was announced that Aberdeen University was to study the effect of the 'black gold' boom. Harper failed to glitter against Airdrie at Broomfield. The following week, Aberdeen accepted Everton's gold, and Harper went to Goodison Park for a reported £200,000.

There are two clubs in England with a tradition of great centre-forwards. One of them is Newcastle United, with Hughie Gallacher, Jackie Millburn and Malcolm Macdonald. The other is Everton, where the tradition started with Bill 'Dixie' Dean, who banged and headed in a record number of goals around the same time as Benny Yorston was doing the same thing for the Dons; it was continued by Tommy Lawton, another spearhead in the traditional English mould. The Goodison crowd's love of number 9s was not restricted on grounds of nationality or style, however, for they had revered Alex Young, the 'Golden Vision', the former Hearts player who had helped them to the league title in 1963. After Liverpool's success in the mid-1960s, the goalscoring exploits of another centre-forward, the young Joe Royle, had played a major role in winning the 1970 championship and restoring what Evertonians regarded as the natural order on Merseyside. That team, founded on the midfield talents of Kendall, Harvey and Ball, looked set for a period of prolonged success, but had in fact disintegrated surprisingly quickly, and the club once again found itself being overtaken by a resurgent Liverpool. Harper therefore went to a club which demanded instant success, the definition of which meant winning major trophies or, at the very least, beating Liverpool. It was a situation not unlike that of Rangers, who had gone through a succession of players and managers in a vain attempt to beat city rivals led by a charismatic and seemingly invincible manager. At least Jock Stein would acknowledge defeat, even if he did blame the referee. You could score more goals than Shankly's side, you could even finish up with more points, but you could never beat them.

Harper was by no means a failure at Goodison, but he was not the runaway success which the club and the fans demanded, and he was never given the chance to make the centre-forward position his own. In January 1974, after little more than a year, he returned to Scotland, to rejoin his old manager, Eddie Turnbull, at Easter Road. It was typical of him that, on his return to Pittodrie the following season, he should score with a free-kick near the end to equalise, and force the rebound for Alex Cropley to score the winner in injury-time.

All was forgiven in April 1976, when the King finally returned to reclaim his crown. It is odd how some players of undoubted ability only flourish with one club. George Hamilton, another player for whom the Pittodrie fans had a special affection, also failed to play at his best in the capital when he was transferred to Hearts, and did not recover his true form until he returned north.

The fans had to wait all summer before seeing their hero back in a red jersey. They had been warned not to expect instant success, under all the 'It's great to be back' headlines. They believed the headlines rather than the warnings, and they were right. Harper made his return on 14 August in a League Cup game against Kilmarnock, was made captain for the day in Miller's absence, and scored with a header in the fourth minute. Success hardly comes more instantly than that. Deeside, according to the following Monday's paper, welcomed the royal family. For Dons fans, the King had come back over the water, and their welcome could not have been more ecstatic. Nor was it to prove a false dawn, for the Dons went on to win the trophy which Ally MacLeod had promised by beating Celtic in the final of the League Cup in November. Harper failed to score in that game, but had a hand in both goals. Another chapter had been written in the Joe Harper legend, and the prologue in the Ally MacLeod legend. Argentina was still two years away, and for the time being club and manager could bask in the glory of victory, and reflect on what a wonderful game football was.

It continued to be wonderful until after New Year, when Ally's revolution ran out of steam, points were frittered away, and, as in 1971, Celtic overtook the Dons to win the championship. On this occasion, however, no blame could be laid at Harper's door. He continued to score freely throughout the season, and, if he did celebrate Hogmanay, it only served to inspire him, for he scored a hat-trick on New Year's Day, just as Benny Yorston had done on 1 January 1930, and he never scored a better.

Frost had made underfoot conditions tricky, which suited a striker of Harper's build, and he took full advantage against the tall Hearts defenders. Twice in the first half he went on mission impossible in the opposition penalty area, surrounded by markers, with his back to goal, yet finding space to turn and shoot and be back in the centre circle while the Hearts defenders were still trying to work out how he had done it. For the first, he shot on the turn after a deft piece of ball-juggling; for the second, he flicked the ball over his shoulder and the head of the centre-half, Gallacher, before wheeling round to volley the ball past Cruickshank. He provided the cross for the Drew Jarvie goal which ended the first half and completed his hat-trick in the second half. In those 90 minutes we saw all the qualities which made Harper such an effective striker: close control, anticipation, speed of reaction and accuracy with either foot. We also saw the flair and the sheer cheek which made him a great entertainer.

He continued to show those qualities for the rest of that season and the following one, scoring a total of almost 60 goals over the course of the two seasons, and making a Dons team without Harper unthinkable. Managers may come and go, and indeed came and went – MacLeod went, McNeill came and went, Ferguson came – but King Joey had made himself as much a part of Pittodrie as the Beach End which adored him. But, early in the 1979–80 season, the unthinkable happened. Harper sustained a serious knee injury in November and missed the rest of the season in which the Dons finally won the title they had been so close to at the beginning of the 1970s.

He missed most of the following season, too, but returned to the team for an Aberdeenshire Cup final at the end of April 1981. Aberdeen beat Buckie Thistle 5–1. It was hardly the most attractive of opposition, nor was it the trophy Dons fans wanted to win above all others, and the fact that 5,000 turned out could only have been due to the drawing power of Harper. Their only disappointment was his failure to score, but in every other way he showed that he was ready to return to the first team.

On 1 May, the sports page of the *Press and Journal* had headlines reading: 'Sexton sacked' – Dave Sexton, the Manchester United manager – and, more cheerfully, 'Harper poised for return'. His comeback was welcomed for his personality as much as for his footballing ability, with a lament for the lack of characters in the modern game. This was at a time when Aberdeen had players like Miller, McLeish and Strachan in the team. The characters always played at least ten years ago. When Harper started, they weren't making them like Charlie Cooke any more – which was true – and when Cooke played, where were the George Hamiltons?

Wherever they were, the Dons could have done with them that day, for they lost 2–0 to Kilmarnock at Pittodrie, and Harper's career ended not with a bang, but with a typical end-of-season performance. The report stated that he had 'few chances to shine', and that 'the scarcity of openings resulted in him trying too hard on the rare occasions he was afforded a glimpse of the target'. The team that day was: Leighton, Kennedy, Rougvie, Watson (Jarvie), McLeish, Miller, Simpson, McGhee, Harper, Angus (Harrow), Hewitt. None of the players who had played in his first game, against the other Ayrshire club, remained; only Kennedy and Jarvie had been in the team when he had returned to Pittodrie.

Outside the club, things had also moved on. The Situations Vacant pages carried advertisements for 'downhole fishing operators', which had nothing to do with fishing, and 'hyperbaric welders', which had nothing to do with bars. A group called Adam and the Ants were top of the album charts. On television, Val Doonican was on at 8.20 that Saturday evening. Oh well, maybe things hadn't moved on that much.

On the Saturday, the *Press and Journal* had welcomed him back. On the Tuesday, it asked: 'Is King Joey's Reign Over?' He said he would accept another contract if the club offered him one, but the club declined. His reign was over.

He remains, however, in the memory of all the fans who saw him, and in the record books as Aberdeen's top scorer. But he did more than just score goals. He scored clever goals, he scored cheeky goals, and he loved to score them. He was not the most disciplined player the Dons have ever had, and certainly not the fittest; perhaps his lack of physical perfection helped the fans to identify with him. When he scored, it was as though one of them had scored. The image which remains in the mind is of King Joey on his knees in front of his loyal subjects, leading the rejoicing. The Dons have had more skilful players, but not that many. They may find a player to score more goals for them, although in a defensively minded age that looks increasingly doubtful. But they will never have a more popular.

Ferenc Puskas

Ferenc Puskas, more than any other player, had his career defined, at least in British eyes, by a single moment. It was the moment he delivered a little piece of magic. In that moment he became the first foreign player to be recognised by every British football fan, and the first foreign name to be acknowledged as a byword for virtuosity, alongside the likes of Stanley Matthews, Tom Finney or Alex James.

That moment came in November 1953, when Hungary played England at Wembley. They came to an England which still regarded 'foreigners' with deep suspicion and not a little disdain. The 1945 result had confirmed England's sense of superiority over the rest of the world; this was further reinforced, in Coronation year, by the conquest of Everest (by a New Zealander and a Nepalese), and had been dented not at all by the 1950 result, when that mighty footballing nation, the USA, had defeated England in the World Cup. That had been dismissed as a freak result on foreign soil, in a competition which awarded a 'World Cup' to the winner as a consolation for being the next best after England.

Defeat at home, however, was not to be contemplated. Wembley was, to the football nation, as potent a symbol of English supremacy as the Tower was to the nation at large. The occasional incursion from the rebellious Scots might be tolerated, and even an occasional sneaky win by the Welsh or Irish, but to every nation beyond these shores Wembley was an impregnable fortress. Puskas didn't fire the first shot – the walls had already been breached, with the score at 2–1 and England desperately hanging on to a retrievable deficit – but his was the direct hit which blew the stronghold apart.

He received the ball in a crowded penalty area, and showed enough of the ball to Billy Wright, England's captain, to tempt him into a rash tackle. In the words of Geoffrey Green in *The Times*, Wright duly arrived where he thought the ball was, 'like a fire engine going to the wrong fire', while Puskas pulled the ball back with the sole of his boot, swivelled, and fired the ball into the roof of the net. To a nation which had never taken foreign football seriously, and which was accustomed to a limited range of techniques, it was a stunning moment. It wasn't just that England were 3–1 down, with the match clearly beyond recall. It was the fact that the lead had been achieved in a manner beyond the reach of any English, or British, player or team. The England team had been made to look pedestrian, and Billy Wright, the golden-haired, clean-cut captain, symbol of all that was good and admirable in English manhood, had been made to look a right diddy. England's conception of itself as the supreme footballing nation crumbled in that instant, and Ferenc Puskas became instantly famous.

To a nation less insular than the English, neither the result nor the manner of its achievement should have come as any surprise, and the name of Puskas would already have been celebrated. After all, the Hungarians had been unbeaten in international football since 1950, and had won the 1952 Olympic competition in some style, beating the holders, Sweden, 6–0 in the semi-final and Yugoslavia 2–0 in the final, and finishing with a total of 20 goals for and only two against. Puskas had scored two against Turkey, one against Sweden, and one of the two goals in the final. Not that you would have known it if you had been reading the British newspapers. *The Times* merely reported the result of the final with no match report. It was not a competition which interested the British press or public very much, offering as it did scant hope of British success: 'The British attitude leaves the least range of choice, while others, such as Brazil, Chile, Sweden, Russia, Finland, Yugoslavia and Austria are able to draw upon players who in fact represent their full national strength. Sweden won in 1948, when they were challenged by Uruguay and Brazil. Most intriguing will be the appearance of Soviet Russia, who have been undergoing intensive training in the Caucasus.' The correspondent managed to give a nice hint of Iron Curtain skulduggery in his preview, combining a contemporary McCarthyite suspicion of all things Red and Eastern European (What the hell are they up to in those goddam Caucasus?) with good old-fashioned British disdain for excessive effort (Intensive training? Sounds like cheating to me, old boy). He also managed to name seven teams without including the eventual winners, who by that time had been unbeaten for two years.

The paper's boxing correspondent did rather better. His analysis of the reasons for American success may have been a little facile ('The success of the five Americans, all of them negroes, could be explained by their clear superiority as boxers, backed up by a stiff punch') but he did pick out as a particularly impressive fighter Patterson, who won the middleweight gold medal at 18 years of age. Floyd Patterson was to go on to become the youngest heavyweight champion just a few years later, sensibly waiting until Rocky Marciano had retired. The man who was to take the heavyweight title from him temporarily was also at the Helsinki games, fighting, or rather not fighting, in the heavyweight final, which 'ended in pandemonium when Johannsen of Sweden was disqualified for not entering sufficiently into a fight with Sanders'. The man who was to take the title from him permanently, the fearsome Sonny Liston, was probably in jail. He usually was.

There is no equivalent of a world title for a footballer, but from time to time one player is universally acknowledged as the greatest player in the world – Pele in the 1960s, Cruyff in the 1970s, Maradona in the 1980s. But, before them all, came Puskas, and, until the emergence of the stars of the Brazil side on the World Cup stage of 1958 and the European dominance of the Real Madrid side led by Di Stefano, he had no rival.

Puskas was born on 2 April 1927 in Budapest and, like almost all the great players, showed his promise early, making his début for the Budapest side Kispest when he was only 16, and for the Hungarian national side just two years later in 1945. By 1948 he was the leading goalscorer for Kispest in the Hungarian league. The following year the club mutated into Honved, the Hungarian army team, and formed the nucleus of the country's national team. Puskas was given the rank of major, but we can assume that his military duties, along with those of his team-mates, were less than onerous. It was their status as soldiers, rather than professional footballers, that allowed them to compete in the 1952 Olympics, which was to be their springboard to world domination. Very nearly.

Very nearly, because, although they were only to lose one game in the next few years, it was the one game that really mattered, the World Cup final. Until that point, everything had gone to plan, with a string of impressive international results convincing even the English press that they might be worthy opponents for England. Heralding 'A Great Match in Prospect', *The Times* on 12 November declined to forecast the result: 'Here, then, are two great giants poised for a battle, the outcome of which none can foretell with any degree of certainty . . . England will use the long through pass, hit first time as often as possible and preferably at the right moment. The Hungarians, like the Austrians and South Americans, put their faith in short, swift passing, often carried out at bewildering pace and dexterity.'

I like that 'preferably'. The English tactics were, basically, 'kick it up the park', 'get rid o' it', or some variant familiar to anyone who has ever seen junior football. In modern jargon, it was 'route one' versus 'the passing game'. There was still a feeling that all this 'short, swift passing' was trickery for trickery's sake, all flicks and footwork signifying nothing, and that it would be put in its place by good honest English strength and endeavour, not to mention natural superiority. It was a nation that had just had a coronation, and had not yet given up its empire, although it was beginning to fray a bit round the edges.

It was also a nation obsessed, or possibly severely afflicted by, constipation, judging by the number of advertisements for California Syrup of Figs – 'When that little extra help is needed' – and similar products. Elsewhere in the paper, Tenova self-supporting socks were advertised as 'the most comfortable in the world' (at seven shillings and sixpence the pair, a goodly chunk of a week's wages, they should have been). It was hard to imagine that a nation which could produce this Rolls-Royce of socks could prove inferior in any way to some Eastern European chappies.

Any doubts about English supremacy disappeared within the first minute, when Hidegkuti scored, and, adding another two for his hat-trick, passed into the language. He had already achieved a measure of fame as the first deep-lying centre-forward, and his performance at Wembley made him almost as much of a household word as Puskas. Partly this was due to the novelty of his positional play, at a time when the traditional line-up was regarded as immutable, and the influence he had on English football, most notably with Manchester City and Don Revie. It may also have been the Wembley hat-trick – always a potent symbol in English sport – but partly it may have had something to do with the name. 'Hidegkuti' was exotic, yet pronounceable, in a way that 'Kocsis' was not. Kocsis was the other half of the main strike force, and was not far behind Puskas, with a contribution of 75 goals out of the 158 they scored between them. Yet when the *Weekly News* (a publication which appeared weekly but contained no news whatsoever) included a Hungarian name in its comic football column 'Fun and Games by Andy James', the name was Hidegkuti, not Puskas or Kocsis. The only other name I can remember was Wan Fittit, a centre-forward of limited ability who could only kick with one foot. I may be mistaken, but I think there was a goalkeeper with only one leg. What I am sure of is that Wan's father worked as a salt packet inserter in the local potato crisp factory, and that Hidegkuti was the family budgie.

Puskas scored another goal from a free-kick, and Kocsis added his usual goal to make up the six. If the English press had been slow to recognise the superiority of the Hungarians before the game, there was unstinting admiration for them afterwards. *The Times* hailed 'A New Conception of Football', and reported that England 'found themselves strangers in a strange world, a world of flitting red spirits, for such did the Hungarians seem as they moved at devastating pace with superb skill and powerful finish in their cherry bright shirts'. They succeeded with 'a mixture of exquisite short passing and the long English game'.

It seemed entirely appropriate that the paper which carried the report of this monumental defeat should also carry a review of a new book about the Charge of the Light Brigade, featuring another comprehensive defeat by an Eastern European enemy. On this occasion, however, it was the victorious enemy rather than the glorious dead who were honoured. The preview of the following Saturday's games lamented the departure of the invaders: 'Football in these islands is going to be like dry bread and water for the next few weeks while the flavour of the banquet provided by the Hungarians . . . still lingers on.'

Two typical English sides, West Bromwich Albion and Wolves, led the league with a powerful, direct style of play which had given them success on the domestic scene. Wolves, managed by the uncompromising Stan Cullis, were to continue to win trophies throughout the 1950s, with three championships and an FA Cup win in this period. The lesson which the Hungarians had taught the English national side had not been totally lost on English club managers, however. Matt Busby was in the process of dismantling a successful but ageing side, and building the team which would achieve fame as the Busby Babes and restore some respect for English football in Europe. Looking back from an era when the league is dominated by the hegemony of powerful big-city clubs, the top of the First Division in the autumn of 1953 has an unfamiliar, almost quaint, look, with Huddersfield Town and Burnley in third and fourth place respectively. Of the teams which finished that 1953–54 season in the top half of the First Division, only Manchester United and Chelsea are still playing in the top division.

If any English supporter thought that Hungary had caught England on a bad day, there was an even worse one to follow. In May 1954, the teams met again in Budapest, and England were beaten 7–1, with Puskas again scoring two of the goals. The only consolation for England was that almost any other side would have suffered a similar result against the team which was undoubtedly the best in the world, and would surely be crowned as champions in the World Cup finals, to be played in Switzerland that summer.

The results in the preliminary round did nothing to dispel that view; Hungary beat South Korea 9–0 and West Germany 8–3. South Korea were a genuinely weak team, but West Germany had deliberately fielded a weak side, calculating (correctly, as it turned out) that they could beat Turkey in the play-off for a quarter-final place, while avoiding Brazil in that round. The Germans had displayed the strategic acumen which was to stand them in such good stead in later World Cups. What was impressive here was their range of tactics: concealing their hand – an entirely legitimate if somewhat cynical tactic; relying on a later victory at the expense of an earlier – a risky one; and crocking the opposition's best player – wholly cynical and very effective. Somewhere between conceding eight goals, Liebrich, the German centre-half, kicked Puskas on the ankle, and the man who should have been the outstanding player of the tournament did not play again until the final.

That he played at all owed as much to his dominant position in the Hungarian squad as it did to his brilliance as a player. The team had already proved that even Puskas was not indispensable by reaching the final without him, and in spectacular fashion. They beat Uruguay 4–2 in one of the finest games ever played in the World Cup, and defeated Brazil by the same score in one of the toughest, the infamous 'Battle of Berne'.

In reaching the final, they had scored 25 goals in four games. This scoring rate was exceptional by any standards, but reflected the overall trend of a tournament which produced 140 goals in 26 games, at an average of over five per game.

The scoring rate of previous competitions had hovered around an entertaining four; after Switzerland it was to decline steadily, dipping below three per game in Chile, 1962, and dropping to a miserable two per game in Italy, 1990. The 1994 tournament brought a welcome rise in the scoring rate after 40 years of increasingly defensive tactics, but the average was still well under three per game, and the final was decided on penalties after two hours without a goal. The 1998 finals maintained the scoring rate of 1994, with the bonus of some goals in the final itself, but, for all the skills of Zidane, France's success was still founded on defensive solidity rather than attacking brilliance. The 1950s were a golden age for goals, in international as in club football.

Hungary epitomised the footballing *Zeitgeist*. They regularly conceded two or three goals, but this hardly mattered as long as they were scoring at least four. It was a philosophy that was to cost them dear in the final. There are those who claim that the return of Puskas to the team caused them to lose the game. This can only be a matter for conjecture, and they're probably still arguing about it in the bars of Buda and the great plains of Hungary. ('What do you think of this horse, Sandor, is it not a fine animal?' 'Fine animal, Zoltan? By my Magyar forefathers, it is as lame as Puskas in the 1954 final.') But what his inclusion did demonstrate was the remarkable consistency in selection which had been a major factor in the team's success; the only change from the side which had won the Olympic tournament two years earlier was the replacement of Palotas by Toth. The Olympic champions, who had swept all before them in Europe, and had now beaten the best of the South Americans, appeared to be ready to become world champions.

They started off in their usual manner, with Puskas apparently vindicating his selection by scoring after only six minutes. When Czibor scored another two minutes later, the final appeared to be turning into a coronation rather than a contest. It took only another eight minutes for that lead to be squandered, and the contest resumed. Typically, Hungary threw everything into attack, but found the German defence a very different proposition to the one which had conceded eight goals in their earlier meeting. Turek, the German goalkeeper, was in brilliant form, and had the additional, priceless, benefit of luck, with the woodwork coming to his rescue when he was beaten. When that happens in a cup-tie, you just know that the underdogs are going to score, and, with only seven minutes to go, that is exactly what happened.

The Hungarians now showed that they had spirit as well as skill. Puskas had the ball in the net within two minutes, but the goal was controversially disallowed for offside. ('Pish! Sandor. You know as much of horses as you know of football. For what kind of lame man can score two goals in a World Cup final? And two he did score, were it not for the blind English dog of a linesman. Would that all my horses were so lame.') There was a final shot from Czibor, brilliantly saved yet again by Turek, and Hungary had lost the match that mattered most.

After that blow, they carried on their winning ways, and looked forward to the next World Cup. Puskas had already shown the extent of his influence on tactics and selection by effectively naming himself in the team for the final. In this respect he foreshadowed Beckenbauer and Cruyff, who were to be such dominant influences for West Germany and Holland 20 years later. In September 1954, it was rumoured that he would be manager and sole selector of Hungary, following his promotion from major to lieutenant-colonel. It did not come to pass, but there can be little doubt that Mandl, the new manager, could only have managed with the consent of Puskas.

He displayed the extent of his powers, and his petulance, in a friendly match between West Bromwich Albion and Honved the following month. He was given a great reception by the Midlands crowd, but their adulation turned to annoyance at his displays of temper, directed at his own team. When Tichy, the young centre-forward, failed to blend with his colleagues, Puskas sent him off and replaced him with a substitute (allowed at that time in friendly matches). As a player in the army team, Tichy was probably dreading a court-martial after the game, and a few years in a labour camp. Whatever punishment he did receive – possibly a couple of weeks of latrine duty – it did not permanently blight his career. He went on to become one of the outstanding players of the 1962 World Cup.

The Scottish public were to see the better side of Puskas's nature in December, when Hungary played Scotland at Hampden. Excitement had been building for some time at the prospect of taking on the best team in the world, along with a certain amount of apprehension at what Hungary might do to us. In the World Cup, Scotland had played rather better than expected against Austria, but had been humiliated by Uruguay. The beginnings of realism in relation to Scotland's place in world football were starting to seep into the Scottish psyche, and even into Scottish journalism. In the *Press and Journal*, James Forbes reported that, while a win 'would give a great fillip to Scots soccer . . . even a creditable show, with a deficit of no more than a couple of goals, would be a tonic'.

This was hardly fighting talk, but it proved to be a realistic assessment of the best Scotland could hope for. The team's performance in restricting the scoreline to 4–2 justified that old favourite headline from 1415 and 1745: 'Gallant Scottish Team Goes Down Fighting'. No doubt there was a measure of satisfaction that the defeat was a smaller one than England had suffered, which made it a kind of victory. There was no doubt in James Forbes's mind about the star performer: 'Puskas, as captain, was the key man, and I cannot recall him wasting a pass.'

The skills appreciated by the Hampden crowd that night were, for the first time, seen by an Aberdeen audience, for that was the night that television came to the North-East. Its arrival had been heralded for weeks in the local press, with detailed, six-step programmes for turning on the device, including setting contrast and brightness controls. That night, any Aberdonian with 60 guineas to spend and the patience to get the horizontal hold just right could have watched Puskas, Hidegkuti and co in the comfort of his own home, as the game was broadcast as a test transmission.

Those who were unable or unwilling to fork out such a substantial sum were still able to see the game in the less comfortable surroundings of the pavements outside electrical-goods showrooms. Considering the size of the screens and the quality of picture, it is doubtful if they could have seen much from this vantage point, but the lure of seeing something for nothing proved predictably irresistible for large numbers of Aberdonians. The window of one shop caved in when more than 200 people on the pavement pressed forward to see the screen.

Scotland played a return game in Budapest the following May, and again performed better than England had done, going down 3–1 in an honourable defeat. The fairly narrow margin may have owed something to Puskas's form: 'The most disappointing Hungarian was Puskas, who has regained his former waistline but has lost some of his skill.' This is nonsense, of course. Skill is always there; it is just that a lack of fitness or motivation may make it hard to find at the right time. The report hints at the recurring weight problems which Puskas suffered throughout his career. Sluggishness through carrying too much or fatigue caused by too rapid a weight loss may have affected his form at any time. Speed of thought rather than movement was his greatest asset, however. If he could have been bothered, he'd have moved as fast as he needed to. Lack of motivation was probably the key factor; faced by opponents he knew he could beat in his sleep, he just didn't see the point of waking up.

At that stage of his career, he probably needed the incentive of another World Cup to produce his best. With no European competition at club or international level, Honved and Hungary were in danger of becoming the Harlem Globetrotters of football, forever parading their talents abroad in exhibition games. In the spring of 1955 it must have seemed a long, long time until the next World Cup finals in 1958, with nothing much in between but the formality of a few qualifying games.

In November 1956, I was old enough to know that something terrible was going on in Hungary, but my only vivid memory is of a newspaper front page – I think it was the *Sunday Mail* – with the story, which turned out to be no more than the hint of a rumour, that Puskas was dead. I don't remember the details of the story, but I remember how sad I felt. That says something about the standards of journalism and the priorities of a football-daft schoolboy, but it also conveys how big a star he was at the time. For the popular press, a story about Hungary had to have a Puskas angle.

He was actually on tour with Honved in November 1956. When the abortive revolution was quelled, the Hungarian Football Association refused permission for the club to visit South America, and ordered the team to return to Hungary for 'rest and training'. No doubt justifiably suspicious of what this might entail, such as a permanent rest or training in Siberia, the club beat a Casablanca select 7–4 (even the scores were starting to resemble those of the Harlem Globetrotters) and announced that the tour was to go on.

The team never did return for that 'rest and training'. In May 1957 it was reported that Puskas was homesick and had telephoned his former team-mate, Josef Boszik, who was a member of parliament, to ask for a promise that he would not be punished if he were to return home. 'I know I have behaved badly in running away, but I cannot forget I am a Hungarian and have played 84 times for my country,' he was reported as saying. Even allowing for a loss in translation, this doesn't ring very true, and only a few weeks later it was reported that he was to join Inter Milan, and would be free to play for them from September 1957. This report proved to be no more reliable than the statement from Budapest; in fact he spent the next year in Austria, but failed to get a playing permit, and did not resume his football career until 1958, when he joined Real Madrid.

He was over 30, and had been out of football for almost two years. He had to lose 16 kilos in six weeks before he could start playing. Football, as well as his waistline, had expanded considerably in that time. The European Cup had established itself as the ultimate ambition of every major European club, and Real Madrid, having won the trophy in each of its first three years, was indisputably the greatest club in Europe. It was a club which could afford to dispense with players, however great their reputation, if they did not meet the Real standard; Didi, the Brazilian midfield player who had dominated the 1958 World Cup, had not lasted long.

Above all, any newcomer had to win the approval of Alfredo di Stefano, the presiding genius of the club, without threatening to usurp his authority. Kopa, the brilliant Frenchman who had played for Reims against Real in the first European Cup final, had been accepted into the side, but had to fill a more peripheral role. Di Stefano played a deep-lying centre-forward role similar to that played by Hidegkuti, so that Puskas would have had no difficulty coming to terms with the tactical requirements of his new colleagues; he simply had to do what he had been doing all those years for Hungary. But it must have been difficult for the former major to revert to NCO status – 'Just go and bang in a couple of goals this half, Corporal, there's a good chap' – knowing that, if he did not bang in the required number of goals, he would be out on his ear. The Puskas name may have been part of history, but the glory he trailed from the great days of Hungary had to match the current glory of Real Madrid.

He did not disappoint. Whatever difficulties he may have encountered in adjusting to a new country, a new club and a whole new way of life, the prospect of a return to Hungary and a few years in a labour camp, weighed against a few million pesetas, probably concentrated the mind wonderfully. Whatever he had lost in pace, his speed of thought and anticipation remained as sharp as ever. He helped Real towards their fourth successive European Cup final in 1959 with goals in the earlier rounds. He was to go on to score 35 times in 39 European games, but, just as his 83 goals for Hungary were overshadowed by that one goal at Wembley, the others for Real were eclipsed by the four he scored at Hampden on that May evening in 1960.

Real Madrid *v* Frankfurt Eintracht was an eagerly anticipated European Cup final for several reasons. It was the first to take place in Britain; Real's reputation had grown with each successive European Cup, along with the status of the competition; there was di Stefano, del Sol and Gento; there was Puskas himself, still fondly remembered for his exploits with Hungary, and even more fondly remembered by the Glasgow crowd for his demolition of England. It was also the first to be televised live in Britain. The great age of communal television-watching, from the early- to the mid-1950s, was over. The great emptier of cinemas and divider of communities had originally brought people together, as neighbours gathered round the one telly in the block to watch the major events and personalities of the day: royal events, to the hushed and reverent tones of Richard Dimbleby; the FA Cup final, to the excited accompaniment of Kenneth Wolstenholme; the Prime Minister; Muffin the Mule. It had been a brief period, for within a couple of years nearly everyone had their own box, and nobody came round to watch the games any more.

There was one exception, my dad's friend, Shirran. Shirran rejected the whole post-war era, and a good chunk of the pre-war period as well. He didn't have a radio, never mind a TV, and only read the racing pages of newspapers. Thus protected, he remained convinced that the Celtic team of the 1920s, Bassett's Liquorice Allsorts, Gigli the opera singer and Player's Navy Cut were the undisputed greatest in their respective fields, and that all forms of telecommunication were the works of the devil. Not that he rated God too highly either. However scornful of all things modern, he did not disdain the opportunity to see the game on our telly. The fact that Shirran had stirred himself to come over to our house on a Wednesday (his usual nights were Tuesday and Saturday) provided the final proof that this really was A Great Occasion, even if he was only going to use it as a further opportunity to pour scorn on all things foreign and modern.

Eintracht, who had demolished Rangers in the semi-final by an aggregate 12–4 and thus ensured the support of at least half the crowd, were expected to provide testing opposition. When they took the lead after 19 minutes, it looked as though they might be more than that, but Real were ahead on the half-hour mark through two di Stefano goals, and just before half-time scored their third with a wonderful strike from Puskas. From a position almost on the bye-line, he 'hit the roof of the net with an awesome left-foot shot'. Well, if it was awesome it had to be his left foot. And it was awesome.

The second half turned into a coronation, notwithstanding a couple of goals from Eintracht, for Real gave the impression that they could score whenever they pleased. Puskas scored with a penalty, completed his hat-trick with a header from a Gento cross, and got his fourth with a typical shot on the turn which found the tightest of spaces at the angle of bar and post. I missed the wonder of di Stefano's third goal, when he gathered the ball in the centre circle and ran through the middle of the Eintracht defence, because I had to go to the lavvie. There were no instant replays then. When I was told that I had missed a goal even better than those I had already seen, I learned a valuable lesson in continence.

After all those years of hearing and revering the name, it was the first time I had seen Puskas play, apart from a few fleeting glimpses on news-reels. I had not yet learned the truth universally acknowledged, that the quality of a sporting contest is usually in inverse proportion to expecta-tion. This time the event exceeded what had been expected. Puskas and Real were confirmed as legends, and a myth was created around the European Cup. The huge Glasgow crowd, 135,000-strong, showed its appreciation unreservedly, and created another myth around the sporting, fitba'-daft Glasgow crowd. They certainly loved Real and their fitba' that night, but as that post-war crowd has dwindled, so has Glasgow's enthusiasm for anything other than the Old Firm and their tribal warfare. In 1976 the only other European Cup Final to be held at Hampden, between Bayern Munich and Saint-Etienne, attracted a crowd of just 55,000.

The European Cup has somehow retained the glamour created for it that night. Despite bribery scandals and the statistical probability that it will be a defensive, low-scoring game, the final is still a game to look forward to in the hope that it will provide the best football of the year. Every so often, it produces a final or a winner that sustains that hope for another few seasons: Real were followed by Benfica and Eusebio; there was the exhilarating victory by Celtic in 1967; Manchester United and George Best the following year; the total football of Johann Cruyff's Ajax in the 1970s, and the more recent Dutch-inspired virtuosity of AC Milan.

Real Madrid's reign as European champions was to last only a few more months, for they were beaten in the first round of the following season's competition by their old rivals, Barcelona, who featured two of Puskas's former team-mates, Czibor and Kocsis. They reached the final, and scored a goal each, but could not prevent Benfica from taking the cup outside Spain for the first time. The following season, it was Real's turn to face Benfica in the final; this time it was a hat-trick from Puskas which proved insufficient to beat Benfica, who came from behind to score five goals and retain their title. It was a match which was arguably greater than the Hampden final, for it added competitiveness and drama to the skill and flair of the 1960 game. Puskas had reached his peak then, but a Puskas past his best was still good enough to win five Spanish championships with Real, and finish as the leading goalscorer in the Spanish league in four seasons out of five. He also played for Spain in the 1962 World Cup.

He was to play in Glasgow once more, for Real against Rangers in the preliminary round of the 1963–64 European Cup. Real contented themselves with a 1–0 win at Ibrox, before thrashing the Pride of Scotland 6–0 in the second leg. If the game at Ibrox was unmemorable, Puskas probably remembered less of the ensuing evening, as he followed Jim Baxter to a party in Drumchapel. Now, it *is* possible that the intention was to introduce Puskas to the traditional Scottish fare of tea and scones ('Will ye no' try ma home-made raspberry jeely, Mr Puskas?'); it is also possible that it was an elegant affair with canapés and chilled white wine ('I think you'll find that the flinty quality of this Chablis complements the earthy flavours of the smoked salmon admirably, Ferenc'); but, knowing the reputation of Baxter and Drumchapel, it is more probable that it offered Puskas the traditional Scottish fare of McEwans, Tennents and Bells. If the story is true, it is a miracle that he managed to get back to Madrid in time for the second leg.

If it is not true, it still says something of the men and the age they lived in. Puskas looked as though he enjoyed life, and indeed laid great stress on the importance of comradeship to the success of the great Hungarian team. Looking back on the fortieth anniversary of the Wembley victory, he said: 'We had some very good players, but what was more important was that we were all friends, almost like a family.' Baxter had a reputation for liking a bevvy, and from his shape it is clear that Puskas was no ascetic. But it is also significant that they could even be imagined going to a party in Drumchapel. Footballers, even the greatest, were still in the real world, not a pop-star world of models and nightclubs. George Best had already played for Manchester United, but he had not yet been invented. In its own way, the Drumchapel party represented an age of lost innocence, although I don't suppose any of the participants looked on it like that at the time. Nor, I imagine, did the neighbours.

Whatever happened in Glasgow, or didn't happen, or can't be remembered, Puskas recovered in time to win another finalist's medal in that season's European Cup, losing 3–1 to Inter Milan. He retired in 1966, but was not in the Real side which won the trophy that year.

His next entry onto the European stage was in the 1971 final, when he managed the Panathinaikos side which lost 2–0 to Ajax. The emerging Dutch team, featuring a teenage prodigy called Johann Cruyff, had been beaten by the old guard of AC Milan in the 1969 final. Now Ajax, following the success of Feyenoord in 1970, were establishing Dutch football as the dominant power in Europe, just as Hungarian football had been in the 1950s. Like Hungary, the national side would beat Brazil on the way to the World Cup final before falling to West Germany at the last hurdle.

In Cruyff, Puskas must have seen much of himself. The success in that 1971 final confirmed him as the major European star; by 1974, following three successive European championships and his outstanding perfor-mances in the World Cup, he was widely regarded as the best player in the world. Just as Puskas had been, Cruyff was a tactician as well as a personal inspiration to his club and national sides. Like Puskas before him, he sought success in Spain, but he was never able to do for Barcelona what Puskas had done for Real, taking them no further than the semi-final stage of the European Cup. He scored goals – some great goals, some important goals – though never as many as Puskas, but by the 1970s the great days of goalscoring had long gone. He was harder working, more athletic, and could kick the ball with both feet.

But nothing Cruyff did, or ever could have done, could possibly equal the impact of that tubby little man showing the ball in that packed penalty area, dragging it back, swivelling and shooting in a movement so smoothly executed it could hardly be followed, and sending a million schoolboys into the garden and onto the streets to practise it. And no match Cruyff took part in, no matter how important, could have changed how a nation thought about the game, in the way that the Wembley and Hampden games had done. Why, after the 1960 European Cup final, even Shirran had to concede that Puskas was 'nae bad', and awarded us all an extra liquorice allsort in honour of the performance. It was that good. And, if you'd known how parsimonious Shirran was with praise and sweeties, you'd realise how good that was.

Denis Law

'Who was the greatest player to . . .?' is a great way of starting an argument. Denis Law would have his supporters as Scotland's greatest player, but there would be plenty of other contenders, from the Wembley Wizard days of James and Gallacher to the post-war period and on to the modern era, although serious discussion would have to stop at Kenny Dalglish. If we try to measure the respective merits statistically, then Dalglish is out on his own in number of caps, but as a goalscorer his 30 for Scotland came from 102 appearances, whereas Law scored the same number from only 55 games.

'Ah, but . . . it was easier to score in Law's day, and Dalglish was never really a striker, and then there was Jimmy McGrory, but goals were easier to score in his day' and on and on. What is beyond argument is that Denis Law was the greatest player ever to come from Aberdeen. The only people I ever heard argue against that proposition were Shirran, who was reluctant to concede that anybody born after 1920 and who did not wear a Celtic jersey could have any merit whatsoever, and Broonser, who thought that he was the greatest player ever to come out of the granite city. As Broonser had some difficulty getting into the school team, his arguments were not to be taken too seriously. Shirran, for all his grumbling, could never come up with a plausible alternative. So Law was, unarguably, the greatest, and that is why he was a hero. He is also the only one of my heroes I passed a ball to.

He was born in Aberdeen in 1940, and made his first appearance in the sports pages as early as 1952, when he played for Aberdeen Primary Schools against Arbroath in the Scottish Primary Schools Cup competition. The *Green Final* billed it as the 'Midgets' Cup-tie', and reported that Aberdeen were 2–0 up within a few minutes. Then Law got his first mention, in the capitals awarded to goalscorers: 'The home team were in control, and LAW added a third . . . Some brilliant leading-up play by Smith ended with LAW shooting a fourth goal.' He scored the fifth in the second half, and completed his side's scoring with the eighth goal. Strangely, the headline was 'Fleming's Hat-trick', with no reference to Law's four. Whatever else young Master Fleming did in his career, he remains one of the few people to grab a headline away from Denis Law.

The nuclear age was already under way, although the dangers of dabbling with the atom were a trifle understated. US troops taking part in atomic warfare manoeuvres were warned that they would feel a 'sudden, fairly strong blast of air', and that they would be 'required to turn away from the burst and wait for three seconds before looking towards the fire ball. Those who fail to obey this instruction may be unable to see for a few minutes. This is much the same effect as you get from watching the explosion of a photographer's flash bulb, although it could be considerably magnified.' Nothing to worry about there, then.

Two years on, there was growing concern about the dangers of nuclear warfare, but rationing had ended, and all was right with the world, as long as it didn't end suddenly. What was happening in the sports pages was much more interesting. Matt Busby, who was to play such a significant role in Law's career, wrote in a weekly column that 'big transfer fees were on the way out'. He would prove himself wrong some eight years later by paying a British record fee to bring Law back from Italy. More astutely, he advocated the importance of ball control, good passing and positional play, against the 'get rid of it' and 'kick and rush' tactics. He had absorbed the lessons of the Hungarian victory over England the previous year, and was in the process of passing on those lessons to the young players who were to become the Busby Babes.

Meanwhile, the player who was to join him had graduated to the Aberdeen Secondary Schools Select side, and appeared for them at centre-forward against Dundee Schools. It seems to have been a fairly typical performance: 'Law was shooting hard and often, but McDonald in the Dundee goal positioned and handled well.' Dundee won 3–1 to end Aberdeen's interest in the competition and leave the young Law with a schoolboy international cap as his only remaining aim in schools football.

Before he could achieve that goal, Huddersfield Town stepped in. In March 1955, under the headline 'Schoolboy Star May Go Straight to Seniors', the junior football column in the *Evening Express* reported that several junior clubs would be disappointed to hear of the interest shown by senior clubs such as Wolverhampton Wanderers and Huddersfield Town, 'clubs noted for their ability to bring on young players'. The report remarked on Law's goal-scoring feats in schools football, including eight in a game (mercifully, it didn't mention the opposition) and his confidence in his own ability, exemplified by his ambition to win a schoolboy cap. Clearly, the qualities that he brought to the senior game were already there.

What is noteworthy is that the report mentioned the possibility that he might 'skip the juvenile and junior grades'. At that time most senior players still came into the professional game through the lower ranks. It was thought exceptional that Law should take the direct route, yet within a few years most professionals were signed straight from school, and the junior game became a branch line on the way to nowhere, rather than a stop on the route to glory.

The photograph used to illustrate the story was the now familiar one of the myopic schoolboy peering through National Health glasses. He had been recommended to Huddersfield Town by the brother of Andy Beattie, the manager. Whatever it was that had impressed his brother was not immediately obvious to Andy. What he saw was a skinny schoolboy in glasses, accompanied by two older youths – Law's big brothers – and was aghast to discover that it was the squinting, bespectacled shrimp he was expected to sign.

At this distance, Huddersfield may seem a strange choice of club for an Aberdeen youngster to join, but Law was not the only one; he joined at about the same time as Gordon Low, another Powis schoolboy, and there were already another couple of Aberdonians on the playing staff. At that time Huddersfield were a First Division side with a proud record: they had finished in third place the previous season, after a single season in the Second in 1952–53, their only period out of Division One since 1920, and they still carried something of the aura of the side managed by Herbert Chapman, which had won three successive league titles in the 1920s.

They were, however, a club in decline, and were relegated in 1956. The following season, as they struggled to regain their first-division status, the opportunity was there for young players to claim a place in the team. By this time the young apprentice had grown, dispensed with the glasses, and impressed the management enough to give him a chance in the first team. He made his début against Notts County on Boxing Day 1956 (perhaps the management felt that a 16-year-old had more chance of being sober) and scored in a 3–0 victory. He retained his place for the next game, and was a 'prominent attacker' in the 1–1 draw with Fulham.

This was the year Elvis made his breakthrough, and popular music was never the same again, for better or worse, depending on your musical taste. In January he recorded 'Heartbreak Hotel'; by the end of the year he had made his first film, *Love Me Tender*, and was just about the most famous person in the world. Every teenage boy in the land was slicking his hair back, and trying to curl his lip, and was socially dead if he didn't know the words of 'Hound Dog'.

Football was changing as well. The first European Cup had been played, and won by Real Madrid. There was controversy over the possible introduction of substitutes. They had already been used in friendly games against foreign teams. As usual, the feeling was that foreign clubs didn't play fair, but the economic argument appeared to be the decisive factor, according to the local press: 'There is something to be said for both sides of the question, but as far as ordinary league and cup matches are concerned, it is doubtful if clubs will ever agree. If substitutes were allowed it would mean additional expenditure in wages for players at each match.' Now there was an argument to appeal to club chairmen. Nevertheless, substitutes were permitted from 1965–66 and hang the expense.

Within a couple of months of his début, Denis Law was some way from world fame, but he was well known in Huddersfield and weel kent in Aiberdeen, which is a good start. As tales of his exploits were reported in the local press, letters came in demanding that 'Aberdeen procure, at any cost, the Huddersfield prodigy, Aberdeen-born Denis Law'.

This kind of response had been triggered by statements such as 'Denis is a soccer genius', from that master of hyperbole, Bill Shankly, who had been Huddersfield's coach when Law was signed, and had since taken over as manager. Just a few weeks after his début, he was being described as 'the best inside-forward discovery since the war' in the Aberdeen papers. Shankly had yet to achieve fame, but more weight would have been given to the opinion of Matt Busby, who had just achieved his second championship with Manchester United, and his first with the Babes. He was inclined to understatement rather than exaggeration, and when he described Law as a 'wonderful prospect' after watching him in action in a cup-tie against Sheffield United, people listened.

All this praise was being heaped on a player who had not yet turned professional. I don't know if it was the first time that the local press had used the term 'soccer genius', but it certainly wasn't the last. The young lads so described usually end up playing for Montrose or Forres Mechanics. On this occasion it just happened to be close to the truth. There is no harm in extravagant praise as long as no one believes it. If Law did believe what was being said about him, it didn't show in his performances, and he retained his place until the end of the season, when he missed the last two games through injury.

He was still injured at the beginning of the next season, and suffered recurring problems which prevented him from re-establishing his place in the first team until November 1957. He has recalled how Shankly would refuse to speak to players on the injured list; they became non-persons as surely as any dissident in the Soviet Union. 'Denis who? – Never heard o' 'im.' When his photo appeared in the Green Final again, it could have been a different person, for the old school photo with the glasses had been replaced with a picture of the young modern professional, showing the influence of Elvis with hair swept back and up into a quiff.

He continued his prodigious rate of progress by making his international début the following year. He became the youngest person to play for Scotland, in the game against Wales in October 1958, when he was just 18. With little going on in Aberdeen to excite the sports fans, it was an opportunity for the local press to exercise a little parochialism by concentrating on Law's performance.

There was no difficulty with the main news. A visitor who had been dropped blindfold into the city would have been in no doubt that he was in Scotland. One headline read 'Big Lum Danger to Bairns', about a large chimney which constituted a risk (fairly remote) to some children, while another proclaimed 'Soorocks and Neeps on the School Road'. God knows what that was about. Elsewhere, teenagers, a relatively new phenomenon regarded as more of a menace than the H-bomb, were terrorising tenants. I blame the soorocks.

In the sports pages, the news was of a teenage terror of a different sort. The preview to the international match commented on the 'formidable reputation' which Law had built over the previous couple of seasons. Matt Busby had been appointed Scotland team manager, and had changed the preparations from the usual 'lapping' to actually working with the ball. This was clearly regarded as fairly revolutionary; probably only someone of Busby's stature would have got away with it. The prevailing theory at the time was that if you kept the ball away from players in training they would be 'hungrier' for it in the match. Busby's methods proved effective, as Scotland won 3–0, and Law scored on his début. The *Press and Journal* praised his performance: 'Law has come to stay in the Scots side. He played with the natural skill and aplomb of a veteran . . . as dangerous off the ball as he was in possession.' This was an opinion which would be endorsed by Danny Blanchflower after a bruising encounter with a young Law eager to impress his personality and his studmarks on opponents. Perhaps he wasn't such a different sort of teenage terror after all.

Elsewhere, there was praise for a future colleague of Law's, as Bobby Charlton, only slightly older than the Scot, inspired England's win over Czechoslovakia, and was described as a 'great inside-forward'.

As Law's reputation continued to grow, while Huddersfield remained in the Second Division, it was clear that his future would lie elsewhere. When the move did come, in March 1960, it was to Manchester City, for a British record transfer fee of £53,000.

The revelation of the 1960 European Cup final had still to take place, but interest was growing, with the progress of Rangers to the quarter-finals, where they had already beaten Sparta Rotterdam 3–2 away and were due to meet them at Ibrox. *The Times*, previewing the match, warned: 'We shall not expect a classic match of the higher graces.' A Belgian writer described Rangers as 'the robust fighters of the Clyde', and after Rotterdam had won the Ibrox match 1–0, offered the forthright opinion: 'Not only are they heavy of limb, but heavy of brain also.' He said it, not me. Despite all this extra weight, Rangers won the replay, which gave the robust fighters of the Clyde the opportunity to be humiliated by Eintracht in the semi.

Manchester City were clearly hoping for some lightness of limb and quickness of brain, but they got a robust fighter as well. His stay was a short one and, whatever he gave them, it wasn't any trophies, though he did set a record which isn't in any of the record books. He scored all six of his side's goals against Luton in a fourth-round FA Cup tie to equal the cup record, only for the match to be abandoned with the score at 6–2. Luton won the replay 3–1, with Law scoring City's goal, to become the only player to score seven goals in a cup-tie and finish on the losing side.

If he thought that was crazy, worse was to follow, for in June 1961 he was transferred to Torino for £100,000, give or take a few million lire. Following the success of John Charles at Juventus, Italian clubs were falling over themselves to buy British players. Joe Baker joined Law in Turin from Hibs, Jimmy Greaves went to AC Milan. None lasted long. Law chafed against the discipline on and off the field, and found himself in trouble with the club as well as the referees. Yet he was popular with the supporters, as he always had been and always would be, and distinguished himself by appearing for an Italian League side.

To confirm how highly he was regarded in Italy, and especially Turin, he was wanted by Torino's city rivals, Juventus, but he refused to sign. There were reports of a transfer to Manchester United in May 1962, and the transfer went through in July for another British record of £115,000. Law declared himself delighted. 'I had always hoped to play for United on my return from Italy.' It's what they all say. ('Since I was a kid I have dreamed of playing for Rangers/Raith Rovers/Ross County'), but in Law's case it might just have been true. Their record since the war had given them a glamour few other British clubs could match, and while Matt Busby remained in charge they retained the aura of winners, whatever their current form.

In one way it is surprising that Busby, who had expressed his distaste for paying large transfer fees, should have been so willing to pay a record amount; in another it is surprising that he did not sign a player he regarded so highly when he had been available a couple of years earlier at half the price. Perhaps at that stage he had still hoped to rebuild the side shattered at Munich by using the same methods of bringing through young players. In 1960 it had looked as though the policy might work, with United in the top half of the table. By the end of the 1961–62 season they finished in the bottom half of a table which was headed by Ipswich and Burnley, and were in need of a quick fix at any price, while they remained one of the few clubs which could afford to pay it. It was time to replace the aura with the substance.

The high price did not guarantee a quick fix, however, as the club flirted with relegation, ensuring their safety only in the last game of the season. The FA Cup was a different matter. Law's goals helped them to the final, where they faced Leicester City, who were the team in form, fourth top to United's fourth bottom in the league. On the day, however, class mattered more than consistency. Law, after scoring United's first goal, inspired a 3–1 victory to give United their first trophy since Munich and himself his first winner's medal. The following season saw United challenging for the league title, and Law challenging referees. He had his first appearance before a disciplinary hearing in November, following a brawl at Villa Park. He received a 28-day suspension. It would not be his last.

It was around this time that, after reading so much about him and seeing him on TV, I first saw him play. The only time I had seen him play a whole game on TV had been the Scotland *v* England game the previous year. Scotland had recovered from the humiliation of the 9–3 defeat of the previous season, and had finally broken the 'Hampden Hoodoo' of a quarter-century's failure to beat England by winning 2–0. Law hadn't scored, but he had picked up everything in midfield, and created a buzz of excitement in the crowd every time he was in possession. Even so, I remember being slightly disappointed that he didn't hold the ball longer, and beat more people. That was what great players did. That was what Charlie Cooke would have done. There was a body of opinion in Aberdeen that considered Cooke a better player than Law. Partly this was because they could see Cooke every week, and they couldn't see Law, but it was also 'I kent his faither', a feeling that a local boy from Powis School couldn't be that good. The image of the small boy squinting through the National Health glasses had lodged itself in the local imagination, and had never been replaced by the athletic figure known to English and Italian crowds until that Hampden performance, which finally established him with the Scottish fans. The BBC sports programme presenters were ecstatic about the team's performance that night. Peter Thomson's glasses gleamed as never before, and George Davidson, brimming over with excitement, and possibly much else besides, reported in his summary that the Scotland attack had 'moved like a well-oiled jigsaw puzzle'.

Then I got the chance to see the real thing. It happened unexpectedly. Scotland were playing Wales in a midweek match at Hampden, and it was my dad's half-day. I should have been at school, but it was only games afternoon, and my dad said he'd give me a note, which would guarantee immunity from prosecution, so off we went on the train to Glasgow. It was a cold, clear November day, and the heating on the train was turned up full blast, so that the windows steamed up. It wasn't quite cold enough for the heating to pack up, so the best British Rail could do was to produce an uncomfortable contrast between the inside and outside temperatures.

The whole country seemed to be in the grip of Beatlemania, with stories of their most trivial doings snatching headlines from the really important news, like Aberdeen bus fares going up a penny. Gerry and the Pacemakers had made their contribution to football by recording 'You'll Never Walk Alone'. There was concern about falling standards and crowds in Scottish football, which was, as usual, in crisis.

The national side was not doing too badly, however. Following the defeat of England, there had been a series of good results, most notably a 6–2 win in Spain. Scotland were scoring so freely that George Davidson missed one of the goals in his commentary. The ball landed snugly in the corner of the net – 'And it's hit the side netting. Bad luck, Scotland.' The crowd roared, the players congratulated each other, the opposition looked miserable. Still he couldn't see why it wasn't a goal-kick, and thought that the referee had given a free-kick on the halfway line – 'I'm not sure what's happening. The referee seems to have spotted some infringement earlier on.' Only when he saw that the kick was exactly on the centre spot, and that both sides were lined up in battle formation on either side of the line, did he realise what had happened, and start to get excited, just as the excitement on the terraces was dying down – 'It must be a goal. It's a goal for Scotland! Scotland have scored! A goal for Scotland!'

Law had scored the first four goals in a 6–1 win over Norway, having previously scored all three in a 4–3 defeat in June, and was expected to perform similar feats against Wales. He did score, an unspectacular but typical close-range effort, to give Scotland a 2–1 win, but I don't remember much more of him. We were near the front, and he seemed so far away most of the time. The old North Terracing at Hampden went down to below pitch level, so that from the front you could only get a decent view of the near touchline, and my memories of the game are mainly of Dave Mackay's throw-ins. In those days, demarcation ruled; defending was for defenders, attacking for forwards, and throw-ins were strictly a wing-half's job. I also remember Willie Henderson tormenting the Welsh full-back, twisting this way and that until the back didn't know if he was on the pitch or in the cludgie. And I remember Roy Vernon, the Welsh inside-forward, stamping on Mackay's leg. Mackay didn't retaliate, but gave him a glare that indicated that the trespass would not be forgiven. It struck me at the time that, apart from being unfair and malicious, it was also a very stupid act; if I ever wanted to stamp on someone's leg, I think I'd make damn sure it wasn't Dave Mackay's.

This last impression seems to have been fairly typical of the match. James Forbes had been on the train, and I remember thinking how purple he looked. He must have gone even more purple when he wrote his report: 'The referee was to blame for the Hampden fiasco. The fans pay to see football, not a hacking match . . . one of the scrappiest, ill-mannered internationals I've seen.' Law's performance was described as 'not one of his best, but he got his customary goal'. It was a goal announced in the usual fashion: the upraised arm, with the sleeve gripped in the palm of the hand.

The next time I saw him was in the international against England in April 1964. By this time Manchester United were back near the top of the league, although they were still one season away from regaining the championship. Law was on his way to 30 goals for the season, had been voted European Footballer of the Year and had established himself, according to James Forbes, as 'undoubtedly the greatest Scots footballer of the decade . . . a brilliant all-round player with the ability to snap impossible chances'. That was the preview. The appraisal after the game was 'disappointing'. The only memorable thing about the match, apart from the sensation of being in a crowd of 133,253, was the brilliant header from Gilzean which gave Scotland their third successive win over England, their first such run since 1884.

The following year hopes were high that this run could be extended further. For some reason that now seems terribly obscure – call it youthful enthusiasm – I made the pilgrimage to Wembley. The fact that it involved two successive nights in a railway compartment bothered me not at all. The annual call to the spirit of Bruce and Wallace and the biennial call to the spirit of James and Gallacher were enough to send us happy band of brothers on our way. Somewhere round about York, in the middle of the night, it didn't seem quite such a good idea, but some spring sunshine in a Trafalgar Square with more Scotsmen than pigeons and the purchase of tartan caps in traditional hand-woven nylon restored our spirits.

Seeing Wembley made me realise what a dump Hampden was. On the way up to the terracing, there was no pee running down the stairs, although one or two Scots were doing their best to remedy the situation and make themselves feel more at home. On the terracing, there was room to get a decent view of the pitch, and there was cover overhead. A couple of Scottish supporters saw this addition to the amenities as an opportunity to overcome the disadvantage of being unable to stand for a whole 90 minutes, or at all. They clambered along the roof stanchions to allow themselves a birds-eye view of the match, while maintaining a prone position; a perfect solution to their problem, apart from the possibility of plunging to certain death. Broonser looked up at them. I saw a glint of admiration and envy in his eyes, but he did nothing about it. That time.

As the kick-off approached, a nearby supporter produced a bottle of whisky from inside his jacket, like a conjuror. The miracle in this case was not that he had managed to secrete it unseen about his person, but that it had survived an overnight journey and a whole morning in the streets of London. Before opening it, he held it before him, in pride at his achievement and anticipation of his pleasure. Just then, there was some movement in the crowd to accommodate some late arrivals. He was jostled, and the bottle slipped from his fingers. I'd never seen anyone dumbstruck before. The power of speech had been slipping away from him anyway, as had the power of movement, but this tragedy left him in an open-mouthed trance. At the end of the game he was taken away to the

British Museum, and stands there still, labelled 'Scottish Football Supporter, circa 1965'. No, I exaggerate, but smell is the sense that evokes most powerfully the remembrance of things past, and the smell of whisky still recalls for me the sights and sounds of Wembley on that day.

The match itself was a fairly scrappy affair. England scored twice through Charlton and Greaves, but Law reduced the arrears before half-time with one of the strangest of goals. Long-range efforts were Charlton's speciality rather than Law's, who scored most of his goals from inside the penalty area. When he tried a shot from well outside the box, it looked to me as though he had run out of ideas. It was not even a particularly well-struck shot, skidding along the wet turf rather than flying through the air. Banks, in the English goal, had a clear sight of it, but may have been deceived by a change of direction as it bounced in front of him. Rather than go down to gather what looked like a straightforward shot, he stayed upright and ineffectually stuck out a foot to try to stop the ball, which was only deflected into the goal. That raised our spirits for half-time, even if it did seem a bit like cheating to get one back like that. Still, they all count, and it enabled Law to equal Lawrie Reilly's record of 22 goals for Scotland.

Substitutes were not allowed until the following season. Ray Wilson, England's left-back, had been injured in the first half and had failed to appear for the second. When Roger Byrne, the right-back, was injured, England were reduced to nine men, and it was against a severely depleted team that Scotland were eventually able to scrape a 2–2 draw. Despite four goals, it had been a scrappy, unsatisfactory game and I was beginning to wonder if I'd ever see a decent international. On the way back, the train was the traditional three hours late, and, walking home from the station after two nights without sleep and with a silly tartan hat on my head announcing to the world 'Here is an eejit', I wondered if it was worth it. Call it the cynicism of youth.

In October there was the serious business of World Cup qualification; my country needed me, and my dad was paying the fare, so I went to Glasgow again in midweek to see Scotland play Poland. Others felt the same way, for the crowd of 107,500 was a record for a floodlit game in Britain. Scotland had made a good start in their qualifying group, but had still to play Italy, the favourites, so a victory over Poland was vital. Scotland's recent form had not been convincing, with a 3–2 defeat by Northern Ireland at the beginning of the month. With the prospect of the games against Italy, and the reward of playing in the World Cup in England, the crowd was buzzing. The programme and souvenir vendors were in good voice:

'O-FISH-ELL! O-FISH-ELL! O-FISH-ELL PROGREMME!'

'WERRA CULL-ERS! RERRA TAR-TEN!'

The team bus pulled up as we made our way to the enclosure under the main stand, and a starstruck crowd gathered to watch the players get off, and intone the names.

'Rerr's Greig.'

'Aye, rerr's Greig.'

'Rerr's Wee Wullie.'

'Aye, Wee Wullie.'

'Rerr's wee Bremner, wi' ra rid heid.'

'Aye, wee Bremner. He's kinna shoart in the leg, is he no' bu'?'

'Aye, he's a wee terrier bu'.'

The last man to emerge, like the sheriff getting off the western stage, was Jock Stein, who was temporarily in charge of the team. By this time he had acquired almost mythical status as a manager, on the strength of his record of continuous success with Dunfermline, Hibs and Celtic. Possibly because of his connection with the last-named club, there remained some sceptics, and two of them were with us.

'Aw, rerr's big Ba'heid!'

The match proved that everything Stein touched did not necessarily turn to gold. Scotland started brilliantly, with Willie Johnston making an outstanding début on the left wing. He was so quick and so assured that you wondered what he was on. Years later, we would find out. With the service coming from him and Henderson on the other wing, it seemed that Law and Gilzean must score, but it was one of those nights when Law never quite connected, usually arriving a fraction early, and Gilzean likewise couldn't quite find his touch. Eventually McNeill scored from a corner. Still, considering Scotland's obvious superiority, we assumed that the second half would offer plenty of opportunities to add to the scoreline.

It did – for the Poles. Whatever big Ba'heid said to Scotland at half-time, it was useless. Scotland were played off the park, and Poland deservedly won 2–1. It was a long journey back to Aberdeen that night.

The summer of '66 looked like being a miserable one, with the big party on in England, and Scotland not invited. Summer started early, however, when The Lovin' Spoonful released 'Daydream' in April, and made everything seem a lot better. Scotland had a last chance to prove their superiority in the traditional international that month. With the big show just a few weeks away, the fixture was already looking a little out of time, but it still generated enough excitement to make it worth seeing. I saw the match from the old North Stand at Hampden, which gave a splendid view of the pitch as long as the cloud level wasn't too low and you didn't mind watching a game between two teams of worker ants.

At least it was an international worth seeing this time. Scotland were always chasing the game after England had taken an early lead, but it had all the excitement that chases should have. Two goals from Jimmy Johnstone, worming his way irresistibly into the penalty area, had brought the score back to 4–2. Law's persistence had paved the way for the first one. Then, in the second half, he scored one of the great Hampden goals, twisting in mid-air to head the ball so fiercely it would have travelled all the way to Mount Florida if the net hadn't got in the way. This was the signal for a final spirited, but unsuccessful, assault on the English goal, so it ended 4–3, but it had been an exciting defeat rather than a depressing draw, and we went home happy.

In his match report, James Forbes praised Law's contribution ('the one forward prepared to take the battle into enemy territory') and Bremner's effort, while doubting his class ('still doesn't look an international player to me'); echoes, there, of 'too shoart in the leg'. He also didn't think that England could win the World Cup ('too many flaws in their make-up'). Well, there were a few of us who thought that. Shortly afterwards, Ramsey announced the World Cup squad of 40 players, including the surprise choice of Martin Peters, a highly versatile player who would play such a vital role in England's victory. Ramsey was nearer than most of us thought to making good the flaws in the team's make-up.

If playing for Scotland was a ticket to failure, Manchester United had proved to be a highway to success. They had followed the 1963 Cup success with the league championship in 1964–65, helped by 28 goals from Law and the precocious skills of George Best. The addition of George Best had given them one of the most talented and exciting club forward lines of all time. In April 1966, the ultimate prize of the European Cup was still a possibility, but the brilliance of their quarter-final victory over Benfica was to be dimmed by a dour Partizan Belgrade in the semi-final. Another league title in 1966–67 was to give them another opportunity to win the trophy that Matt Busby prized most of all.

They won it, memorably, by beating Benfica at Wembley, but they won it without Law. A declining goal tally bore testimony to the cumulative effects of injuries suffered by this most combative of players in the harshest of environments – the opposition's penalty area. He had missed most of the games in the earlier rounds, either through suspension or injury. It was a half-fit Law who played in the first leg of the semi-final against Real Madrid, and by the time of the return leg he had accepted that his season was over.

The following year Elvis returned to performing live from the wasted years of Hollywood, and sounded and looked as good as ever; he was, emphatically, still the King. At Old Trafford, Law held a similar position and, restored to fitness, returned to claim his crown. The goals no longer flowed as freely as in the years when he could be relied on for at least 20 a season, and maybe 30, but to the United fans he was still the King. United were beginning to fray a little round the edges, but were still a force in Europe; they looked as though they might retain the trophy, but went out at the semi-final stage to AC Milan. What looked like an equaliser from Law was disallowed. Argumentative as ever, he complained bitterly that the ball had crossed the line, and a quarter of a century later was complaining still.

By 1970 the team, with many of the players ageing and Best increasingly wayward, was unmistakably in decline. Before they were relegated, however, there was one last flurry, in the autumn of 1971, and it was during this Indian summer that I saw Law play for Manchester United. It was at Crystal Palace. United were in the middle of a run of form, and Law was clearly enjoying every minute of it, alert to every opportunity, constantly on the move, arguing with the referee, arguing with the linesmen, arguing with his opponents and challenging for everything. It had been rumoured that he was one of the names in Jack Charlton's infamous 'little black book', and it was easy to see why. He scored a great breakaway goal, beating the goalkeeper on the edge of the penalty area, and squeezing the ball past a defender and in off the post. The arm went up in the familiar salute, and I was sorry I hadn't seen more of him in his prime.

I was to see him once more, at Hampden, the night that Broonser peed in a pie stall. I must emphasise that it was not being used as a pie stall at the time; having been vacated by the pie vendor, it was occupied by needy spectators as an improvised urinal, in the manner of advancing forces occupying enemy trenches. There was no immediate danger to public health, but the incident should serve as a warning to anyone wishing to take advantage of the stadium catering facilities.

In July 1973 Law had been transferred back to Manchester City. While his old colleagues struggled, he had enjoyed a renaissance, to such an extent that he found himself back in contention for a place in the Scotland squad, and bound for the 1974 World Cup in West Germany. Before that, he had league business to complete. It was probably his most famous goal, the back-heeler that defeated his old club in the Manchester derby and sent them into the Second Division. It was a goal executed out of professional duty, the one goal that did not prompt the familiar raised-arm salute. It ended his league career with a kind of symmetry, for it had been a penalty won by him in the Manchester derby of 1963 that had kept United up and sent City down.

He was as energetic and enthusiastic as ever on his return to the Scotland team, the familiar blond head always the focus of attention, the arm forever raised, demanding the ball. He did enough in the games before the World Cup to merit selection for the opening match against Zaire. He should have been there in 1962, when he had been at his youthful best, and Scotland had a team capable of making some progress in the competition – they had only just failed to qualify in a play-off against Czechoslovakia, the eventual finalists. Had it not been for that disastrous second half against Poland, he might have been there in 1966, in his prime, and capable of being one of the outstanding players in the tournament. There was no chance of that now, and he spent most of the game trying to recall past glories by scoring from one of his trademark overhead kicks. He failed, but seemed to enjoy himself, and he had at last, at the very last, played in the World Cup. Unlike Elvis, who had started his career at about the same time, Denis knew it was time to get out, while the memories were all good ones. Scotland played creditably, and Broonser said the view from the roof of the stadium was magic, although he had encountered some problems in explaining things to the local Polizei.

What is less well known is the part he played in the World Cup final of 1961. The final was played every Sunday afternoon. There were lesser games every other day, but the Big One had to be on Sunday, because it was the parkie's day off. The only decent pitch was a large grassy area, presided over by a fearsome park-keeper with a large stick and a club foot. He didn't prevent play on other days – when he emerged from his hut, waving his stick, there was still time for a good half-dozen goals – but his presence did reduce the status of mid-week fixtures.

The Sunday World Cup was the big one, conducted with all due ceremony: picking the teams; choosing the ball; laying the pitch, the most vital of all. Seven paces was the agreed standard width of goal. But whose paces? A small goalkeeper produced a narrower target; he also gave considerable scope for negotiating a lower height for the imaginary bar. I believe that this tradition has had some influence on Scotland's reputation for producing duff goalkeepers; the best ones have all looked like jockeys.

The goal-lines were also imaginary, which gave further scope for negotiation; it was an excellent training ground for trade union leaders and corporate lawyers. A path alongside one side of the pitch formed one sideline, but, with no clear point of reference and acres of grass, the other sideline scarcely existed at all; good for stamina, bad for close ball control, great for time-wasting. One goal was set in front of an advertising hoarding for the latest film at the ABC Cinema – *Ice Cold in Alex* or *A Town Called Alice*, or whatever – which usually gave the team facing that goal John Mills or Jack Hawkins as a target when drawing a bead on goal.

The match had started cautiously, and it was well into the second minute before the first goal was scored, a speculative lob by a boy called Lavvie. Don't ask. After that, play opened up, and the score stood at 17–14, or thereabouts, when a thunderous volley from Lavvie flew past the imaginary upright that stretched upwards in an imaginary line from the pile of jerseys. He claimed a goal, but eventually accepted that it had struck the post, a compromise that satisfied his pride without conceding a goal. He was a good player, but a soft touch.

The ball landed behind the goal on another pitch, where a group of lads in their 20s played. Lavvie noticed that one of them looked like Denis Law. Law was a god. Law was in Italy. We were us. We were on the links in Aberdeen. This was the kind of remark from Lavvie which had done much to reduce his credibility, and made it easy to refute his claims. He was, as usual, talking shite.

But when the fair-haired figure moved, there was no mistaking who it was. He was athletic, he was brilliant; he was, as usual, suspended. On enforced leave from Torino, he was having a kick-around with a few old mates. Our game stopped as we gazed in wonder. The ball was crossed in front of their makeshift goal. There was the leap, the hang in the air, the twist, and suddenly the ball was flying towards the group of boys, much faster than from Lavvie's thunderous shot. While the others were still taking in the enormity of it all, one boy reacted, passed the ball back to Law, and disappeared; nothing was going to sully the shoe that had passed the ball to Denis Law.

The effect on his team's World Cup chances were catastrophic. It was his job to shout, 'Last goal the winner!' when the situation demanded. He had the knack of raising the shout when the opposition had just scored, and felt invincible. It was his only talent, but it had rescued many a lost cause. That week the shout never came, and the cup was lost.

It's why Scotland teams in those days kept playing as though they had a chance, whatever the score; they were waiting for the shout. Then they could go for it. Alas, it was a rule unrecognised by FIFA, and referees have no romantic souls. Denis did. He'd have gone for the last goal, the way he went for everything. That's why he was a real hero. That's why the shoe that had passed the ball to him remained untouched until the next World Cup, a whole week later.

The Wingers

The wingers. A dying breed, according to some; extinct, according to others. There has been no sighting at Pittodrie since the departure of Peter Weir. Not in a red jersey at any rate. The last to be seen in the Premier Division was the late Davie Cooper, who, even in his footballing dotage, could still accomplish more with a few deft touches than a whole battalion of midfield toilers. Even he had abandoned his left-wing beat for a deeper role, but let's not quibble; the man was an artist, and he has had no obvious successor in Scottish football.

A winger, in the purest example of the breed, should have as his sole aim in life the total humiliation of the full-back and the perfection of the subsequent cross. If you want to identify him, you ask first if his instinct is to beat a defender rather than pass. If it is, then he might be a winger. You then ask if he beats the defender outside rather than inside. If he does, then he's probably a winger. If he always goes on the outside, and the defender knows it, and still can't do anything to stop him, then he's a real winger. If he goes back and beats the defender again, just for the hell of it, he's a tanner ba' player. He should have no interest in the sort of midfield scuffling which can only demean his artistry. In the modern game, such players are deemed to be luxuries, and if they appear at all it is in cross-bred rather than thoroughbred form. We are all the poorer for that.

One of the earliest examples to be seen at Pittodrie was Willie Lennie, who graced the left wing from 1905 to 1913. He was a player who could run at, through and round defences, and the reports of the period make frequent mentions of his runs. It was a time when dribbling was more generally favoured than it is now, but he owed much, as any winger did, to the service he received from his inside-forwards, in his case Charlie O'Hagan and Pat Travers.

In the late-1920s and early-1930s, Andy Love was a part of the famous 'Love, Cheyne, Yorston, McDermid and Smith' forward line. Again, the partnership with his inside-forward, Alex Cheyne, was an important factor, just as his service from the wing was a vital part of Benny Yorston's goalscoring success. Apart from providing Yorston with many of his chances, Love took a fair number himself, 83 in 237 games.

Adam McLean, from his left-wing beat, had performed a similar service for Jimmy McGrory in helping him to set his scoring records for Celtic.

He arrived at Pittodrie in October 1931, shortly before the sudden departure of Yorston, and did not have time to establish a similarly productive relationship with the Aberdeen centre-forward, but his vast experience was to provide invaluable support to the young Willie Mills on his introduction to the team.

Love's replacement on the right wing was a Welshman, Jack Benyon. A less prolific goalscorer than Love (37 in 140 games), he performed the basic function of a winger, to get past the full-back and cross accurately, with great consistency, and was a popular member of the Dons side of the 1930s. He died tragically of peritonitis on the club tour of South Africa in 1937, following a bout of appendicitis.

His counterpart on the left wing was Billy Strauss, of the fast and powerful rather than tricky school of wingers, noted mainly for his shooting power. He scored in each round of the 1936–37 cup run, but was injured in the semi-final and so was unable to play in the final. His importance to the Dons team of that season can be judged by his scoring record, a remarkable 30 goals from 34 appearances. His Aberdeen career was interrupted by the war, and it was some time before the Dons again had a winger who could create havoc with defences and excitement for the spectators.

When that player did arrive, it was at the tail-end of his career, and consequently Dons fans did not see the best of him. What they did see was nevertheless good enough to ensure him of a place in the Pittodrie Hall of Fame (has anyone ever been there? what's it like?), and an enduring place in the memory of all the fans who were fortunate enough to see him play. Tommy Pearson did not arrive at Pittodrie until he was 35, but his skill and trickery, in particular his famous 'double shuffle', made him effective enough to be retained for another five years. Even when he was no longer able to hold down a first-team place, his entertainment value was sufficiently high to ensure crowds of several thousand at reserve matches.

In looking at trends in football attendances, it is sometimes forgotten that crowds at post-war reserve games were numbered in the thousands rather than the hundreds, whereas modern first-team crowds are boosted by relatively large travelling supports. Travelling long distances to support your team was a less attractive proposition before the invention of the aluminium can. Cases of 'screwtaps' were so heavy, and a bottle stuck in each pocket simply ruined the line of a jacket. Cans were much less likely to inflict lasting damage on the tailor's art.

There has also been the growth of private transport, the five-day week and a greater degree of affluence, all of which have made it much easier for fans to follow their teams to away fixtures, with the consequent decline in reserve-match attendances. The empty stadium at a modern reserve match lends the proceedings an air of unreality which cannot make the transition to first-team football easy for the young player stepping for the first time into Archie MacPherson's 'seething cauldron'. Perhaps it is time to reconsider the reserve programme. All of which is a long way from Tommy Pearson. When he was playing in the reserves, Pittodrie was the place to be, and it was a poorer place without him.

When he retired his place on the left wing was occupied by Jack Hather, who had taken what was at that time the unusual route for an Englishman of playing in the Scottish League. Aberdeen had never minded where the players came from, as long as they were good enough, and were pioneers in reversing the southward flow of players long before the Prince of Darkness arrived at Ibrox. George Anderson, the goalkeeper from 1914 to 1922, was, like Hather, a native of north-east England; Jack Benyon was a Welshman, as was Don Emery, while Billy Strauss was from South Africa. It was his absence through injury in the Cup final which undermined the club's challenge for the trophy in 1937, and it was another South African, Stan Williams, who scored the winner in the 1947 final. From the 1960s onwards a string of foreign players have enriched and enlivened proceedings at Pittodrie; and sometimes not.

Jack Hather most certainly enlivened proceedings throughout the 1950s with his runs down the left wing. His greatest attribute was undoubtedly his pace, the standard Hather move being to belt down the wing past the full-back and whack the ball into the middle for Paddy Buckley or Harry Yorston. He would also, on occasion, cut inside to have a shot himself, and in 351 games ran up the very respectable total of 104 goals. As a goalscoring winger he was overshadowed by Graham Leggat, but then so was everyone else. Where he would never be overshadowed, so we thought, was the matter of sheer pace. Was there ever a winger as fast as Hather? Well, actually, there was. A man called Gento, who played for Real Madrid. But we only saw him on television, a grey, fuzzy figure flitting across a 17-inch screen, so he could to some extent be classed along with the Lone Ranger in the credibility stakes. No one could run that fast with a ball at his feet; no one could run that fast with his feet touching the ground. As for the old 'Hi-yo Silver!' man, no one could be so stupid as to get tied up every single episode. Eventually we learned that the Real Madrid players were mortal; they simply belonged to a different class of human being, playing a different game. Eventually Ronald Reagan became president, and made the Lone Ranger look pretty smart.

While Hather was scorching the earth down the left touchline, George Mulhall had to bide his time, but when the moment came for Hather to retire he proved a more than adequate replacement, and won a Scotland cap soon after becoming a regular member of the Aberdeen side in 1959. If he was not quite as fast as Hather, he had more variety in his play, and, like Hather, was a regular goalscorer, with 42 in 150 appearances. He was transferred to Sunderland in 1962 for what was then a substantial fee of £23,000, and went on to have a successful career in England.

There was a bit of a dearth of wingers after that, until Jimmy Wilson arrived in 1965. In signing him, Bobby Turnbull was following a fashion for diminutive wingers that had been started by Willie Henderson at Rangers and continued so gloriously at Parkhead by Jimmy Johnstone. Suddenly every team had to have a wee winger, and it all started to get a bit ridiculous, with wingers getting smaller and smaller; street vendors outside football grounds started to sell opera glasses as a sideline ('Werra cull-ers! Werra gless-es! Seerra wing-ers!'). Jimmy Wilson wasn't actually as wee as all that, and he injected some much-needed life into the Dons attack when he arrived.

It was the year after his arrival that England – the 'wingless wonders' – won the World Cup, and the death of the winger was first announced. The report, as it turned out, was exaggerated, but sightings of the winger did become rarer as 4-2-4 evolved into 4-3-3, and wingers had to become 'wide men' or some such aberration to justify their precarious existence.

Aberdeen's outstanding, almost their only, winger of the 1970s was Arthur Graham, yet another Bobby Calder discovery, who will always be remembered as the 17-year-old who won a Scottish Cup-winner's medal after only a handful of games. After such a brilliant start, his subsequent career, although by no means unsuccessful, appeared to be something of an anticlimax. He was an effective player, but without the artistry of the true winger.

For that we had to wait for Peter Weir. He was signed from St Mirren in 1981. He added the final touch to the team which Alex Ferguson had assembled over the previous seasons, and raised it from a successful Scottish team to one which could compete with, and beat, the best in Europe. Along with Gordon Strachan, he was the man who provided the cutting edge to the solid steel which ran through the side from Willie Miller to Mark McGhee. He was a pure winger, operating almost exclusively along the left touchline, beating defenders with control and pace, and crossing with great accuracy. He cut inside often enough to create uncertainty in the full-back's mind, and when he did, could create havoc in the heart of the opposing defence. This was never better demonstrated than in the game against Ipswich, already described in the chapter on Gordon Strachan. His only concession to the demands of the modern game for all-action, all-purpose players was to lie a little deeper than some of his predecessors would have done, to make himself available for the pass from the defender, and thus to contribute to the midfield play, rather than confine himself to the ritual humiliation of the full-back. If his contribution was inconsistent, that was only to be expected of the type of player he was. If his contribution was sometimes marginal, it was always accurate, elegant and distinctive.

Since then the nearest Aberdeen have had to wingers have been Joe Miller and Stephen Glass. Miller was, along with Paul Wright and Steve Gray, one of a trio of young players who promised to extend the trophy-winning tradition which Alex Ferguson had established, but the promise they had shown in the youth team was never quite fulfilled. On his return to Aberdeen from Celtic, Miller suffered from playing in a side in decline. The one ray of light in what has been a long, dark night of the soul for Dons fans has been the emergence of Stephen Glass. He shone too brightly to be contained in a struggling side, and if he does develop into one of the great wingers, it will be at St James's Park rather than Pittodrie.

There are two notable absentees from this review of Dons wingers. Alex Jackson was an Aberdeen player for only a single season. In any other case, I would have regarded that as too fleeting an acquaintance with Pittodrie to qualify for inclusion in this volume, but he was something else; he was a Wembley Wizard, and for this alone he had to be included.

If the Wembley Wizards are heroes whose praises have been sung rather too loudly and too long, Graham Leggat is one of the unsung heroes of Scottish football, at least in those benighted regions south of Stonehaven. If you didn't see him, take it from me: he was the greatest.

Alex Jackson

In 1924 James Ramsay MacDonald formed Britain's first Labour government, and Lossiemouth gave Britain a prime minister. That government was to last less than a year, with the Conservatives back in office by October. Civilisation As We Know It was safe, at least until the next election.

Alex Jackson's Aberdeen career started that year and was similarly brief, lasting but a single season, from August until the following April. By 1929 Labour were back in power, and MacDonald back at 10 Downing Street. By then we knew that Pittodrie had given the nation a Wembley Wizard. There have been many prime ministers, and will be many more, but there were only, and only ever will be, 11 Wembley Wizards. Alex Jackson was not only one of them, he was the Wizard who scored three goals against England. MacDonald, the victor of 1924 and 1929, was to become the villain of 1931; Jackson was to remain a hero for as long as Scots love football and love to beat England.

For those of us who think of the US soccer league as a last lucrative haven for ageing European stars, the start of Jackson's Aberdeen career seems strange, but it was not so unusual then. Having begun his professional career with Dumbarton, he had gone to the United States, along with his brother, Walter, to play for a team called Bethlehem FC in Pennsylvania. Quite a few Scots players had gone to America to try their luck in the professional soccer league, and among them was Jock Hume, the former Dons full-back. On Hume's recommendation, Aberdeen signed the Jackson brothers when they found America had not, after all, turned out to be the promised land. So, for a combined fee of less than £1,000, they arrived in Aberdeen on 19 August 1924.

The next day, the *Press and Journal* announced: 'Aberdeen's New Forwards Play Tonight.' Walter and Alex Jackson, it reported, were down to play for the 'A' team against Highland League opponents Elgin City, despite having only just arrived from America after a journey which, at that time, would have involved several days' travelling by train and ocean liner. The report is revealing about the management of the club, and the treatment of players: 'The directors have included them in the team, although it is recognised that they may not be in the best of fettle.' On 2 August Aberdeen had appointed a new manager, 'Mr P. Travers', in succession to Jimmy Philip, who had guided the club through the first 21 years of its existence. Perhaps the directors wanted to keep the new man in his place; it is evident that he was not in sole charge of team selection.

As the press heralded the start of Paddy Travers's career in football management, it also announced the end of another sporting career, that of Harold Abrahams, who had recently won the gold medal in the 100 metres at the Paris Olympics – the *Chariots of Fire* games.

There must have been a great fear of the red tide lapping up the Dee, for every other issue of the local paper seemed to carry an article warning of the 'Tyranny of Bolshevism', or some such menace. There was no need to worry as long as that eternal bastion of free enterprise, Morrison's Economic Stores, was there, offering in its 'Gigantic Emporium full of Wonderful Sights' over £150,000 worth of merchandise from all parts of the world, including aluminium goods, tweed blankets and, for some unfathomable reason, 496 Austrian melodeons; to some, these would have represented a far greater threat from the east than any number of Bolsheviks. Professional entertainment was being provided, as always, by Harry Gordon at the Pavilion, while the Tivoli was advertising a show called *Bonk!*. Happy days.

The opening of the grouse season was reported as prominently as the start of the football season, with a half page in the Saturday paper of 'typical scenes from the moors'. Alongside reports of Highland games and other events was announced: 'Today will see a general resumption of the football season in Scotland. Nowhere is there to be found anything but optimism for the success of the season.' The 'air of quiet confidence' so beloved of a later generation had not yet been identified, but it was there nonetheless. There was no mention of the Jacksons, who were still *en route* from America.

Elsewhere in the paper there was a mention of the place the brothers had just left, with news of 1,200 emigrants heading from the Clyde 'for the west'. If it was the Wild West they wanted, they would have been as well looking back east, for the following week the headlines announced 'Oldmeldrum's Wild Hooligans', above a report of a policeman ambushed and a sergeant locked up in his own police station. If that wasn't enough to convince the emigrants that they were bound for a better place, there was a report of a man *v* horse race: 'At the end of the fifth lap of the six days' man *v* horse race at the Crystal Palace yesterday, the positions of the contestants were officially stated as follows: man: 309 miles 206 yards; horse: 289 miles 1,610 yards. The distance covered by Mr Hart yesterday was 61 miles against 54 miles by the horse. The pedestrian has thus increased his lead to approximately 19 miles.' I swear that this is true, or at least that it is an accurate transcript of a report in the local newspaper. One can only conclude that the horse, which was not named, had a little more sense than Mr Hart.

On the subject of more orthodox sporting contests, the football reporter considered that Aberdeen's chances of repeating the previous season's victory against Rangers were 'decidedly rosy'. He considered that the inclusion of the brothers Jackson would remedy the defects which had been apparent in the failure of the forwards against Falkirk the previous week. He was evidently no lover of tanner ba' players: 'It is calculated that effectiveness will substitute ornamentation,' he wrote approvingly, with particular reference to Alex Jackson's 'penetrative power'. He had impressed the fans and the reporter in the game against Elgin City with his speed and accurate crossing.

There was a crowd of 23,000 for the visit of the Robust Fighters of the Clyde, about average for a Rangers game in the 1920s, including a large contingent of visiting supporters who had travelled by special train and motor coach. The Aberdeen team that day was: Blackwell, Hutton, Forsyth; Pirie, J. Jackson, McLachlan; A. Jackson, Milne, W. Jackson, Rankine, Smith. Even this line-up did not exhaust the club's supply of Jacksons, for W.K. of that ilk made his début later in the season to give the Dons no fewer than four of them in the same side, which must be some kind of record.

As far as the most famous of them is concerned, his début was described as no more than 'promising', and he received few mentions in the report of a match which saw Aberdeen struggling to get the better of their opponents before going down 1–0. This was not unexpected at a time when Rangers were the dominant force in Scottish football – in the 20 seasons between the wars, Aberdeen only recorded four home victories against them – but it was a disappointment to those who had thought that the Dons were assembling a team which might at last challenge for honours. Jackson's promised 'penetrative power' was insufficient to pierce a Rangers defence which stubbornly clung on to their narrow lead to take both points back to Ibrox. Does this sound eerily familiar?

The Jackson brothers were given more opportunities to shine the following week, against Ayr United at Somerset Park. The *Press and Journal* reported that 'thrills and goals were plentiful', as indeed they were in a 3–3 draw. All the Aberdeen goals were labelled Jackson, with Walter getting two and Alex the other, when Smith crossed for him 'to jump a great height into the air and head the ball downwards into the net'.

He seems to have been more at home in the west, for his next goals did not come until the visit to Firhill on 27 September, when he scored two against Partick Thistle and laid on the other for Walter with an accurate cross. His goals came from a rebound from the goalkeeper, and a header from a Smith cross. He continued to score the occasional goal, but his influence on games seems to have been sporadic, flitting in and out of games as wingers often do, rather than dominating them, and this inconsistency was reflected in the team's results.

It was not until the last home game of 1924 that he established his reputation with an outstanding display against Third Lanark. He was described as 'the most dangerous raider on the field', with two goals of his own and a string of crosses which produced Aberdeen's first goal and a number of missed opportunities. He scored the side's second goal with a shot from the edge of the penalty area, and got the third with a header. For a winger, an unusually high proportion of his goals were headers, reflecting not only his height but also his propensity for departing from his orthodox right-wing beat to arrive in the penalty area at the opportune moment; something similar was to be seen 30 years later in the play of Graham Leggat.

Jackson did not stay long enough at Pittodrie to establish a reputation as a prolific goalscorer – his tally was a relatively modest eight from 40 appearances – but, like Leggat, he was to be remembered for the brilliance of his goals. In that game against Third Lanark, which Aberdeen won 3–1, he narrowly missed scoring a hat-trick when he shot just over the bar after a 'wonderful dribble', but he was finally to etch his image on the collective memory of the crowd with his last goal for the club, in the game against Hamilton Accies on 1 April 1925. The newspaper headline referred not to the result, but to 'A. Jackson's Brilliant Goal', and the report is worth quoting in its entirety: 'It was one of the best-taken goals seen on the ground for some time, and raised the spectators to a high pitch of enthusiasm. Receiving just inside his own half of the field, he beat first

Thomson and then Hunter, and then, cutting in close to goal, drew at Sommerville and then flashed the ball into the net. It was a wonderful effort, and one of the best goals ever scored on the ground.'

Jackson's was a brilliant flame, but one which was to flicker only briefly at Pittodrie, and the report ended prophetically: 'The game finished in semi-darkness.'

He played his last game for Aberdeen on 25 April, the final game of the 1924–25 season, against Motherwell at Pittodrie. The Rothesay Co-optimists were playing at His Majesty's; if they did not appeal, and it is hard to imagine that they did, Bud Flanagan was offering more popular entertainment at the Tivoli. The BBC made few concessions to popular tastes, with classical music at 3.30, interspersed with talks of an uplifting and educational nature. There was always the cinema for some light relief, with the Playhouse showing *The White Moth*, La Scala *Lure of the Yukon*, and the Cinema House and the Grand Central *Three Women*.

It was announced that Ford had just made 250,000 cars in Britain, but if you couldn't afford one, you only needed a tanner to console yourself with a packet of ten Waverley cigarettes. If you had enough left over for a flutter, the man to bet with was James McLean, 'The Turf Accountant with 30 telephones'. There again, if he could afford all those telephones, perhaps he wasn't the man to bet with, and certainly not if you were relying on newspaper tipsters.

For some reason, the press was always reporting on lunacy in Scotland. At that particular time it appears there was less of it, the reason for the decline (or improvement, depending how you look at it) being given as 'the effect of weak whisky'.

At least the Dons supporters no longer needed a dram to steady their nerves, for Aberdeen, having flirted with relegation for much of the season (another familiar story), had secured their position in the First Division. The team that lined up against Motherwell was: Blackwell, D. Bruce, Forsyth; J. Jackson, Hutton, MacLachlan; A. Jackson, R. Bruce, W. Jackson, W.K. Jackson, Smith. The two goals which defeated Motherwell were scored by Jacksons – Mr McLean would have given you very poor odds on that, since few other names appeared on the teamsheet – but Alex had already scored his last goal for the club. Nevertheless, he 'revealed much brilliance on the wing and his individual runs delighted the crowd'.

He had already won three international caps, and had attracted such attention that a club like Aberdeen could not hope to retain his services for long. He was transferred to Huddersfield in the close season for £5,000, a club record at the time. He won a league championship medal in his first season with his new club and, typically, scored the two goals against West Ham which secured the title. It was the Yorkshire club's third successive league title but, with the departure of their manager, Herbert

Chapman, to Arsenal, it was to be their last. They remained a major force in the English game for the rest of the decade, however, with Jackson continuing to enhance his reputation as one of the finest wingers in the country.

Thus he found himself selected for the Scotland team to face England at Wembley on 31 March 1928. The Scots were hardly in a rich vein of form, having drawn with Wales and lost to Northern Ireland in the Home International Championship, virtually the only international competition which existed at the time; indeed it was not until the following year that Scotland played its first game against 'foreign' opposition, with a 7–3 victory against Norway, at the start of a European tour which took in games against Germany (1–1) and Holland (won 2–0). Internationals followed at fairly regular intervals after that, but only the home internationals counted, and of those, only the game against England really mattered.

And so it was with the usual high hopes, but with no great degree of confidence, that the Scottish fans made the third of what was to become the traditional biennial pilgrimage to the fabled Twin Towers (the stadium had only been opened in 1923). Apart from the team's indifferent form, the Scots were widely regarded as too small to compete with the more powerful English side. With the exception of Jackson, the only way the other forwards could be guaranteed a view of the game was by playing, as they were hardly tall enough to see over the wee men with the big bunnets or huge tartan tammies who seemed to form the bulk of the crowd. As the *Daily Mirror* had it, they were 'the lightest and smallest attack the land of the thistle has ever had in a match of this sort'. All of this helped to fuel the David and Goliath myth of the brave wee nation overcoming the might of the hated oppressor.

On the Monday after the match, the *Sporting Chronicle* bemoaned England's 'Biggest International Disaster for 46 Years', but the *Press and Journal* was not going to get carried away with the tide of euphoria that was sweeping the rest of North Britain. The sports page carried two football columns, one headed 'Rugby' and the other 'Association', with 'Heriots Win Scottish Championship' given equal prominence alongside 'Scots Great Triumph at Wembley'. The reporter did not stint in his praise of the footballers, however: 'Saturday's game provided on the part of the Scots one of the finest and most thrilling exhibitions of football ever seen in an international match, and will be memorable for the amazing cleverness of the Scottish attack which, at times in the second period, simply toyed with a defence that ordinarily would be classed as very capable.' The local paper was never one to miss a local angle, noting that the 70,000 spectators included 'several thousands of enthusiasts who had travelled from Scotland on two special trains from Aberdeen'.

For the record, the team was — no, wait: if you think you can remember the Wembley Wizards team you committed to memory all those years ago, or even last week, here's your chance; close your eyes now, and see if you got them right before you read the next paragraph. If you don't know their names, read on; it will be a handy reference for the next time somebody challenges you to name the Wembley Wizards. If you don't give a toss, just skip the next paragraph, but be warned — you are no true Son or Daughter of the Land of the Thistle.

The team was: J.D. Harkness (Queen's Park), Nelson (Cardiff City) and Law (Chelsea); Gibson (Aston Villa), Bradshaw (Bury) and McMullan (Manchester City) (captain); Jackson (Huddersfield Town), Dunn (Hibs), Gallacher (Newcastle United), James (Preston North End) and Morton (Rangers).

Jackson and his colleagues gave an early warning of what was to come when he headed the first goal from a cross by Alan Morton (the 'Wee Blue Devil'), following a passing move by McMullan and James. 'This success aroused tremendous enthusiasm among the Scottish supporters, and the accuracy of the movement amazed everybody,' according to the report, which referred to England as 'the Saxons', giving the impression that they waved shields in the air and kept up their shinpads with cross-garters outside their stockings. The photographs show them in fairly conventional football attire, with long, baggy shorts and no shields whatsoever. Shinpads remained essential protection in an age of robust tackling and boots with rock-hard toecaps. Whatever faced him that day, however, Jackson was undaunted.

The mature Jackson had retained his youthful flair for the unorthodox and unexpected, but he had added to it the ability to dominate an opponent and a match. Time and again he 'bamboozled' or 'glided past' Jones, his hapless opponent, to lay on a series of crosses or to shoot for goal — he had clearly passed the test to graduate as a Real Winger — until in the second half he scored Scotland's third and his own second goal with a replica of the first, a header from a James–Morton passing move. He was involved in the fourth goal, starting with a pass to Dunn, and providing the cross from which Gallacher shot, for James to score from the rebound. He completed his hat-trick with the final goal, this time with a shot from yet another Morton cross.

That 5–1 win was Scotland's most famous victory, but the fact that it remains so, after all these years, says something about the development of the game in Scotland. Ever willing to look back to a mythical world of hills, glens, but'n'bens and tartan warriors rather than to confront contemporary reality, we have revered the Wizards as representing the ideal of Scottish football (wee men with skill) and our true status in the game (the best). This notion sustained us through the decades of failure that were to follow, until Jock Stein, when he took over the national side, at last reminded us that we were a small nation of limited resources, and should tailor our expectations accordingly. Until then we had put down defeats against England to the 'Hampden Hoodoo', the 'Wembley Hoodoo', or whatever other explanation could be found, apart from the inconceivable notion that they might just have a better team, and that, with a population ten times as large, this was only to be expected.

This is not to denigrate the Wizards' performance, but merely to state that for too long it gave us a false image of our worth as a football nation. Like any sporting performance, it must be set in perspective, and part of that perspective is that, however good the Scots were that day, it was a poor England team that they beat; the sides were, after all, competing to avoid the wooden spoon, with England already having been defeated by Wales and Northern Ireland. Like so many of our legends, that of the Wembley Wizards looks less impressive when the mists have cleared.

None of this can take anything away from the performance of Alex Jackson. Nor was he finished for the season; on the Monday following the international, he scored the only goal of the game for Huddersfield in their FA Cup semi-final victory over Sheffield United, thus ensuring another trip to Wembley for the final. It was not to prove a victorious return, for Huddersfield were beaten 3–1 by Blackburn Rovers. Jackson did have the consolation of scoring his side's goal, and it was not a wholly unsuccessful occasion for alumni of Pittodrie, for one of the Blackburn defenders was that other Dons legend, Jock Hutton, who had been in the Dons team in which Jackson had played. Perhaps it was a game more suited to his style of play, for Blackburn's first goal was scored when the Huddersfield goal-keeper was bundled into the net with the ball in his hands. This seems to have set a trend for Lancashire teams in cup finals, for Nat Lofthouse was to do the same for Bolton Wanderers some 30 years later in their final against Manchester United.

The FA Cup final had not yet taken its place as the climax of the season, and Huddersfield, and Jackson, still had the opportunity to win the league championship. But the strain of fighting on two fronts told on them, as it has on so many teams chasing the elusive 'double', and they were eventually defeated by the combined weight of their fixture list and Dixie Dean's goals for Everton – this was the season that he scored his record 60 league goals. It was to be Huddersfield's last real tilt at glory, and they gradually slid down the table into obscurity.

Jackson did not go down with them. In 1930 he was transferred to Chelsea. A move to the bright lights somehow seemed appropriate for him. He ended his career in even more glamorous surroundings, playing in France for Nice, and was finished with football before he was 30.

From the game's earliest years, football fans have created legends out of players. If his skill had not been sufficient, Alex Jackson created a legend on that day at Wembley in 1928, and secured his place as one of Scottish football's 'immortals'. I don't know why Scottish football has 'immortals'; no other nation seems to have them. Bill Shankly's words of congratulation to Jock Stein when Celtic won the European Cup were: 'Jock, you're immortal.' Perhaps it is something to do with the 'Immortal Memory' of Burns Nichts. In Jackson's case, it was cruelly inappropriate, for he was to die in a road accident at the age of only 41, while serving with the army in Egypt. All we have left are the reports, the memories of those who saw him, and the photographs. Most of the pictures of footballers of the period show the stern, defiant faces of men confronting the enemy. Jackson is reputed to have played with dash and style, and this is reflected in his photographs. In his football strip he looks lithe and athletic; in his portraits he dares to smile. With his slicked-back hair he has the air of a crooner or a silent film star, rather than a footballer, and reflects the gaiety of the Jazz Age rather than the stern reality of unemployment and general strikes and national governments. He looks young, at a time when other players looked old. He was one of those players who brought enjoyment to the game and transmitted it to the spectators; watching him, they could forget reality for 90 minutes. He gave the spectators their money's worth. He was an entertainer; he was a Real Winger and he played the Real Game.

Graham Leggat

Older readers won't thank me for saying it, and younger ones won't believe me, but I'm afraid it's true: as you get older, you get more and more like the old farts you used to laugh about when you were a kid. You go on about how dear everything is, and how you used to be able to go out to the pictures and the pub and have a pie supper on the way home, and still have two bob change out of half a crown; and you go on about how you can't hear the words of the songs any more, and there's no melody, and they can't sing, not like Bing Crosby, or Lonnie Donnegan, or Johnny Rotten. And the football – what football? They can't play any more; can't trap the ball, can't pass, not like Alex James, or Billy Steel, or Jim Baxter. And they've no wingers any more; not like Alan Morton, or Willie Waddell, or Graham Leggat.

But here is where I must stop, and insist, and repeat: Graham Leggat really was the greatest. I cannot prove it, in the way that anyone with a video can demonstrate beyond question that Pele was the greatest footballer who ever kicked a ball, for Leggat played in the days before the close-up and the action replay. If any of his games are preserved on film, he will appear only as a grey dot moving against a grey background, while a newsreel film will only show a glimpse of play, before the brief close-up of the goalkeeper picking the ball out of the net and the detailed shot of the celebrating fans, including the boy with the 'ricketie', who seemed to have attended every match covered by Pathé News from 1930 onwards. Like Peter Pan and Oor Wullie, he never grew up, but I suppose football fans never do. For most of them, each season brings only disappointment, yet they cling to the belief that glory is only just around the corner. There is always another goal, another game, another season.

In 1955 I really was that fan, without the 'ricketie' (did anyone ever really use them, or did Pathé just dish them out for the newsreels?) but with a Dons scarf which reached down to my knees, and the Dons really were the champions, not of some fantasy league, but of the real league, of Scotland. I had just missed seeing them win it, but that hardly mattered, because I was going to see every single game from now on, and the Dons were going to win them all, and were going to be champions again in 1955–56 and, well, for ever. And if Fred Martin was the first of those giants I could identify, because he was in goal, Graham Leggat was the first hero, and because of that he will always be the greatest.

He was the first hero because he was different. He beat the back, he crossed the ball; so did other wingers. He scored goals; so did other wingers, but not as many, and not as good. His goals were different. He looked different. The other players looked like your uncles, with plastered-down hair and off-centre partings and a general appearance of having been around since the dawn of time; Leggat looked like your older brother, with a quiff that suggested he might just have heard of rock'n'roll. He looked like Terry Dene a couple of years before Terry Dene was invented.

For those too old or too young to remember the said Mr Dene, he was one of a horde of otherwise blameless British teenagers who were renamed and dressed up to resemble real rock'n'roll stars. In time we were to discover that Terry Dene wasn't rock'n'roll, and in fact wasn't even Terry Dene, but how were we to know that at the time? After all, if somebody could be called Elvis Presley, they could certainly be called Terry Dene. And if Tommy Steele never felt more like singin' the blues, never felt more like cryin' all night, these, we concluded, must be the blues, even if he had copied the song from a real blues singer like Guy Mitchell.

But all that was in the future when Leggat started his career in the Indian summer of 1953, in the days before rock'n'roll. He had been mentioned in the local press a couple of years earlier, when his sporting abilities had been praised: 'Graham Leggat, a 17-year-old pupil at Central School, is one of the most promising all-round athletes in Aberdeen. Last Saturday he won the boys' singles event in the Aberdeen Secondary Schools tennis tournament. In Grade cricket in the season just closed young Leggat played so well for Balmoral that he was chosen for an Aberdeenshire Association select team. He also found time to play football, and in the early weeks of the season his performances on the wing for Torry FPs had junior and senior agents watching him.'

He had planned to go to Jordanhill PT College, but had opted instead for a career in professional football, and joined Aberdeen in August 1953, after a season with local junior side Banks o' Dee.

On 7 September the temperature had been 78°F at Dyce, and there had been sunbathing on the beach. Elsewhere, Neville Duke had set a new world air speed record of 727.6mph. The Dons had been considerably more pedestrian in suffering a 3–0 defeat by St Mirren, and there were calls for changes in the team. These were answered by the introduction of Graham Leggat, a youngster 'who had been showing good form for the reserves'.

His first-team début was against Stirling Albion at Annfield. The side was: Morrison, Mitchell, Caldwell; Harris, Young, Allister; Leggat, Yorston, Buckley, Hamilton, Hather. Stirling Albion were never the most distinguished of opposition, but they were distinguished enough that day to win 1–0, and inflict a fourth successive defeat on Aberdeen. Amid general condemnation of the Dons, there were some words of praise from Norman MacDonald, the *Press and Journal* reporter: 'Graham Leggat . . . was keen and lively in the opening stages, but did not receive enough of the ball to show his real worth . . . The former Banks o' Dee player has a good idea of the game.'

Playing football certainly sounded a better idea than swimming from the Don to the Dee, which was what H. Lambert Wilson became the first man to do. It took him an hour and three-quarters for the two-mile swim, having taken 18 years to get round to the idea after doing the swim in the opposite direction. When he wasn't in the water, Mr Wilson was the leader of the orchestra at His Majesty's Theatre. On a lower theatrical plane, the Tivoli was advertising *Making Whoopee*, starring Jack Milroy, who never failed to make me laugh. ('*She's my peerie weerie, weerie, weerie winkle, – My jeelie and my jam . . .*') Corny, but I loved it, and so did the Aberdeen audiences. The weekend radio programmes offered the inevitable Scottish dance music, but at 6.30 there was *Sportsreel* to bring you up to date with the football results. The paper had no details of weekend TV programmes. The cinema offered new releases like *From Here to Eternity*, which was more or less how I felt after the first ten minutes of the dreaded Saturday-night accordions.

The Standard Eight was advertised as the new low-price car for under £500 – £481 and seven shillings to be exact – with a top speed of 60mph. A child's coat could be had for 15s 11d, in good grey flannel. But there was a snag: it had a velvet collar. And there was a further snag: Prince

Charles had one just like it. There's not much to be said for growing up, but there is always the consolation that you no longer have to dress like the heir apparent unless you are the sort who really wants to; the sort of boring old fart you used to laugh at when you were a kid, in fact.

The following Saturday Leggat retained his place in the side and made the opening for Yorston to score the goal against Dundee which secured a point for the Dons. A draw was better than nothing, and certainly better than the 3–0 defeat inflicted by Celtic the following week. This was a real curiosity of a game, for Celtic's three goals were all scored by Bobby Collins from penalties conceded by Jimmy Mitchell. Not surprisingly, public criticism of the club continued.

The Dons had to wait until October to record their first league win of the season, and give Leggat his first win bonus, with a 2–1 victory over Partick Thistle at Pittodrie. Mitchell's own-goal was insufficient to maintain the Dons' losing sequence, but at least kept up the run of goals for which he could claim personal responsibility. If it was not the best of times for Mitchell, Leggat was beginning to look like an idea whose time had come, for the match also marked his first goal in senior football, from a 'judicious pass' by Buckley. According to the report, it capped an excellent display by the young winger. 'On a day in which chances were wasted with reckless prodigality, Leggat seized his opportunity with the coolness and assurance of a veteran.'

He scored again the following week, the first goal in a 5–0 defeat of Airdrie, a score which, for some mysterious reason, never failed to prompt the headline: 'Dons Go Nap'. The faint praise which had attended his first couple of games had now become fulsome: 'There is a sparkle and intelligence about Leggat's play which augurs well for this lad's football future. And there seems to have been an improvement in Yorston's play since the advent of Leggat.'

He must have enjoyed playing against Partick Thistle, for he scored another two goals against them in the Dons' 6–3 victory at Firhill on 9 January. Praise was again showered upon him: 'The award for the most distinguished service must go to Graham Leggat. The right-winger was full of dash and courage and his two goals were first-rate efforts. The first, the result of a Hamilton–Hather move, saw Leggat, with the coolness of a veteran, drive the ball into the narrow space between the keeper and the post. Number two was a neat piece of opportunism.'

His first hat-trick came the following month, in the 5–3 victory over Clyde. The first of his goals was a spectacular diving header, and his overall display prompted yet more journalistic praise, which by now was becoming lavish: 'The outside-right was lively, speedy and intelligent, and his clever hat-trick in the first 49 minutes unquestionably paved the way for Aberdeen's 5–3 victory. Leggat is a young player with a bright future.'

He continued on his scoring ways, helping the Dons to climb back to a halfway position in the league, which was respectable after such a dismal start, and to reach the Cup final, where they lost, yet again, to Celtic. There was the consolation of having defeated the Robust Fighters of the Clyde 6–0 in the semi-final, proving that Aberdeen could beat the Old Firm in Glasgow. Leggat finished the season as the club's second-top scorer with 19 goals from 31 appearances, an excellent performance by any standards, but a remarkable one for a teenage winger in his first season. The following season his scoring rate declined to 13 from 36 appearances, but that hardly mattered as Aberdeen sorted out their defensive problems and conceded only 26 goals on their way to the league title.

It was season 1955–56 which was to be his personal *annus mirabilis*, as he averaged a goal a game with 29 from 29 appearances, including the winner in the League Cup final against St Mirren, gained his first international cap, and scored against England. He started the league campaign with two goals in a 6–2 rout of Hibs, 'Famous Five' and all, and went on from there. I saw that game from the stand, with my father, but by October I was adjudged big enough to go on my own and take my place behind the goal. Certain precautions had to be taken, of course, the main one being to ensure that I was warm enough. With vests, shirts and jerseys, I was clad in enough layers to have survived a day and a half in the North Sea, never mind an hour and a half at Pittodrie, and that was in October. With the onset of winter came the real humiliation: the scarf warmed in front of the fire, crossed over the chest and pinned behind the back. The chest was deemed to be of prime importance, and had to be kept warm at all costs. The head, too, was fairly important, considering what went on in there, and was encased in something that looked like a flying helmet, so that the all-important ears could also be protected.

Protection from the elements became less important as you worked your way down from the chest. Your feet were used for walking and kicking, activities of marginal usefulness, and were granted the fairly minimal protection of shiny wellies, but knees were used for nothing at all, as far as mothers could see, and were therefore left completely bare between the shorts and the wellies until adolescence was reluctantly conceded to have begun, but by that time most of us were suffering from permafrost of the knees. As for Those Bits, they mattered not at all, and were left to take their chances swinging about inside a pair of somewhat draughty underpants, for these were the days before Y-fronts.

Broonser's mother took this sartorial philosophy to extremes, even by the standards of the day, and, with an exaggerated respect for learning and brainpower, felt compelled to protect her son's brain and ears with a balaclava and woolly hat as well as the flying helmet. We could have told her that, if the resistance of his brain to learning was anything to go by, it could withstand any amount of cold; as far as his ears were concerned, he never listened to anything anyway, but neither did his mother, so there was no point telling her. The result was that on a cold day Broonser finished each game looking like a Rangers supporter, with a large expanse of blue legs and a red face peeping out from a frost-covered balaclava. His appearance invited a certain amount of ridicule, but his mother had devised a system of overlapping, tucking-in and safety-pinning that would have defeated Houdini.

Farce turned to tragedy on the coldest day of that winter, however; winters were really cold then, for those were the days before central heating, when you woke up to frosted window panes. They were the days before the Gulf Stream. It was invented by my secondary-school geography teacher, and winters were never the same after that. The snow no longer came over the top of your wellies, as it had before. There was no snow on this particular day, but a cold east wind from beyond Peterhead promised there would be plenty to come. Broonser's mother had taken the extra precaution of putting some warmed cotton-wool in his ears, just in case. It was a dull game, and it gave us some distraction to watch his knees getting bluer, and his face redder. He keeled over about ten minutes into the second half, and was carried off on a stretcher. I suppose I should have gone with him, but the Dons had a corner, and by the time it had been cleared, Broonser had disappeared to wherever stretcher cases disappeared to.

His mother was beginning to get worried when she got the phone call from the hospital: 'I'm afraid it's serious, Mrs Brown. Gangrene of the knees had set in, and we've had to amputate.'

'Oh no.'

'That's not all. His head suffered badly from overheating, and his brains were, well, I don't know how to say this, but they were, to all intents and purposes, cooked.'

'Oh no.'

Broonser's mother was a woman of few words, most of which were 'no', but she gathered herself and her vocabulary sufficiently to ask the really vital question: 'Fit aboot his ears?'

'A bit singed round the edges, but they'll be okay.'

'Thank God for that.'

Of course, it didn't really happen like that. It couldn't have: Broonser didn't have a phone. None of us did. Broonser didn't even have an inside lavvy, never mind a phone. Now the kids feel deprived if they haven't got a phone they can take into one of their lavvies, and if you take the call, it sounds as though someone's pissing in your ear.

The mundane fact is that we survived the rigours of our first winter of spectating, and in the springtime were able to look forward to the big game of the season – the Scotland *v* England international at Hampden. Anticipation was heightened by the selection of two Dons – Archie Glen and, for his first international, Graham Leggat.

That match came on 14 April 1956. Leggat had run into form, with a hat-trick against Hearts the previous week, prompting the headline: 'Leggat's Form Bodes Ill For Roger Byrne [the Manchester United and England left-back who was due to face Leggat at Hampden].' The first goal against Hearts had been scored 22 seconds after the kick-off, followed by an opportunist strike in 40 minutes, and a clever lob (one of his trademarks) ten minutes from the end.

On the morning of the international, the Scottish press was as confident as ever; to be otherwise was unpatriotic, regardless of the 7–2 thrashing inflicted on us by England the previous year. Norman MacDonald, in an echo of James Forbes' remarks on Fred Martin the previous year, prophesied that 'Leggat has only to produce his club form to be a success'. It was to be hoped that this optimism would not have the catastrophic effect on Leggat that it had had on Martin. MacDonald was to prove more prescient than his colleague, though, for he went on to provide a shrewd analysis of Leggat's abilities: 'His main value lies in his aptitude for materialising on the right spot at the psychological moment, and it would be a mistake if he were to stick religiously to the touchline.'

On the Monday after the match he was able to report that Leggat's goal had 'his signature written all over it'. It had come in 61 minutes, when Hewie, the Charlton left-back, had moved upfield. 'Leggat, sensing the possibilities of the situation, stole quietly to the inside-left position on the edge of the penalty area when the ball came over. He brought it down smartly, and cutely lobbed it over the head of Matthews, the England keeper, who had stepped out of his goal.' It was a goal fit to win any match, and it almost did, but, just when we thought that Scotland had at last broken the Hampden Hoodoo, Johnny Haynes equalised for England in injury-time, and we could continue to curse Scotland's bad luck, a much more satisfying way to spend the rest of the year than gloating over victory.

It was a goal which typified so many of Leggat's qualities: his reading of the game, his positional sense, his goalscorer's instincts, the accuracy of his finishing. Many of his goals were scored from the inside-left position, an unusual move for a winger in those days, and many came from lobs or chips, when most players would have been tempted to blast the ball towards the net. It was a goal which was broadcast to the nation; now everyone would know that Graham Leggat was the greatest. I remember it, because I saw it on a 17-inch black-and-white screen, sitting cross-legged on the floor of our living-room with half the street in serried ranks behind me, in a miniature version of the Beach End. I remember the roar when the goal went in, and I remember the roar when the screen went blank. There was still a degree of pride in having a TV, and the humiliation of having the TV which broke down in front of about 50 neighbours while Scotland were in the lead would have been too much to bear. Apart from that, there was the distinct possibility that the house would be wrecked, for a Scotsman who has partaken of strong drink and has just been deprived of the pleasure of seeing England being beaten is not easily mollified. But luck was on our side, for there was among our number an electrician who spotted that the small boy sitting nearest the set had kicked out the plug in his excitement at seeing Leggat score for Scotland. Electricity and order were restored, and the remainder of the match was watched with good humour, growing tension and, ultimately, disappointment as England's equaliser went in. For that, at least, the small boy could not be blamed, and the crowd dispersed with our house intact.

By the next year, nearly everyone had a TV, and it never happened quite like that again. Leggat never had a season quite like that again. In 1956–57 he scored a total of 16 goals from 31 appearances. The fact that this was sufficient to make him Aberdeen's top scorer by a comfortable margin was an indication of the club's decline, as they slipped from the runners-up position of the previous season to sixth in the league, and suffered an early exit from the Scottish Cup at the hands of Falkirk. That defeat was not quite as ignominious as it sounds, for Falkirk were to go on to win the Cup that year, beating Kilmarnock in one of the less glamorous finals, distinguished in my mind only by the way a spectator jumped up in front of the TV camera and totally obscured the televised view of the winning goal.

For the Dons, winning goals were in short supply the following season, as they slumped still further to 12th place in the league. Their cause was not helped by the absence of Leggat for a large part of the season with a broken leg. Nevertheless, he still managed to finish the season as the club's second-top scorer, with 15 goals from only 24 appearances. There was to be no opportunity to regain his place as the club's leading scorer, for 1957–58 was to be his last as an Aberdeen player. He had been reluctant to re-sign at the start of the season, and the continued decline in the team's performances, together with his own misfortune, did nothing to diminish his disaffection with the club. It was symptomatic of the club's disarray that, when he returned to the team, he was as likely to be picked at centre-forward or inside-right as in his most effective position of outside-right.

The RAF wasn't sure what to do with him either. On 9 April he was pictured leaving for his National Service with RAF Cardington. Within 48 hours he was discharged on medical grounds. If he wasn't fit enough for the air force, he was still fit enough for Aberdeen FC, and he was at centre-forward for the game against Queen of the South on 12 April. Aberdeen lost 4–3, a result which prompted the *Press and Journal* to report that the club was facing a crisis, and that 'drastic action' would have to be taken before the start of the new season.

The following Wednesday, with Leggat at inside-right, they faced a Hearts side who were already champions, and lost 4–0. There was no disgrace in being defeated by one of the most dominant and attractive of the post-war sides, with experienced players such as Conn, Bauld and Wardhaugh, along with emerging talent such as Dave Mackay and Alex Young. Nevertheless, it was a measure of how far Aberdeen's fortunes had declined in just a couple of seasons that such a result should be expected and acceptable.

After that, defeat at Ibrox in the last game of the season was regarded as almost unavoidable, and so it proved to be, by a humiliating 5–0 margin. It was also inevitable that it would be Leggat's final match for the Dons. He played his last game at inside-right to his young successor on the wing, Dickie Ewen. The team was: Morrison, Walker, Hogg; Burns, Clunie, Glen; Ewen, Leggat, Davidson, Wishart, Hather. Of the team in which he had started his career just five years previously, only Morrison and Hather played in this last game; of the side which had triumphed in the league in 1955, only Glen, Wishart and Hather remained. The Dons looked different; the old jerseys with collars had been replaced by V-neck, short-sleeved 'continental' jerseys; the old, high-lacing boots with massive toecaps were giving way to the modern, low-cut 'continental' boot.

It was not only on the field that changes had occurred. Televised highlights of league games were being shown regularly on *Sportsreel* on Saturday nights, even if the cameras were not always focused properly or even pointing in the right direction. There was one memorable Kilmarnock *v* Rangers game when the camera somehow slipped to show the players from the knees down. There was a controversial penalty-area incident during the game, involving almost all the players and the referee, which produced the bizarre image of an empty foreground, with 40-odd feet crammed along the top of the screen.

Unfortunately, the cameras at Broadcasting House never failed to get Billy Cotton in focus, and he had to be endured earlier on Saturday evening, forever shouting 'Wakey! Wakey!' quite unmercifully before we could get our weekly fix of football with Peter Thomson and George Davidson. Earlier still on Saturday evening, the BBC had acknowledged the arrival of rock'n'roll with *Six-Five Special* – 'Over the points, over the points,' sang Don Lang with His Frantic Five, while Tommy Steele, Britain's first rock'n'roll star, was already showing the first signs of respectability and middle age by appearing in films like *The Duke Wore Jeans*. For the real thing we still had to look to America. Danny and the Juniors had promised us that 'Rock'n'Roll is Here to Stay', and we believed them, especially when Buddy Holly arrived. Sadly, he was to be gone the following year. The music didn't die that day on 3 February 1959, but it would never be as young again.

The 1958 news had been dominated by another February plane crash, when a team and an ideal had died. The team was Manchester United; the ideal was eternal youth, for these were the Busby Babes. As far back as I could remember, they had represented all that was good in the game: they were brilliant, they were the best, they were the youngest, they were the Babes, they would always be the best, they would never grow old. They would never grow old because old people had always been old, like your grandparents, in the same way as your mother and father had always been the age they were, and always would be. Munich put an end to all that. After those first, unbelievable radio bulletins, came the confirmation of the television pictures, and the realisation of what mortality meant. Even then, right at the end, there was Duncan Edwards, the greatest of them all, hanging on to life. Surely he would fight and never lose. But the medical bulletins got worse, his kidneys failed, and he slipped away, like the *Titanic* slipping towards its fate.

After that, the game seemed pretty pointless for a while, and the rest of the season was an anticlimax. When Leggat went, he was only going to Fulham; it wasn't the end of the world, and his last game didn't have the impact for me it might otherwise have had. By the time it came along, he must have been 'demob happy'. According to the report, he 'worked hard at times and gave big Sam Baird one or two anxious moments, but the old dash and shot just wasn't there'.

He had asked for a transfer the previous week. Whatever a club may say in public about keeping its best players, there is little it can do to retain someone who genuinely wants to go. Leggat started the following season as a Fulham player, and was an instant success, according to the *Green Final* report: 'Leggat quickly made his mark in English football, scoring a goal after a brilliant run and laying on another to help Fulham to a 4–0 halftime lead over Stoke.' The poor management of his former club was shown, not in allowing him to go, but in selling him for £16,000, which even in those days was a tiny fee for a player of such talent. It could be said that Leggat, too, showed misjudgement in going to a club like Fulham, when he had the skill to play for one of the more glamorous clubs. Possibly he thought that, if it was good enough for Johnny Haynes, England's best inside-forward, it was good enough for him, and with Haynes in the team there was always the chance of success and the certainty of a few free jars of Brylcreem. The fact is that one man, even one as good as Haynes, does not make a team, and apart from him Fulham's best-known player was the other inside-forward, Jimmy Hill, yes, *that* Jimmy Hill; the snag was that he was famous for his beard and his leadership of the players' union in their fight to abolish the maximum wage, rather than for his football skills. He was successful in abolishing the maximum wage, enabling Haynes to become the first £100-a-week player. He was less successful in advancing Fulham's cause, and throughout Leggat's career they were a club trying to hang on to their First Division status, rather than vying for honours.

The result was that he achieved less in terms of winners' medals and international honours than was promised by the brilliant start he had made to his career. The international selectors had, with their usual Old Firm bias, quite disgracefully preferred Alex Scott of Rangers on many occasions. Then, at the start of the 1960s, came Willie Henderson, whose genius, I must reluctantly admit, could not be overlooked.

Leggat, too, was a genius, but in a totally different way. He was a Real Winger, who could do all the things a Real Winger is supposed to do, but he was also a player ahead of his time, who used his nominal wing position as a base from which to launch guerrilla attacks, rather than simply provide the ammunition for the full-frontal assault by the centre-forward. He had the goalscorer's gift of seeing the chink in the enemy's armour, and of choosing the right weapon for the kill – the full-blooded shot, the finely judged lob, whatever would beat the goalkeeper.

His goal against England epitomised all those qualities, but he will be remembered best by all who saw it for the one he scored against St Mirren on 11 February, 1956. The *Press and Journal* described it thus: 'This confident youngster with the twinkle in his feet must have had an even brighter twinkle in his eye when he scored the fourth goal. When the Aberdeen team was awarded a free-kick on the left side of the penalty area, the Paisley defence, as usual, formed a solid phalanx in front of the taker. Leggat collected the ball, looked round casually, stepped forward and in one movement placed and toed the ball over the astonished St Mirren players' heads into the net. It was the cheekiest goal that has been seen at Pittodrie for many a day . . . and introduced a delightfully lighthearted touch to what had threatened to be a dull game.' The *Green Final* headlined the goal as 'Leggat Foxed 'Em With Clever 'Un'.

I remember it slightly differently. It was a cold, grey February day, the wind blustery and the ground hard and bumpy. As he ran up to take the kick, the ball was blown from the spot where he had placed it. He bent down to replace it and, without looking up or drawing his foot back, flicked it over the heads of the defensive wall and behind Jim Lornie in the St Mirren goal; Lornie had relaxed his guard while the ball was being replaced, and the first intimation he had of what had happened was the roar from the crowd when the ball landed in the net behind him.

That's how I remember it, and there is no means of checking exactly what did happen, for these were the days before televised highlights and action replays. All we have are the match reports, not always completely reliable, and the recollections of those who were there, some 15,000 or so then, and, with the passage of time, rather less than that by now. Their memories can hardly be relied on so long after the event, but ask them which Pittodrie goal they remember best, and that will be the one. Each of them will have a slightly different version of events, but they will all remember the glow it brought to light up a dull February afternoon, and after all this time it is the memory that matters rather than the facts. It was one of those rare moments when the Real Game visited Pittodrie. In the Monday-morning playground games, free-kicks would be contrived so that the moment could be relived.

The afternoon wasn't the only thing that was lit up, for those were the days before government health warnings, and the goal was taken as a cue for the Woodbines and the Capstans to emerge for a vast communal smoke in celebration of the goal. A buzz went round the crowd for the rest of the game, as the fans, almost oblivious to the action still in progress, discussed what they had just seen, and reconstructed the events they had just witnessed, to be recollected in the tranquillity of their homes or the turmoil of the bars. They had to check with each other what had happened, for it was something so original and unexpected, in the days before elaborate free-kick routines and rehearsed set-pieces; it was to be a quarter of a century before a crowd would find itself one step ahead of a German defence in predicting what Strachan and McMaster were going to do.

They were the days before floodlights, when midwinter games started early to allow 90 minutes' play in daylight. Even so, on a dull day dusk would begin to descend some time in the second half, and play at the far end would melt into a shadow display, punctuated with the thud of the ball and the roars of the crowd. This was one of those afternoons, and from the Beach End the crowd under the cover at the King Street End had merged into an all-consuming blackness, forming a backdrop for the white stripes of the St Mirren players and the white shorts of the Dons.

They were the days before the all-seated, all-covered stadium, before there was even a cover over the Beach End. From that end, behind the goal, a small boy stood and gazed into the gathering darkness, replaying in his mind the wonder that he had seen, while around him the buzz of the crowd continued, and, at the far end, matches were struck and cigarettes glowed in the dark, like so many harbour lights.